Lyn Meyers
Dist Governor
Leono Dist 23 A

Dist Governor
Bob Cormier - 23 B

Juliane Shulosky
Council Sec - Treas

Best wish
CC Stan Doutar

Ed. Welch,
Thanks for being
with us today
Mark

Thanks for making
our convention a great
Success.

DG Ken Tucker
23 C

Thanks for
joining us!
Neal Winter
TD Carolyn Messier

# A Brief History of Lionism in Connecticut 2007 Edition

Author/Manager: Frank P. Mauro, PCC
Co-Author:     Richard Foote, PDG
Editor:         Joel J. Ragovin, PDG
Art and Graphics: Lion Dan "Zeno" Hadjstylianos
Publishing:     Dan Uitti, PDG

Published by the State Council Connecticut Lions Multiple District 23

ISBN-13: 978-0-9708430-8-1

Published by Multiple District 23
in association with DaSum Company LLC


Printed in the United States of America

Printed on Recycled Paper




Published December 2007

This book is dedicated to PID Otto Strobino
and the Lions of Multiple District 23

## Melvin Jones

Melvin Jones, founder of the International Association of Lions Clubs, was born at Fort Thomas, Arizona on January 13, 1879, where his father was an Army Captain. He remained there until he was seven years old, after which time the family moved to a farm just north of the army installation.

He received his early education in Arizona and Missouri. In 1894 Melvin went on to study at the Union Business College in Quincy, Illinois. Upon graduation, he continued on to Law School and in 1899 received his law degree from Chaddock College in Quincy.

At age 20, following graduation, he moved to Chicago. At age twenty-one he began to study voice at the Apollo Club of Chicago. As a tenor, he was devoted to classical music and became quite famous in Chicago.

In the following year be began to work at the office of Johnson and Higgins Insurance Brokers.

In 1912, he opened his own insurance firm - "The Melvin Jones Insurance Agency." Soon thereafter, he joined the Business Circle of Chicago.

In 1914, while serving as Secretary of the Business Circle, he began contacting independent clubs and associations throughout the country in an effort to interest them in the formation of a service club association. He had the full support of his own club in this undertaking.

On June 7, 1917, delegates representing many of these clubs met at the LaSalle Hotel in Chicago and formed the International Association of Lions Clubs, which was later incorporated in the State of Illinois. At this time, Melvin Jones was elected Secretary of the association, and later became its only Secretary General.

Through the years, Melvin Jones was honored by many countries with numerous awards and citations.

Melvin Jones' first wife, Rose Amanda Freeman, passed away in June 1954 and two years later he married Lillian M. Radigan.

Melvin Jones died on June 1, 1961 at the age of eighty-two in Flossmoor, Illinois, a suburb of Chicago. As a tribute to this great Lion and the life of service he lived, the board of directors abolished for all time the office of Secretary General, which he held with great honor and distinction.

## Joseph M. McLoughlin, Past International President

In June 1977, the Lions Clubs International Convention was held in New Orleans, Louisiana. It was at this convention that Joseph M. McLoughlin of Stamford, Connecticut was elected as the Association's 61st President.

At the conclusion of his presidency, he was asked to serve as the President of The Lions Clubs International Foundation, and he served that position with distinction as well.

Past President McLoughlin was the president of a lumber company and a real estate development firm.

A member of the Springdale (Stamford) Lions Club since 1956, he held every major office in the club and District. In 1970, he was elected to serve a two-year term as International Director of the Association.

Both he and his wife Betty have been honored as Melvin Jones Fellows. For his outstanding service on behalf of Lionism, Past President McLoughlin has received thirteen International President's Awards, three Extension Awards, and the Master Key Award. He has also received the "Ambassador of Good Will Award" for his commitment to the Association and its worldwide service efforts.

During his term as President, his theme was, "Lionism, People Caring For People" which motivated Lions across the globe to extend the hand of friendship and service to people everywhere.

Past President McLoughlin, the only individual from Connecticut to serve as our association's President, passed away after a lengthy illness.

PID Scott Storms

## Past International Director Scott Storms

Scott A. Storms, of Windsor Locks, Connecticut, USA, was elected to serve a two-year term as a director of The International Association of Lions Clubs at the association's 84th International Convention, held in Indianapolis, Indiana, USA, July 2-July 6, 2001.

Past Director Storms is an attorney.

A member of the Windsor Locks Lions Club since 1973, Past Director Storms has held many offices within the association, including club president, cabinet secretary/treasurer, Leadership Development chair, multiple district council chair and district governor. In addition, he has served as president of the Connecticut Lions Eye Research Foundation, Campaign SightFirst Sector Coordinator for Connecticut and Rhode Island and as a presenter at three USA/Canada Lions Leadership Forums.

In recognition of his service to the association, Past Director Storms has received numerous awards including the 100% Club President Award, the 100% District Governor's Award, the District Governor's Excellence Award, the Guiding Lion Award, the Rebuilding Lion Award, an Extension Award, three International President's Certificates of Appreciation, the International President's Leadership Award, three International President's Awards and the Ambassador of Good Will Award, the highest honor the association bestows upon its members. He is also a Master Key Member, a Connecticut Knight of the Blind and a Progressive Melvin Jones Fellow.

In addition to his Lion activities, Past Director Storms is active in numerous professional and community organizations. He is a member of the Connecticut and Massachusetts Bar Associations and an Eagle Scout and Merit Badge Counselor for the Boy Scouts of America. He has also served as a member of various boards and commissions for the Town of Windsor Locks, including chair of the Board of Education.

Past Director Storms and his wife, Dale, also a Lion and Melvin Jones Fellow, have two sons.

PID Otto P. Strobino
(1926 - 2007)

## Past International Director Otto Strobino

Otto Strobino of Cheshire was elected to serve a two year term as a director of the International Association of Lions Clubs at the associations 73rd International Convention held in St Louis, Missouri July 11-15, 1990.

PID Otto was a Life Member of the New Britain Lions Club where he had been a member since 1957. He held many positions with the association including club president, zone chairman, deputy district governor, district governor, and project director of the publication of the Connecticut Lions history. He was also responsible for the establishment of both the Lions Memorial Forest at the University of Connecticut and the Temporal Bone Bank in Connecticut. In addition he served as an appointee to the board from July 1994 through July 1995, and from July 2000 through July 2001. He also served as National/Multiple National Coordinator for Campaign Sight First, and served a two-year term as the President of the Connecticut Lions Eye Research Foundation.

In recognition of his many contributions to the Association, PID Otto received numerous awards, including the 100% President's Award, the 100% District Governor Award, three rebuilding Lions awards, four extension awards, five International Presidents Appreciation Awards, a Presidential Leadership award, five International President's awards, and the Ambassador of Good Will Award, the highest honor bestowed upon a member of the association. He was also a Progressive Melvin Jones Fellow and sponsored over ninety members. In addition he served as chairman of the Lead Gifts Committee for Campaign Sight First II.

PID Otto's wife Agnes can best be described as "The wind beneath his wings" and was usually found by his side during most Lion's events. Otto and Agnes had two children and five grand children.

His life was one of giving of himself for the betterment of mankind. Although he had recently celebrated his 80th birthday, he felt that his work was not yet finished, and did not have time to pause and reflect on a life filled with accomplishment in service to mankind. His death left a void that will not be easily filled.

## PID Harold Ashley

Harold Ashley, from Waterbury, was elected to serve a two-year term International Director of The International Association of Lions Clubs after his election at the 31$^{st}$ Convention held in New York on July 26-29, 1948.

Harold Ashley is well known in our state as the founder and first president of the Connecticut Lions Eye Research Foundation.

## PID Joseph W. Ganim

Joseph Ganim, from Trumbull, was elected to serve a two-year term International Director of The International Association of Lions Clubs after his election at the 47$^{th}$ Convention held in Toronto, Canada on July 8-11, 1964.

Joseph Ganim earned a Master Key Award for his tireless endeavor to invite new members to join the cause. His work also helped to create and build new Lions Clubs throughout

## PID Joseph L. Raub

Joseph Raub, from New London, served a two-year term as International Director of The International Association of Lions Clubs after his election at the 63$^{rd}$ Convention held in Chicago, Illinois on July 2-5, 1980.

During his years of Lionism, he promoted the idea of Lions Leadership training. He initiated the annual New England Leadership Seminars that are held each year in the fall. This inititative was among the successes that encouraged the first USA/Canada Forums. He also encouraged the statewide Train-the-trainer seminar series that would further encourage higher level Lion Leaders to train more leaders.

## The History of Lionism in Connecticut Committee

Shown are the members of the History of Lionism in Connecticut Committee. In the back row from the left are Mary Krogh, PDG; Bob Gyle, PCC; Mike Granatuck, PDG; Joe Porier, PDG; Dr. Stephen Polezonis, DG; George Ondrick, PDG; Dave Burgess, PCC; Dick Foote, PDG; Blanche Sewell; Syd Schulman, PCC. Seated are Joel Ragovin, PDG; Sue Ragovin; Frank Mauro, PCC; Keith Weurthner, PDG; Dan Uitti, PDG. Not shown are Terri Bousquet; Collette Anderson; George Salpietro; Carolyn A. Messier, PCC; Meryl Aronin; Eric C. Jacobson, PDG; James Bennett, PDG; John Gagain, PDG; Alan Daninhirsch, PCC; Richard C. Stathers, PDG; Judy Daninhirsch; Ralph Dolan; George "Curt" Fitch, PDG; Mary Krogh, PDG; Marie Salpietro; Rose Marie Spatafore, DG; Julianne Shilosky, DG; Robert Weiss, IPDG, Paul Maxwell, IPDG and Lion Dan "Zeno" Hadjstylianos.

# Acknowledgements

History is a record of the past, and bringing the past to life allows this record to live on forever. Bringing life to this work required the involvement of the many who devoted countless hours to the task. These are individuals whose reward was not financial, but something far more valuable; a sense of great accomplishment, which, of course, is nothing less than priceless.

This was a team effort, involving numerous individuals who assisted with the essential steps that ultimately lead to the publishing and distribution of this work. We cannot fully express our gratitude to the Lions team for their generosity of time, faith, talent and superb guidance. Without them, we would not have been able to surmount the tragedy of the passing of Past International Director, Otto Strobino who was the project director.

We are most grateful to Past Council Chairman Frank P. Mauro for stepping forward and assuming the most challenging role of project director following PID Otto Strobino's death in March, 2007. His leadership during a most difficult period allowed us to expeditiously bring this project to conclusion.

Every book must have editing, a massive undertaking. How fortunate we were to have the golden pens of Past District Governor Joel J. Ragovin and his wife, Lion Sue. The fruit of their labor is obvious, their creativity unequaled. Once the editing is finished, then comes the second massive undertaking, publishing. Again good fortune was on our side. Past District Governor Daniel A. Uitti's innate talent, his computer expertise and his profound knowledge of publishing made all our lives a little easier. Lions Joel, Sue and Dan, we cannot thank you enough.

The appendix of a book is challenging. Past District Governor W. Keith Wuerthner accepted that challenge. For the task of compiling facts and figures with meticulous accuracy, there is no equal. To you Lion Keith, our profound thanks and appreciation.

To our steering committee, Past Council Chairmen Sydney T. Schulman and Robert B. Gyle III, thank you for your thoughts, your ideas and most of all, your encouragement through many difficult times.

As with any writing, such as this, there are committees within committees. Our sincere appreciation and profound thanks to the General Committee members not previously mentioned: Lions Collette Anderson, Terri B. Bousquet, PDG Richard J. Foote, PCC Robert M. Redenz, PDG Robert Weiss, DG Dr. Stephen Polezonis, Dr. Keith Lemire and PDG Arthur Davies. Other members of various committees who contributed writings as well as other duties are: Lions: George Salpietro, PCC Carolyn A. Messier, Blanche Sewell, PCC Michael Granatuk, Meryl Aronin, PDG Eric C Jacobson, PDG James Bennett, PDG John Gagain, PCC Alan Daninhirsch, PDG Richard C. Stathers, Judy Daninhirsch, Ralph Dolan, PDG George "Curt" Fitch, PDG Mary Krogh, Elba Cruz Schulman, Marie Salpietro and Dan "Zeno" Hadjstylianos. A number of non-lions also contributed. Among those was Mona Gillet, who works with the NGO Section of the Department of Public Information at the United Nations.

We cannot forget the many Lions who devoted their time, talent and passion in completing their club's histories. The many hours the club historians devoted to research in an effort to uncover the facts, names, projects and events to insure that their club histories would be accurate and honor the unselfish service of their members are too numerous to calculate. To all the silent Lions, the committee offers a heartfelt thank you.

Our thanks to PID Otto and Agnes Strobino as well as PCC Frank and Lion Shirley Mauro for opening your homes so that our committee could conduct their business. Your hospitality contributed greatly to our ability to complete the task at hand.

The passing of Past International Director Otto Strobino put the publishing of this book in crisis. Throughout this turmoil, Multiple District Council 23 never wavered in its support for the project. For your endorsement and financial support, we are forever grateful.

To Lion Otto Strobino…here is your book.

The ad hoc History Committee

## Preface

A Look Back at the First Edition of the "History of Lionism in Connecticut."

Did You Know. . .
This is the Second Connecticut Lions History Book

Many Lions, Lionesses, Leos and Friends of Lions who are reading this new Connecticut Lions History book, may not realize that this is the second Connecticut Lions History book to be published.

The first book had 321 pages and a golden cover and not many of them are still around today. If you find one in your local public library, take a look at it and see how far we have come since the first book was published in 1986.

In the fall of 1979, Kenneth V. Olson of the New Britain Evening Lions Club, decided to act on an idea that had been on his mind for several years. Why not do a history of Lions in Connecticut? He discussed his idea with another member of his club, Curtis Jennings, who agreed to work with him on this ambitious project.

There would be two primary purposes in writing this history: First, it would record the work done by the Lions in the state to help others who were less fortunate and to make their communities better places in which to live. Secondly, it would contribute to the literature of volunteerism, and thus be a part of the social history of Connecticut.

The proposal had the strong support of Past District Governor Howard V. Wry and Otto P. Strobino, both of the New Britain Lions Club. Lion Otto would become District Governor in 1981. It would be necessary to obtain the support and approval of the Multiple District 23 Council of Governors, as the project would require the cooperation of all Lions Clubs in the state.

The Council gave its approval in 1980, and an ad hoc Committee was appointed to assist and advise. Olson and Jennings were designated the committee's co-chairmen. Other members of the committee included the following: District 23-A – PID Joseph Ganim, PDG Edward Hagerty, Lion John J. Murphy; District 23-B – PDG Nunzio Rosso, District Governor Otto Strobino, who became the Project Manager, and W. Keith Wuerthner, President of the New

Britain Lions Club. Keith served as Secretary-Treasurer to the ad hoc committee; District 23-C – PDG Richard Case, CST Everett Clark and Lion John Kromish.

All of us should be very proud of what we have accomplished since the 80's. We, the Lions of Connecticut have had a magnificent past, but even more importantly, our future is represented by a glowing light, the light of Lionism, which will show us the way to a an even better tomorrow.

## Foreword

State of Connecticut
Office of the Governor

It's Great To Be A Lion! These words were printed on the bumper sticker that was presented to me by my sponsor PDG Bob Gyle when I was installed as a Charter member of the Candlewood Lions Club in June of 1995. At that installation I met PID Otto Strobino whose words were an inspiration to the 40 new Lions and assorted dignitaries and guests who were in attendance.

Over the next decade I would see Lion Otto on numerous occasions and he was always the consummate gentleman and caring individual. Over the years he became a constant for me as he had been for all of Connecticut's Lions for many years. He would mention the fact that he was pleased I adopted "Marshal" a Fidelco guide dog who needed a home. He encouraged my having a CRIS radio show and in 2003 presented me with my Melvin Jones Fellowship.

The Lions have allowed the Governor's office to welcome many Lions dignitaries and invariably it was Lion Otto who would be the gracious host for these meetings. The Lions of Connecticut will miss him and so will I. It is a fitting reminder to all of Connecticut's Lions to have their history preserved in a book that was championed and initiated through his efforts. I am proud to be a Lion and it is great to be a Lion and it's even greater to be Connecticut Lion.

Lion M. Jodi Rell
Governor

# A Lions' Perspective
By Scott A. Storms, PID

Since my election as an International Director in 2001, Lion Dale and I have traveled over 250,000 miles for our Association. In such hot spots as Cut Bank, Montana, Rainbow City, Alabama, and Escalante, Utah (with a population of 850 and two Lions Clubs!), we have met some great Lions and Lionesses, and have seen the wonderful service that members of our Association perform every day for those in need. We are better Lions for it, and indeed are richer for having witnessed how Lions are affecting positive world change...one person at a time.

Whenever we travel and are asked about our state, we reply that we come from a small town in Connecticut, one of the six (6) New England States. We continue by saying that our state and our region are more than places on the map tucked away in the northeast corner of our country ... they are special places, where small town traditions and values are held dear, places where Lions Clubs have flourished as a result of a deeply rooted sense of community spirit, and where the "lend a hand to your neighbor" philosophy and principles of Lionism are part of our daily lives.

As the great anthropologist Margaret Meade once said, "Never doubt that a small group of committed citizens can change the world." I believe that the Lions of the world, and more specifically, the Lions of Connecticut, are members of such a group.

For over 90 years, the Lions of the world have led all others in caring for the blind, the afflicted and the underprivileged. Lions have provided transportation and companionship for our elderly citizens and education and mentoring for our youth. They have responded to catastrophes in distant places and built ballparks in their own backyards. Lions members have clothed the needy and distributed food to local food banks, while collecting used eye glasses that have been sent around the world. Lions Clubs have built bridges over raging waters for transportation and over cultural differences as a means of promoting international understanding among the peoples of the world through youth exchange and other cultural exchanges between our members. Lions and LCIF have built homes for the disabled through Habitat for Humanity, orphanages and schools for displaced youth, and eye banks, hospitals and low vision centers for the visually impaired. We have restored sight to millions through SightFirst and our continuing commitment to meet the challenge of Helen Keller.

In Connecticut, Lions have been serving others for over 85 years. Beginning with the Bridgeport Host Lions Club, our record of achievement and accomplishment is filled with service activities and projects intended to better the quality of life within and without our local communities. In our early years, our Lions busied themselves with providing direct community assistance to local people by supplying milk to under nourished children, aiding the public schools, supporting youth camps and providing eye glasses and eye surgeries to those in need. More recently, while continuing to provide needed community assistance, the support of low vision centers, CRIS radio, eye research at Yale University and the University of Connecticut, FIDELCO Guide Dogs, community based eye screenings, and Special Olympics have further captured the attention of the Connecticut Lions. In the 1990's, the Multiple District was recognized as a leader in the Association's campaign to eradicate preventable blindness around the world, and it is once again answering the call to serve those with eye problems worldwide through Campaign SightFirst II. The Connecticut Lions were honored to serve as a model for the Association's Lions Eye Health Program and have been recognized several times by Lions Clubs International for their continuing commitment to this project.

Our state is also recognized as having a strong tradition of leadership and dedication to our International Association and the peoples of the world. Nine Connecticut Lions have been elected to serve as International Directors and, in 1977, one such Lion, Joseph M. McLaughlin, served as International President.

Whenever and wherever called upon, the Connecticut Lions have stepped up to the challenge of serving their fellow man. In the aftermath of the World Trade Center disaster of September 11, 2001 and again in 2005, after Hurricane Katrina, Connecticut Lions contributed financial support through LCIF as well as expending many volunteer hours at the sites of these disasters by delivering needed services and supplies to those in need.

As Lions, we have left a unique and indelible mark on the lives of the people we touch, and we should never doubt that what we do in our local clubs truly makes a difference! As Helen Keller once said, "Alone we can do so little, together we can do so much." Together, the Connecticut Lions, in concert with others, can and will continue to change the world!

## Transitions In Lionism
Observations of a Connecticut Lion
By PDG Dick Foote

Early Lions members were businessmen and professionals who met in restaurants, usually at noontime. They joined clubs in their own hometown for the most part, or in the city in which they worked. This adherence to a commercial/mercantile milieu is reflected in the words of the lions Code of Ethics "…that I may merit a reputation for quality of service." "…to demand all fair remuneration or profit as my just due, but to accept no profit or success at the price of my own self-respect lost because of unfair advantage taken…" "To remember that in building up my business it is not necessary to tear down another's; to be loyal to my clients or customers and true to myself."

There were, furthermore, concomitant attendance requirements. Missed meetings could be made up under certain specified rules; by visiting another club, attending a sub-committee or Board of Directors meeting of his own club, or visiting the headquarters of The International Association of Lions Clubs in Chicago.

Any of these had to be accomplished within a certain number of days before or after the missed meeting; verified by card or letter to his club's secretary.

With Lions Clubs made up entirely of men, it is not too difficult to imagine meetings of gentlemen in business attire, smoking cigars and drinking brandy. Business and politics could not be discussed during meetings lest the perpetrators be fined, but of course, contacts were made, friendships formed, and great times were had by all. Lions were the acknowledged leaders of their communities, and looked and acted accordingly.

But it was a woman who gave them their direction. Helen Keller, speaking to an assembly of "…strong and brave and kind…" Lions at Cedar Point, Ohio on June 30, 1925, asked them to become "Knights of the Blind in this crusade against darkness." The International Association of Lions Clubs has had vision care as its primary focus ever since.

Lionism was born during the First World War and was in its formative years during the years between the two great wars. Even though there were hard economic times on both sides of the Atlantic, one country was under the heavy-handed rule of a ruthless dictator who spread violence and hate, while at the same time, a nation like ours was able to produce an organization whose very existence depended on people who promoted humanitarian service to their fellow-man.

After the Second World War, times were good. Servicemen who returned home from the war were able to get good jobs, and many of them entered college under the G.I. Bill. They eventually realized that they had more free time to do things that they weren't able to do before they went away. Along with leisure activities and time spent on "Do It Yourself" projects, these men also became involved in church and community activities. Where heretofore these latter two activities were primarily in the realm of the more prominent "business/ professional" class, our nation now witnessed a growth of interest and participation in all aspects of community life by the middle class. Lionism was one of the beneficiaries of this trend.

Things went along quite smoothly for a number of years. Leo and Lioness clubs were organized, signifying Lions International's attempts at becoming more inclusive. For many clubs, projects became larger and more involved in response to perceived community needs. A good share of this growth can be attributed to Connecticut Lions' support for Connecticut Lions Eye Research Foundation, American School for the Deaf, the American Diabetes Foundation, and the Fidelco Guide Dog Foundation, to name a few.

Increased support for such programs required increased help with necessary Lions projects. In 1987, women were granted full rights and privileges of membership in Lions Clubs. Almost immediately, most Connecticut Lioness clubs converted to Lions Clubs. A few years later, former Lioness Club members were able to add their time of service as Lionesses to their Lions years of seniority.

Leo Clubs, as of this writing, are on the rise across the state. These youngsters are proving themselves to be invaluable as helpers to their sponsoring Lions Clubs, at fairs and outings; helping with accumulation of Christmas gifts and toys for Lions' Christmas Basket projects, and still carry on projects of their own; baby-sitting so parents can attend meetings, helping with homework, raising funds foe Fidelco or Habitat For Humanity, to mention a few.

With a changing world, organizations like Lions Clubs, as an international association must change with it. Whether we like it or not, The United States of America, as the founding nation of Lionism, is falling behind in its percentage of total membership. Also, our average age creeps ever upward. But there are hopeful signs on the horizon as well. Events such as the USA/Canada Forum have drawn Lions from both countries closer together; creating new incentives, friendships and enthusiasm.

Campaign SightFirst and Campaign SightFirst II clearly show what Lions can do. Disaster relief in recent years, and Lions' participation in it does the same. The rise of youth involvement throughout the world through the Leo program bodes well for future membership; including a diminution of the "average" age of Lions members.

## Table of Contents

## Table of Photos

# Table of Appendices

## Chapter 1 - Lions Inspiration

## Helen Keller/Mark Twain in Connecticut

Samuel Clemens, whose pen name was "Mark Twain," was a Connecticut resident for much of his later life.

Helen Keller, gave Lionism its mission, was already impressed with his writings, when, at the age of 14, she first met Mark Twain in March, 1895. He was quite impressed with her extraordinary intellect and spirit, and paid tribute to her in his book "Following the Equator." In an article he wrote in the December 1893, issue of the St. Nicholas Magazine, he referred to Miss Keller as "the most marvelous person of her sex that has existed on this earth since Joan of Arc." Thus began a friendship that would last until Twain's death in 1910.

In late 1896, Mark Twain appealed to his friend H.H. Rogers, then head of Standard Oil, to support Keller's education. Rogers quietly paid her way through Radcliffe, where she was admitted in 1904 and Miss Keller graduated magna cum laude four years later.

In the same year that Helen Keller graduated from Radcliffe, Olivia, Mark Twains wife of 34 years, passed away. Twain decided to leave Hartford and purchased a 161 acre estate known as "Innocents at Home," in Redding, Connecticut. There he built a magnificent new home, renamed the estate "Stormfield," and took up residence on June 18, 1908. That winter, Twain invited Miss Keller and her life-long teacher, Anne Sullivan (then Mrs. John Macy), to a party at Stormfield to promote Miss Keller's new book *The World I Live In*. In his *Biography of Mark Twain*, Albert Bigelow Pain recounts the following memories of that party:

"It was fascinating to watch her, and to realize with what a store of knowledge she had lightened the black silence of her physical life. To see Mark Twain and Helen Keller together is something not easily forgotten. When Mrs. Macy communicated his words to her with what seemed a lightening touch of her fingers, her face radiated every shade of his meaning - humorous, serious, pathetic."

One can only imagine the electricity that must have been present in that house in Redding, Connecticut that night between Mark Twain and the young lady he referred to in his letter to H.H. Rogers as "This marvelous child."

Helen Keller moved to Easton, Connecticut in 1936, continuing her connection with our state. She died there on June 1, 1968. In his eulogy at her funeral, Senator Lister Hill said, "She will live on, one of the few, immortal names not born to die. Her spirit will endure as long as man can read and stories can be told of the woman who showed the world there are no boundaries to courage and faith."

Note: Special thanks to Patti Philippon, Collections Manager at the Mark Twain House and Museum, for her assistance with the research for this article.

## The White Cane, and its Place in History

During Lion George Bonham's term as President of the Peoria, Illinois Lions Club in 1930, he witnessed a problem. He watched a blind man in the process of trying to cross a street, only to be left helpless as traffic whirled around him. Futility tapping his black cane on the pavement, the man was totally isolated in the middle of a wide street where drivers had no way of knowing that he could not see them or in any way understand his impairment.

Lion Bonham pondered over the problem. Suddenly he had the answer. Paint the cane white and put a wide band of red around it! When the blind person crosses the street, let him extend it so that everyone can see and be aware of his blindness.

He presented the idea to the Peoria Lions Club, and the members voted unanimously in favor of it. Canes were painted and given to the blind in the city. The Peoria City Council passed an ordinance giving the right of way to a blind person using the white cane.

At the International Convention in Toronto, Ontario in 1931, a resolution was introduced describing the Peoria Illinois Lions Club's White Cane Program.

During World War II, the Veterans Administration set up rehabilitation centers for blind war veterans. Techniques for using white canes were refined at these facilities. The extended cane is moved in a semi circle in rhythm with the user's footsteps, with a light touch on the ground at the end of each ark. This enables the blind person to feel obstacles such as gratings, steps, posts, and walls.

By 1956 every state in the United States passed White Cane safety laws, giving any person using a white cane the right of way at crossings.

In 1964, President Lyndon Johnson issued a proclamation that marked the climax of the campaign by the blind to gain endorsement of their rights as pedestrians. With Johnson's proclamation, the white cane became officially recognized.

. Congress, by a joint resolution approved on October 6, 1964, authorized the President to proclaim October 15, 1964 as White Cane Safety Day.

Many Lions Clubs use the white cane as a part of their fundraising programs for the visually impaired. A lapel pin in the form of a small white cane is given to each contributor.

Today the white cane holds much significance. It is a simple and indispensable tool, which gives greater freedom and mobility to the blind, and allows them to participate and contribute fully to the community in which they live. It is a symbol of independence and, by its presence, increases public awareness about the abilities of people who are visually impaired.

## The "Opening Eyes" Program

Connecticut Lion, Dr. Sue Danberg, a member of the Glastonbury Lions Club, had a vision. She was quite aware of the importance of Special Olympics in the lives of the many who were involved annually. She also became aware of the special needs of this unique group of athletes. Thus, she was instrumental in the formation of a partnership between LCI and Special Olympics. Through her efforts an LCIF grant of 3.3 million dollars allowed for the creation of an "Opening Eyes Program."

Since 2001, during the first weekend of June, the "Opening Eyes Program" has been held at Southern Connecticut University at the Connecticut State Games of the Special Olympics. Each year approximately 231 athletes have their vision tested. Most athletes walked away with a new set of glasses, which are made at the location.

Approximately 20 Lions and 30 eyecare professionals work as a team on each shift during the two-day event. The Lions who attend the event consider involvement in this project as one of their most rewarding experiences as a Lion.

The "Opening Eyes Program" is today sponsored in 45 states across our nation and in 35 countries throughout the world. In Connectiut, it has become a program of the Connecticut Lions Eye Research Foundation, administered by a committee of the foundation.

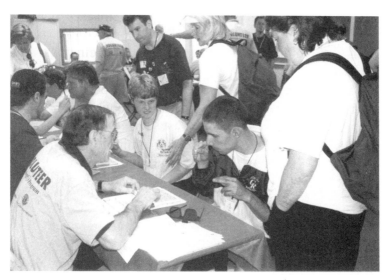

Loren Otter, PDG works as a volunteer at registration desk for the Opening Eyes program in conjunction with the Special Olympics.

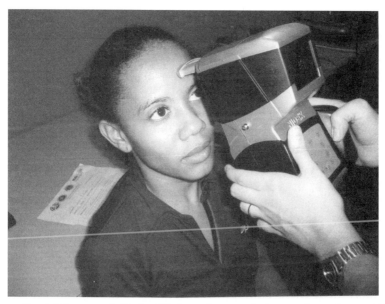

Connecticut Lions and Duke University work in conjunction with the First Lady's program, "Progressando" to provide needed Eye Care during Ophthalmology Mission to the province of El Seybo of the Dominican Republic.

## The Ophthalmology Mission to El Seybo
A Dominican Republic - Connecticut Lions Club Partnership

By Otto Strobino, PID and John R. Gagain Sr., PDG

*Past International Director Otto Strobino began writing the following article. He had actively participated in two advanced ophthalmology missions co-organized by the Lions Clubs of the Dominican Republic and the State of Connecticut. All of this was in cooperation with the President and First Lady of the Dominican Republic. Upon the passing of PID Otto in March 2007, Past District Governor, John R. Gagain Sr. completed the article in honor of PID Otto, and all those who shared his vision for bringing sight to the thousands of underprivileged Dominican citizens.*

Like many American citizens that have decided to spend their family vacation in the sunny tropical destination of Punta Cana in the eastern part of the Dominican Republic, PDG John R. Gagain Sr. and his wife embarked on such a journey in 1995. This was five-years before their son, John Jr., decided to move and live there at the invitation of Dr. Leonel Fernandez, President of the Dominican Republic.

The area was quite beautiful and the people most gracious, but the tourist industry was young and the staff inexperienced. Often food that was served was spoiled, and the sanitation systems were backed up. This, coupled with the sight of armed military on the beach, left visitors with a less than pleasing memory of their visit, enough to decide never to return.

Not until John Jr. met his Dominican wife Erika and decided to spend the rest of his life in the Caribbean country, did John Sr. and his wife decide to visit the Bella Vista Lions Club in Santo Domingo, Dominican Republic in 2003.

PDG Maximo Montero, his wife, Lion Taty and many other Lions held a large community-wide event in honor of then Vice-District Governor Gagain. The Lions thanked him and his wife for thinking of their small club during their visit to the island.

Gagain and Montero met on the Internet prior to the event. The Bella Vista Club was inspired. All were determined, after learning of John Sr.'s first visit, to ensure that this time he would leave with a sense of hospitality and warmth and would want to return to the Dominican Republic.

John Sr. did leave with a deep desire to return the favor. He asked his son John Jr. to begin thinking of how his Governorship of District 23-A could help serve the people of the Dominican Republic in partnership with their Lions Club.

John Jr. began coordinating the efforts of District 23-A with the clubs of the Dominican Republic. This resulted in the development of the first Joint Eye Screening and Ophthalmology Mission co-organized by the Lions of both countries in conjunction with the President's and First Lady's Offices, Duke University, Lumenis Laser, American Airlines, Allergan, the Ministries of Tourism and Public Health, and Elias Santana Hospital.

The First Lady's program, "Progressando," which teaches community and family values to the disadvantaged, began in the impoverished Province of El Seibo in the eastern part of the Dominican Republic, primarily because over 30,000 families had vision problems, which included glaucoma, stigmatism and cataracts among others.

The Lions of District 23-A and the Dominican Republic decided to help Dr. Margarita Cedeno de Fernandez, the First Lady of the Dominican Republic and the people of El Seibo. John Sr., then Governor of District 23-A and Arturo Liriano, then Governor of R1, (the District of El Seibo) signed a cooperative agreement to bring assistance to thousands in need of medical attention.

The First Lady, with much enthusiasm, decided to make the signing of the agreement an official ceremony in her office in Santo Domingo, with the presence of many of the most renowned individuals from public life and media in the Dominican Republic.

The preparations for the first Joint Eye Screening and Ophthalmology Mission was but a beginning. The Lions Clubs of the Dominican Republic and District 23-A agreed to invite His Excellency, Dr. Leonel Fernandez, President of the Dominican Republic to be sworn in as the first standing Head of State and Government to serve as an honorary Lion.

PID Otto Strobino delivered an inspirational speech dedicated to President Fernandez, the Lions, and the people of the Dominican Republic. Lions Otto, John Sr., Maximo Montero, and the Lions of the Dominican Republic pinned President Fernandez and inducted him in as an Honorary Lion. President Fernandez told those that were gathered that it was both an honor and privilege to be sworn in as a member of an organization that holds service, values, ethics, and ideals as its foundation. His heartfelt speech delivered a message that service should be the motto of not only his government, but also those of other countries throughout Latin America and the Caribbean.

The work initiated by the many involved in this humanitarian effort has only begun. Allergan and Lumenis Laser donated equipment valued at thousands of dollars. After the equipment was used, much of it remained so that it could be used for other programs in the Dominican Republic. Not only was this a humanitarian effort for immediate assistance but it also served as a teaching mission so that the country's hospitals and clinics could repeat the task on their own in the future. This great humanitarian effort carried out through the joint efforts of Lions Clubs of two nations with the cooperation of their governments.

In 2005, this effort became a project of the Connecticut Lions Eye Research Foundation with the intent to provide support to PDG Ganain as its permanent chairperson.

## Connecticut Lions Offer Assistance to Katrina Victims

It was perhaps one of the most devastating hurricanes to hit Louisiana and surrounding states. Both rich and poor were impacted by nature's fury, but those without resources, the poorest of the poor, were most severely affected.

Under normal circumstances, when the order came to evacuate, the majority would have driven their families to safety. Many did not have cars. There were few modes of transportation available. They could not obey orders to evacuate, as transportation was not available. For those lucky enough to find transportation, few had sufficient funds to meet the cost of lodging.

Local, state and federal government resources were stretched beyond their capability to assist the poor who were left to fend for themselves without money, without any feasible plan to continue life outside of the affected area. There were pregnant women and very young children, the disabled and the elderly, unable to cope, but forced to do everything possible to survive the devastation, to perhaps live for just one more day in hope that help would come, but for many that day never came. Death was at their doorstep and help was nowhere to be found. They had in effect been abandoned.

The Lions of Connecticut recognized that a need existed, and from each and every District they responded.

In December 2005 and again in April 2006 then District Governor David Burgess led District 23-C in their efforts to bring relief to the victims of hurricanes Katrina and Rita. He personally delivered cash and materials collected by the Lions of the District to the Lake Charles Louisiana Lions Club, and they in turn distributed in excess of 20,000 pounds of needed supplies and $10,000 in cash to the victims. Lion Steve Eaton provided the truck and personally paid for transporting food and materials to the affected areas.

District 23-A responded as well. During Labor Day weekend in September 2005, the Yalesville/Wallingford Lions Club collected goods for victims of Hurricane Katrina. The communities of Yalesville and Wallingford donated food, blankets, water, baby toiletries and clothing valued at over $25,000. There was a three-day event chaired by Past President Sandra Thibodeau with the help of club members, family and friends who gave up their weekend to participate in this project. An area trucking company donated its services delivering the collected goods to the Hartford Armory, and from this central point members of the Army Reserve delivered the goods to New Orleans.

In 2004 Karen Boutin of the East Windsor Lions Club spearheaded a relief project. She was able to unite the clubs of District 23-B to collect tons of supplies, and these in turn were loaded on to four 53-foot trailers and delivered to the affected areas.

The Lions of Connecticut have collectively combined their efforts to serve those in need. The Lions of MD-23 can proudly say that "We serve best when we serve together."

Lion Glenn Boglisch works as a volunteer with District 23-B in their efforts to prepare relief materials and ship them to victims of Hurricane Katrina.

David Burgess, PCC works as a volunteer with District 23-C in their efforts to prepare relief materials and ship them to victims of Hurricane Katrina.

## Chapter 2 - Connecticut & Lions International Projects

## History of the Connecticut Lions Eye Research Foundation

The year was 1953, and the Connecticut Council of Governors had a vision; a vision of a major project that would bring all the clubs of Multiple District 23 together, to act as one to fight blindness.

The Council appointed a committee to investigate several possibilities.

The committee found that there was a huge amount of money directed towards the blind; however, a very small percentage was allocated toward finding the cause of or cure for blindness. Actually only one percent of all monies allocated were being spent on research.

The committee asked the Council for approval to establish the "Connecticut Lions Eye Research Program." This was later changed to the "Connecticut Lions Eye Research Foundation."

During the Connecticut Lions State Convention held at Lake Copake in New York June 6, 1954, the delegates of Multiple District 23 voted to establish an eye research clinic. The facility would be under the auspices of the Yale University Department of Public Health and located at the Yale University School of Medicine in New Haven. It would, however, be necessary for three-quarters of the clubs to agree to contribute at least three dollars per member, but no more than five dollars per member during the next five years. This was accomplished and reported at the Mid Winter Conference on February 12, 1955.

The founding officers were President Harold Ashley, PID; Vice President Richard Case, International Counselor; Secretary, A. Leroy Anderson, International Counselor and Treasurer Spencer B. Hirst, International Counselor.

Several notables were honorary members of the board including Connecticut Governor Abraham Ribicoff; TV show host Ed Sullivan; Vernon Lippard, Dean, Yale University, and Stanley Osbourn, Connecticut Commissioner of Public Health.

A charter for the foundation was issued by the State of Connecticut on July 20th, 1956, designating the Connecticut Lions Eye Research Foundation as a non-profit corporation.

In 1961, Marvin L. Sears, M.D. was hired as a full time Director of Research, and served in that position until July 1993. Today the

Department of Ophthalmology and Visual Science is under the direction of James C. Tsai, M.D., Chairman. M. Bruce Shields, M.D. served as Chairman from 1996 until October of 2006.

It is interesting to note that Yale, during the early years, set aside 100 square feet for a laboratory and provided Dr. Sears with one assistant. Today the research facilities at Yale have a staff of over 25, and are housed in their own multi million-dollar facility, the Boardman Building, which the Connecticut Lions helped to renovate with a $500,000 donation. It is in this building that the Connecticut Lions Eye Research Foundation maintains an office. Research at Yale has resulted in the development of "Timolol" which has been found to be very effective in the treatment of glaucoma. As the foundation grew, our involvement extended into other areas. Through the efforts of Dr. James O'Rourke, the Lions' Eye Center, a second research facility, was created at the University of Connecticut's Farmington Medical Center. In 1974 Dr. O'Rourke announced the launch of a Micro Vascular Retinal Imaging Project using Lions grants. As a result, a screening program for children with juvenile diabetes was developed using the equipment and technology developed from that project.

Through grants from our foundation, organisms recovered from laboratory mice and Australian cattle aided in the development of a cure for river blindness.

Several hospitals in Connecticut have been the beneficiaries of Lions' grants, allowing for example, the purchase of equipment to facilitate various types of eye surgery.

The Foundation, in the beginning, primarily relied on annual club donations and income from "SightSaver" Day (formerly called "Lions Day" or "Candy Day"). When the Foundation needed additional funds for the Boardman Building project, the car raffle was introduced. Since that time, both the memorial card and recognition card programs were introduced, as well as the annual golf tournament.

Today funds are being raised through the 21st Century Fund as well as the "Knight of the Blind" awards. Beginning in 1990, it was the Foundation's hope to raise $2,100,000 by the year 2000. Since that time, the Foundation extended the target date to coincide with the Foundations 50th Anniversary. This money would be the base endowment for a fund that would insure that we would be able to meet the future needs of the blind and visually impaired.

The Connecticut Lions Eye Research Foundation has had a magnificent history, providing funds that have allowed scientists to continue to work so that one day, together, we will find a cure for all forms of preventable blindness.

In this early photo, Dr. Marvin Sears conducts a tour of the Yale Eye Research facilities in New Haven to Lions Club members.

Connecticut Lions are presented with a tour of the Eye Research facilities at the University of Connecticut Medical Center in Farmington.

Sydney Schulman, PCC; Robert Redenz, PCC; Rocky Cingari, PDG; John Gagain, PDG; and Michael Del Re, Jr. PDG gather at the Wall of Benefactors recognition plaque that honors that major donors of the CT Lions Macular Degeneration Research program at the Yale Eye Research facilities in New Haven.

The Connecticut Lions make use of the State of Connecticut Specialty License Plate program to help raise funds for Eye Research programs through the Connecticut Lions Eye Research Foundation.

## History of the CLERF held PGA Event

In August of 1996, the Connecticut Lions Eye Reasearch Foundation hosted an exiting PGA event at the Woodway Country Club in Darien. The event raised approximately $110,000 for the single day event, and attracted several well know professional golfers to our state.

The event began with an early morning shotgun golf tournament, where amatuers teamed up with local section golf teaching professionals. The top sponsors were teamed up with Senior PGA touring pro Larry Nelson, who later became the tour's top money winner in 2000. The Senior PGA renamed itself the Champions Tour in 2002.

After lunch, a Skins Game format tournament began, featuring Golf's great Arnold Palmer, Peter Jacobsen, Mike Hill and David Frost. David Frost was a favorite, since he was the 1994 Greater Hartford Open winner. Mike Hill was the Senior PGA top money winner in 1991. Peter Jacoben later became the Greater Hartford Open winner in 2003; and has always been a favorite in Hartford.

The Skins Game was sponsored by Southern New England Telephone. It attracted a crowd of over 3,000 spectators, who followed the foursome through the game through the early afternoon.

This project was first proposed by Lion John Boscarino of the Windsor Locks Lions Club, who, working in concert with the officers of the Foundation, developed and planned the event for at least two years before hosting a pilot golf event early in 1994, featuring golf legend Arnold Palmer. This smaller event proved that the Connecticut Lions could develop a major event and led to the later skins game format. Lions from all three Districts participated in making these golf events the most successful fundraising activities held by the Foundation since its inception in 1956.

# History of the Lions Low Vision Centers in Connecticut

In 1989, the Lions of District 23-B were approached by the then Executive Director of the Board of Education and Services for the Blind, Past District Governor George Precourt, to enter into a new arena of service for the visually impaired in Connecticut. His proposal was to open a center where visually impaired and legally blind individuals could come for vision rehabilitation and be given aids and devices.

Receiving hundreds of requests at his agency for assistance, by many who had difficulty managing their activities of daily living due to significant vision loss, he recognized the need for individuals who did not meet the criteria of legal blindness, to receive low vision aids and devices. The State of Connecticut was providing services for the legally blind, but by statute, was unable to assist the thousands of other requests. Only an organization like the Lions would be able to answer this need.

Working closely with then District Governor, Scott A. Storms, PID, the Lions of District 23-B put together a committee for the purpose of opening the first low vision rehabilitation center. Fund raising began and a Board of Directors was formed in 1989. Clients, both visually impaired and legally blind, came to the center for evaluation of their activities of daily living, the impact that vision loss was having in their lives and then, without charge, were given aids and devices to assist them. The success was enormous and the impact on the lives of those in need was life changing.

District Governor of 23-A, Raymond Zaleski became interested in this program, and, working with the Bridgeport Lions Club, found a location for a new Low Vision Center in Fairfield County. By late in 1990, the Lions of District 23-A opened the Lions Low Vision Centers of Fairfield and New Haven Counties, on Brewster Street in Bridgeport and soon after in West Haven, Connecticut at BESB's workshop for the blind.

In 1992, in District 23-C, District Governor Kenneth Craig began the groundwork needed to place a center in Eastern Connecticut. In 1993, under District Governor Frank Mauro's leadership, The Lions Low Vision Center of Eastern Connecticut was opened at the Uncas on the Thames Hospital in Norwich, Connecticut. This finally meant that visually impaired people from all over the state could now be helped closer to their homes.

From 1993 until the present, although locations of the Lions Low Vision Centers have changed, the services provided have continued to grow. With the employment of low vision therapists, occupational therapists and vision rehabilitation teachers, thousands of visually impaired have been helped. Many of these people have maintained their dignity, independence and have made the adaptations necessary to continue their activities of daily living.

Our partnership with the Yale School of Ophthalmology has provided residents with a low vision component in their curriculum. Meriden Lion, Dr. David Parke, Professor of Ophthalmology, oversees the Lions Low Vision Center at Yale. His teaching has been invaluable to the residents who have gone through that program over the years.

The Lions Low Vision Centers provide glare control, magnification devices, telescopic devices, lighting, rehabilitation, teaching in the use of aids and devices, adaptive technology, safety, mobility issues, and counseling in adapting to vision loss.

During the years following 1993, satellites have opened with partnerships with local hospitals. Direct partnerships have been established with Yale-New Haven Hospital, Greenwich Hospital, Danbury Hospital, Bridgeport Hospital, New Britain General Hospital and Bristol Hospital. The Niantic Senior Center, the Torrington Senior Center, a mobile Lions bus in District 23-C and the First Congregational Church in Waterbury provide space for our satellites. In 2006, the Lions of 23-B partnered with the Fidelco Guide Dog Foundation to open a satellite on its premises.

There are collectively 11 satellite locations throughout the state. They have been geographically located to make access to them easier for those who need the low vision services.

# History of the District 23-C Lions Low Vision Centers

The District 23-C Low Vision Centers were established with an initial pledge of seed money from the Lyme-Old Lyme Lions Club.

The first organizational meeting was held on September 25, 1992 in Old Lyme. The name "Lions Low Vision Center of Eastern Connecticut" was adopted and bylaws were prepared.

A law firm prepared copies of the bylaws and certificate of incorporation and filed it with the office of the Secretary of State. Lion Harry Best agreed to prepare the 501(c)(3) application.

District Governor Ken Craig prepared grant applications to both Lions Club International Foundation (LCIF) and Connecticut Lions Eye Research Foundation (CLERF). As a result, a grant in the amount of $35,000 was received from LCIF and $12,900 from CLERF.

At a meeting held on December 7, 1992, the following officers were elected to serve until the date of the first annual meeting:

President:  Lion John B. Musgrave
Secretary: Lion Diane (Pettit) Bielski
Treasurer: Lion Harry Best
Directors:  DG Kenneth Craig, IPDG Arthur Davies, PDG William K. Allen II, Zone Chairman Mario Lupone, Lion John A. Collins lll & Lion Dr. Thomas Wagner.

The first Annual meeting of the Lions Low Vision Center of Eastern Connecticut was held at the Kutshers Resort in Monticello, NY on May 22, 1993, where the first board of directors was elected.

The Center was officially opened on April 30, 1994 at the University of Connecticut Health Center, located in the Uncas on the Thames facility in Norwich, CT. The Center was opened with a lease agreement between the Low Vision Center, the state's Board of Education and Services for the Blind (BESB), and the University of Connecticut. Technician Heidi Ross, under contract to BESB, was hired by the center.

The Low Vision Center continued to operate at Uncas on the Thames until it moved to its present on November 27, 1998.

A satellite office was opened in Niantic, CT at the East Lyme Senior Center in August of 1999 to better serve the clients living in the shoreline communities.

In the spring of 2001, the Board of Directors and a committee of interested Lions started what became an annual Golf Tournament. This event provides much needed additional funding for the centers. Also at that time, the Board of Directors and a committee of interested Lions met with the Portland Lions and agreed to take responsibility for their donut booth at the Hebron Lions Fair held in September of each year. This venture also became an annual source of income for the centers.

During this same period, Vice District Governor Diane (Pettit) Bielski met with the District Governor from District 33-A in Massachusetts, about acquiring their ten-year old Sightmobile.

The Board of Directors voted to purchase the Sightmobile, PDG Eric Jacobson wrote a grant, and, with the help of ID Scott Storms, was able to obtain $15,000 from Lions Clubs International Foundation (LCIF) to make the purchase.

The Sightmobile was transferred to the Low Vision Center on November 1, 2002, expanding the availability of services of the center. The vehicle also provided much needed publicity about the centers and has also been utilized by many Lions Clubs for their eye screenings as part of the Lions Eye Health Program (LEHP).

In late 2005, it was determined that due to the increasing cost of maintaining this aging vehicle and with its diminished use in the field, it would be in the best interest of the centers to offer it for sale. It was sold and a new vehicle was purchased.

During the early stages of the development of the centers, there were considerable disagreements between a member of the staff and the board, as well as the questionable support of BESB. Strong leadership, a will to survive, and the knowledge that the visually handicapped in our district desperately needed low vision services, brought our Low Vision Center out of turmoil to totally focus on serving this very vulnerable population.

The Lions Clubs of District 23-C have supported the Low Vision Center since it opened in 1994 with over $250,000 in donations. The Board of Directors' additional fund raising ventures and grants have brought the total amount raised to $340,000 as of April 2004, the tenth anniversary of their Low Vision Centers.

## History of Journey for Sight

The Journey for Sight Walk-a-thon project began in District B and was supported by Lions Clubs International, where banners, and supporting pins and press releases were available to clubs that participated.

The District B Chairmen, Lions Jim Wrinn and Carolyn Messier visited the Griswold Regional Lions Club for a presentation about the project in 1992. At the time, DG Kenneth Craig was spearheading the formation of the Lions Low Vision Center of Eastern Connecticut and was pursuing funding for this project. The Griswold Regional Lions Club, chaired by Lion Marie Salpietro, sponsored the first Journey for Sight Walk-a-thon in District C. During that year, it was presented as a zone-wide project and funds raised were used to support the formation of the Lions Low Vision Center.

The following year it expanded to a region-wide project, due to the interest of the area clubs. In 1994-1995 DG Eric Jacobson adopted the walk as a district project and appointed Lion Marie Salpietro as its first District chairperson. A district committee of interested Lions across the district was formed, many of whom are still on the committee today. Funding was then split 50-50 with 50% designated for a district project and the remaining 50% left to the club's discretion.

Since that time club participation and funds raised has increased yearly, resulting in hundreds of thousands of dollars raised for the district projects, and has become, for some clubs, their major fund raiser. It is also the only district fundraiser and has become a fun day for Lions to get together while making a huge difference.

# History of Connecticut Lions Eyeglass Recycling

Each of our three Districts approaches the collection of thousands of pairs of used eyeglasses differently.

Individual Lions Clubs in District "A" collect used eyeglasses, sort and forward them to the New Jersey Lions Eye Glass Recycling center operated by the New Jersey Lions.

District "B" collects the used eyeglasses at their two regional breakfast events, and ship them to the New Britain Lions Club, which in turn disposes of broken frames, cases and other non-essential items. The glasses are then packed and, as in District "A", shipped to the LCI Recycling Center operated by the New Jersey Lions Clubs. The New Jersey Lions have a contract with the New Jersey Department of Corrections.

Under the contract the inmates of a prison in Avonel, New Jersey work with equipment provided by the New Jersey Lions. The glasses are cleaned and sorted according to optometric scale using machinery that detects the power of the lenses. The glasses are then graded and packed with the appropriate labels.

Virtually all glasses from the New Jersey Recycling Center are sent to third world countries and disaster relief areas. The glasses are usually sent as "accompanying baggage" with medical, optometric, religious or disaster relief missions going to these countries. Occasionally they are sent directly to Lions Clubs where needed, but never sent directly to overseas governments or their agencies.

Some of the clubs in District "C" collect used eye glasses, sort, and ship them directly to a third world nation. Other clubs in the District send eyeglasses that are collected to one of the Lions Clubs International Eyeglass Recycling Centers. The center closest to Connecticut is located in Roanoke, VA.

Clubs shipping eyeglasses to the regional centers sort and remove eyeglass cases, broken frames, loose lenses and sunglasses. Volunteers at the regional centers sort, clean, place eye glasses in pouches, which display the Lions emblem and eyeglass prescription, and ship the glasses according to requests.

As eyeglasses are received, contributing clubs receive a special certificate acknowledging their contributions.

## History of Fidelco Guide Dog Foundation

When Charles and Robbie Kaman founded the Fidelco Guide Dog Foundation in 1981 after more than 20 years of breeding German Shepherd dogs, it was due to a combination of their love of the breed and more importantly, the realization that people with visual disabilities can be free and independent with a Fidelco guide dog by their side.

Since then, Fidelco has placed more than 1,000 trained guide dogs throughout the United States and Canada with men and women who are determined to live a full and productive life.

Fidelco pioneered "In community training" in the United States. Through this process, individuals are trained to use their guide dogs in their homes, neighborhoods, and places of work. Throughout the training, they have the support of their family, friends and co-workers. In-community training also allows the trainer-instructors to carefully evaluate a new client's progress and to make corrections early in the training process. The Fidelco staff has found during their nearly three decades of placing guide dogs, that this training method helps the client become productive during a short period of time.

Fidelco has enjoyed the support of Lions Clubs in Connecticut and throughout the Northeast. Since joining forces with the Lions, 19 guide dogs have been trained and placed through the Lions' "Sponsor a Dog" project. Thirteen Vans, donated by Lions Clubs in Connecticut, Rhode Island and Maine transport guide dogs and instructors/trainers to and from training and placement activities.

The ongoing partnership between Fidelco and Lions is one of the important ways in which Fidelco will continue to meet the needs of people with visual disabilities. An annual Lions open house celebrates the relationship between Fidelco and Lions and the kind of support that only the Lions can provide.

## History of Camp Rising Sun

In 1985, the Willimantic office of the American Cancer Society requested financial assistance for their camping program, which at that time was being held at the Easter Seal camping facility in Hebron. Several Lions visited the facility and agreed that it was deserving of Lions' support.

Initially Camp Rising Sun became a Zone project in 1985, but with growing enthusiasm from Lions from throughout the District, it became a District Project in the late 80's.

Lion Gordon Allan has, from the beginning, been the "wind beneath the wings" of Camp Rising Sun. What started as a Lions contribution of $250, has evolved into Lions gifts totaling more than a third of a million dollars. This would not have been possible without the active involvement and persistence of Lion Gordon who simply would not take "no" for an answer. The fine work being performed at Camp Rising Sun was evident as Lion Gordon persuaded Lions to visit the facility and to see, first hand, campers at work and at play, involved with baseball, arts and crafts, swimming and more. For many campers, this would be their last year, whereas others might find the strength to return time and time again to be with other children who may also look different because of the side effects of cancer, and may also be facing the greatest crisis of their lives. This was home; No one would laugh at them because they looked different. Each gave his or her support to the other, and each year, when possible, looked forward to returning.

Perhaps the following letter from the parent of a child attending Camp Rising Sun will best illustrate how Camp Rising Sun has affected the lives of their participants:


*Tina Saunders*
*Camp Rising Sun*
*American Cancer Society*
*P.O. Box 1004*
*Meriden, CT 06450-1004*


*Dear Tina:*

*When Zack received the notice about the reunion weekend, I realized I had never finished this letter to you. I got caught up with getting Zack back to school this year after being homebound last year but still want to take the opportunity to express my sincerest thanks to all of you at Camp Rising Sun. Zack's cancer is certainly an experience I would have preferred to live without; but it has also been a gift and the camp has been part of that gift. Zack had his first week at the camp last summer and the week was a major turning point in his recovery. When we arrived for the circus performance, I knew I was seeing something important in his face, but I didn't know right away what it was. Something special had happened for him at camp and it was a lasting change that has impacted each member of my family.*

*On Thanksgiving 2002 we were propelled into this whirlwind experience when Zack had a massive seizure in the car, in the middle of who knows where, on our way home from the big annual gathering of food, touch football, and games. Within a matter of days he had surgery to remove a brain tumor with an initial pathology report that was very reassuring, the best possible kind of tumor with a very low recurrence rate. Over the next few weeks, I watched a fatigued Zack in a dazed and confused state, worrying about some loss of vision, yet trying to go about his life as a normal teenager. It was not until several weeks later, at a routine visit to the oncologist, that the word "cancer" became real. The initial pathology report had changed to a curable cancer with a worrisome recurrence rate. It didn't change anything we were doing medically, but it changed forever the way Zack thought about his life, and I think he was filled with anxiety, confusion and anger.*

*I am a clinical psychologist and my husband is a clinical social worker and we've both worked with teenagers. I knew Zack had some tough times ahead as he adjusted so when I saw the flier for Camp Rising' Sun at the oncologist's office, I grabbed it up, and filed it away. I cautiously mentioned it to Zack expecting him to laugh at the idea but he didn't. Although he wouldn't commit to attending he agreed that I could send in the application. Over the next few months it was painful and very frustrating to sit by and watch Zack suffering as his neurological recovery was slow.*

*He denied being depressed but he was struggling academically and was engaging in some risky behaviors. Not surprisingly, with two therapist parents he refused any psychotherapy and nothing I did was helpful. I was banking on the camp and that he would meet some other teenagers who had similar experiences and would provide something I was powerless to give him.*

*Camp was all that I had hoped for and more. When we came to pick him up and first found Zack, he was sitting in the last row of the audience, waiting for the circus performance to begin. He looked teary eyed and I was worried that he had a bad time. My concerns were lowered by his counselors who told me he had done okay. He chose not to participate in the performances but wanted to watch, sitting behind us in silence. I now think he was filled with emotions. During the performance it was all that I could do not to sob, watching both the healthy and more impaired kids and knowing what some of the parents might be feeling. Every child's "ta-da," and smile had so much meaning to me, and I think to Zack as well. I couldn't put my finger on it, but something was happening with Zack and in the ride home it became clear quickly as he shared the week's experiences with us.*

*In the days prior to leaving for camp, Zack had become depressed and very angry but he came back as the sensitive, thoughtful young man that I thought we had lost. His tumor probably was growing for 3 ½ years and caused slow but significant changes in Zack's personality. He had lost his spontaneity, humor, creativity, and passion. Follow that with brain surgery and the changes were profound. As we heard about camp, the activities, food, music he listened to (including Phil Ochs and Bob Dylan), people he met, learning to juggle and that he wanted to go again to camp, I knew some important healing had happened. He told us his three favorite things at camp were the rope swing, the lakeside candle ceremony on the last night, and the talent show. I would have expected him to like the rope swing but the talent show touched something in him, especially when Jessica sang to the camp. He came home more tolerant of people that are different and more willing to take a stand against the cruelty of his peers toward those that are different. Since Zack has a brother who struggles with being*

*"different," this was a very meaningful development for me to
see. The final evening's candle ceremony when all the camp
members shared a thought was special for him. Listening to the
youngest campers to the oldest, each sharing something that was
age appropriate and personally meaningful, whether or not
about their cancer, Zack felt safe and understood.*

*Camp Rising Sun has been a major turning point for Zack. While
it has still been a bumpy road for Zack, he came back from the
camp with hope. He is more social at home, talking and
participating with us, including with his brother. It seems that he
experienced some peace with having had cancer and has opened
up and talked more with me about the hand of cards he's been
dealt. Attending camp rebuilt his sense that he has a future that
he is not alone, and that others have been through something
similar and have done well. I will be forever thankful to you all
for the gift you gave him.*

*Sincerely,*
*Denise Foster*

Dozens of Lions have visited the facility each summer, and
many continued when Camp Rising Sun relocated to Camp Jewell in
the Northwest corner of the state, in the town of Colebrook, in the
1990's.

During his year as District Governor, PCC Angelo Miceli
brought the program to the attention of Lions in District 23-C by
selecting it as a new project during his year as Governor. Today, Lion
Gordon remains a staunch supporter of the camp, and his dream of
continued Lions support is made possible by the work of PCC Angelo
Miceli along with committee members.

## History of the Connecticut Radio Information System

During the latter part of the 70's, there was much discussion concerning the needs of the visually impaired and others with physical limitations.

These individuals want to know what is going on around the world and in their hometown, but cannot now and may never have that ability.

Newspapers are purchased because they offer news in depth. A newspaper offers opinion as well as a three dimensional view of happenings around the world. Newspapers offer advertisements, so that a reader can determine where the best food buys are during a particular week or what is on sale at local department stores. Those who cannot see or hold a daily newspaper are deprived of such information.

In August 1978 "The Connecticut Radio Information Service" was incorporated, and it would not be until June 1990 that it would receive its current name, The "Connecticut Radio Information System."

The very first broadcast took place on November 26, 1979. It was two hours in length and the listening audience totaled 50 individuals in the Hartford area who were provided with special radios. The length of broadcasts gradually increased until February 18th, 1985 when CRIS became a 24 hour-a-day service.

On September 13, 2000, CRIS program services expanded with the initiation of the "CRIS Telephone Reader Service." Now, for the first time, anyone who missed a specific broadcast could hear it in its entirety by calling a toll free number and entering specific codes. This opened a whole now world to those who were employed and were not available to listen to an original broadcast.

CRIS today has its home studio in Windsor, CT and satellite studios in Danbury, Norwich, New Haven and Trumbull. These satellite studios provide reading from local newspapers, and broadcast a few hours in the mornings and evenings. Broadcast for the remainder of a 24-hour day primarily originates from the Windsor studio.

Today, a listener has several options; they can receive the broadcast via a "CRIS" radio or, if there is a cable television hookup in the home, they can have their cable company provide a connection to a conventional FM radio tuned to a specific frequency, and this will be done without charge. And, of course, the telephone reader service is becoming increasingly popular.

CRIS has only a handful of paid staff, who work with the more then 400 volunteers who contribute approximately 18,000 hours of service a year. Financial support is received from listeners, individuals, and organizations such as Lions Clubs, foundations, corporations and the State of Connecticut.

CRIS is widely known as "Connecticut's Talking Newspaper."


## Connecticut Lions Work at the United Nations

Every year, Lions Club members from around the world are invited to a special "Lions Day with the United Nations" program in New York at headquarters.  The event features speakers from the United Nations; luncheon with an Amassador or other significant United Nations dignitary; awards ceremony for the grand prize winner of the Lions International Peace Poster Contest. The event often recieves an address from the Secretary-General of the United Nations. Lions are treated to tours of the United Nations and have an opportunity to learn more about the world organization.  Lion Harriet Raffel works tirelessly each year to promote and arrange for easy bus transportation to Lions that wish to participate in this event.

For Lions, the United Nations is more than a place for diplomats to talk of peace. Lions interest in helping the handicap, providing disaster relief, improving education and the concern of narcotics & substance abuse in our communities are among the many subjects that arise. To find support of these humanitarian goals, Lions Clubs International had taken a leading role in activities during the UN Charter Conference at San Francisco in 1945; and since 1947, Lions Clubs International has been one of the non-governmental organizations holding consultative status to the Economic and Social Council (ECOSOC).

*Article 71 of the Charter of the United Nations states, "The Economic and Social Council may make suitable arrangements for consultation with non-governmental organizations which are concerned with matters within its competence.  Such arrangements may be made with international organizations."*

Lions Clubs International has also found that the United Nations Department of Public Information (DPI) has an interest in developing relationships with Non-government Organizations (NGO). Through this association, the DPI seeks to reach people around the world and help them better understand the work and aims of the United Nations. Again, opportunities arise, where Lions can learn and share information about worldwide concerns.

PID Otto Strobino worked with several committees at the United Nations. These include the NGO/DPI Executive Committee; which operates an annual Conference with the DPI every year in September for all associated NGOs. Otto served on that committee as a member, but also as its Treasurer. PDG Dan Uitti was also elected to serve on that committee, and performed volunteer work with that committee's website and conference website venues.

Through the Conference of NGOs, Lions have worked on substantive committees. PID Otto has served on the Narcotics and Substance Abuse committee, and served as that committee's Chairman. Through this committee, Otto led the committee to collaborate with similar U.N. related organizations in Vienna; organized information programs on the status of various narcotics related activities of the U.N. He encouraged the development of that committee's position statement. During his term, he encouraged the DPI to provide the latest information about the U.N.s work to NGOs. In April 2003, a briefing was developed on the topic *"The Opium Economy in Afghanistan: A Setback for Drug Control."* This briefing was well attended by NGO representatives.

## Chapter 3 - History of the Lionism in District 23-A

## History of the Ansonia Lions Club

The Ansonia Lions Club was chartered in April 1950 under the sponsorship by the Stamford Lions Club. Lion Morton Linett served as the first president.

Christmas time in Ansonia was a special time of year especially at the Derby Nursing Home. It was at that time that the Ansonia Lions made their annual visit, presenting gifts of clothes, cookies and toiletries to the patients, and at the same time serenading the patients by singing Christmas carols. During several of those years, the club chartered a bus, and drove the ambulatory patients around the city allowing them to view the many Christmas displays.

This was a wonderful and altruistic act. In 1993 the project was turned over to the Derby-Shelton Lions Club. The Ansonia Lions since that date have continued their gift of love during their annual visits to the Mariner's Nursing Home in Ansonia.

Fundraising activities during the early years included collections from gumball machines, the eye seal campaigns, Halloween candy sales, light bulb sales, raffles and paper scrap collections. During the later years, the members sold fruit cakes and florescent light bulbs More recently, the Ansonia Lions have raised funds through collections at local super markets.

This club has generously contributed to their community. Along with two other Lions Clubs, the Ansonia Lions contributed $10,000 to the Griffin Hospital for the purchase of eye equipment.

Since their beginnings, the Ansonia Lions have met the needs of the less fortunate by providing eyeglasses when the need existed. LCIF, CLERF, the DARE program, Fidelco, Camp Hemlocks and the Salvation Army have all been recipients annually.

A Tele-Binocular device for testing eyes was donated to the Ansonia School System. Each year scholarships were awarded to both high school and industrial school students.

Other services have included building a ramp for a disabled person, purchasing rocking chairs for their hospital's maternity ward, purchasing a movie projector for the Willis School, purchasing a life guard chair for Colony Park playground and funding three glaucoma screening clinics.

The list goes on and on, as this club has truly served for over half a century.

The members of the club are proud of the many who have served, including Larry Feinberg, who served both as president of the club and member of the District Cabinet, including as Deputy District Governor. He is the one who initiated visits to the convalescent homes and was chairman of the project for 10 years.

Lion C. Tomasella was club president, Zone Chairman and Deputy District Governor. Lion Tomasella has sponsored over 25 members. Others recognized for high achievement were Lion Joseph LaRocco, Lion Michael Impellitteri, Lion Delbert Rau and Lion Thomas Duffy.

## History of the Beacon Falls Lions Club

The Beacon Falls Lions Club, sponsored by the Naugatuck Lions, was chartered February 27, 1953. Frank W. Semplenski Sr. served as the Charter President.

Through the years, the Beacon Falls Lions have served their community through flood relief, annual Red Cross Blood drives and annual picnics for seniors.

This club has paid for eye examinations for children whose parents could not meet the cost. They also paid for eyeglasses when needed. The Beacon Falls Lions have sponsored an explorer scout troop, sponsored the Beacon Falls Boys Basketball Tournament and created a scholarship fund for graduating high school seniors.

The Middle School was the recipient of an eye examination device, and Camp Hemlocks has been the beneficiary of significant funding each year. During the Thanksgiving holiday, the club provided turkeys for needy families.

A scoreboard was purchased for the Laurel Ledge School, and the Lions Quest program was launched for the Beacon Falls School System. In addition the club sponsored an Explorer Scout troop as well as the Beacon Falls Boys Basketball Tournament.

Eye screenings have been sponsored by the club on an ongoing basis and $5,000 was donated to the local library. At the same time $5,000 was pledged for Macular Degeneration.

When the club was informed that a family's house had been destroyed by fire, and the family lost everything, the members voted to provide immediate financial assistance.

Fundraising projects have included light bulb sales, a Memorial Day car wash, raffles, an annual Easter flower sale, pancake breakfast events, entertainment books, the sale of fried dough, a wine tasting event, a town wide mailing, the annual Valentines Day dance and the Duck Race at Volunteer Park.

The club is honored to be the home club of Raymond Shea who served as District Governor 1999-2000 and served as President of the Connecticut Lions Eye Research Foundation from 2001-2003. Joseph A. Poirier served as District Governor 2006-2007, and and went on to serve as Council Chairman during the period 2007-2008. Another Beacon Falls Lions Club member, William Mis was honored to serve as President of the Lions Low Vision Center of New Haven and Fairfield Counties during the period 2003-2005.

As is indicated above, during their more than fifty years, the Beacon Falls Lions Club has had an outstanding history.

## History of the Bethany Lions Club

Under the sponsorship of the Woodbridge Lions, the Bethany Lions Club was chartered on March 6, 1952.

Historically, the club members have played an active role in the life of their town. Many have held high positions in town government and at most times in their history, at least one of the town's selectmen also has served as a club member. In fact, as of the date of this writing, all three selectmen were members of the Bethany Lions Club.

Annual fundraisers include a spring goods and services auction, a spring horse show, a summer letter of solicitation, a holiday poinsettia sale, and a fall car show.

A large percentage of the club's funds are used for projects and services that benefit its local area. The club provides food and energy assistance as well as eyeglasses and examinations to local residents who are in need.

The Bethany Lions Club built and maintained a horse show facility on property owned by the town. The club is responsible for managing the annual Memorial Day ceremony and parade as well as the community tag sales.

These Lions have also provided financial support and manpower for the preservation of town historical sites.

Each spring the organization awards $5,000 in scholarships to town residents who are advancing from High School to College. In the fall, the club members provide a safe and fun-filled Halloween party for children in their town.

During the year the club works with the Red Cross in sponsoring blood drives and they also provide support for the town library, volunteer fire department and ambulance corps.

For over 50 years, the Bethany Lions Club has most certainly made a difference in the town they call their own.

## History of the Bethel Lions Club

One of the oldest Lions Clubs in the Multiple District is the Bethel Lions Club, which was established in 1928. The membership today represents a broad spectrum of the Bethel community. The members for the most part reside in the Bethel/Danbury area and represent a cross section of the community in which they live. The men and women are dedicated to serve the community of Bethel. Many of the members provide services directly to their community by working with the scouts, the churches, the food bank, the volunteer fire department, and the town government. The members are committed to providing financial support for local charitable organizations and Lions programs and dedicate themselves to assure that funds are available.

Over the years the Bethel Lions Club has conducted numerous service projects in the Town of Bethel including constructing and equipping facilities in three town parks. They have a very active eye glass and hearing aid collection program as well as a program to provide eye examinations and eye glasses for needy area residents. One example of this club's dedication to community concerns a Bethel resident who lost his vision in an accident. The club members worked together helping him modify his home and also assisted him in obtaining a guide dog.

The club conducts a bi-annual eye screening to identify area residents with eye problems.

The Bethel Lions have hosted dinners and entertainment evenings for Bethel senior citizens, and has sponsored a Boy Scout troop for 35 years, one that serves youths with special needs. Currently the club supports two Boy Scout troops.

Other youth oriented programs include two annual scholarships awarded to Bethel High School graduating seniors, contributions to Boys and Girls State, and support of the Bethel Police Department's DARE program.

The Bethel Lions have had several types of fundraising events. For several years their greatest fundraiser was a food stand at the Derby Fair. Other events included beerfests, turkey shoots, fishing derbies, Las Vegas nights, tag sales, raffles and a horse show. During the past several years, their major fundraiser has been an annual golf tournament. This has been well supported by local businesses and individuals and has allowed the club to continue its support of local charities as well as many Lion's charities.

These dedicated Lions have served their community for almost 80 years and continue to be an important part of the fabric of this community.

Lions Marty Lawler and Ed Mills work behind
the counter at the Bethel Lions Food Booth.

## History of the Branford Lions Club

In May, 1951, the Branford Lions Club was organized with twenty-eight charter members.

The Branford Lions through the years have involved themselves in several fundraisers including an annual Valentines Day Sweetheart Ball which was continually successful for over 25 years. This event was eventually replaced by the Branford Lions Holiday Basketball Festival which is held annually between Christmas and New Years. Several high schools participate in a two-day round robin competition, and this profitable event has continued for the past 23 years.

A very profitable beer fest was held annually for several years, however, the acceptances of this type of event diminished over the years. The event was replaced by the Branford Summer Festival which is held on the Branford town green during Fathers Day weekend. During the festival, the Branford Lions food tent is a most popular event.

Over the years, the Branford Lions have supported both International and Multiple District charities including CLERF, which has received over $100,000 from the club. They have also contributed annually to support LCIF, Camp Hemlocks as well as Speech and Hearing, the Low Vision Center, Diabetes and Fidelco.

Locally, the club provided funding for ground level access for the physically handicapped at the Blackstone Library. They have supported the local VNA and provided eye-testing machines to all of the town's elementary schools.

Over 30,000 pairs of used eyeglasses have been collected and forwarded for processing.

When the need existed for eye examinations and glasses the Branford Lions responded to those who could not afford to meet the cost.

The Lions Club of Branford is a highly recognized and respected service organization. From time to time they recall with pride the achievements of their distinguished past but also look forward to the future with eager anticipation. Most importantly they do their best to stay firmly grounded in the present and always ready to carry out their mission to serve under the banner of the Lions Club of Branford. These Lions are proud of what they term as the "Lions honor roll."

which consists of eighteen Melvin Jones Fellow, nine Knights of the Blind, and one recipient of the International Presidents Leadership medal.

Branford Lions for years have been involved in the District 23-A cabinet. Members of this club were called upon to fill various positions. Past President Jerry Osochowsky served as District Governor in 1996-1997, and was called upon to serve as President of The Connecticut Lions Eye Research Foundation following the sudden death of Lion Bob Hoxie.

A wonderful past and a promising future, the Branford Lions continue to serve the community they love.

## History of the Bridgeport Host Lions Club

The Bridgeport Lions Club was chartered February 28, 1921. It was not only the first club in Connecticut but the first club as well in all of New England. Soon after its creation, the members were approached by the Visiting Nurse Association for help in developing a permanent fresh air camp for Bridgeport's youth.

Lion member, Peter Davey, who served as Bridgeport's Postmaster, responded by donating 29 acres of woodland in Trumbull. Lumber, roofing and plumbing contractors provided supplies and members used their skills to construct the building.

With its new permanent location, the VNA continued the camp's name as "Camp Hemlocks." The Lions deeded the property to the VNA, which operated it as a fresh air camp until it was sold to the Easter Seal Society for summer programs for disabled children and adults. The Bridgeport Lions Club has had close ties to Hemlocks, a relationship that continues today in the new camp in Hebron.

For several years the club focused on car raffles as fundraisers, until they were given the opportunity to sponsor concerts in the Klein Auditorium with lucrative program advertising books.

With concert and stage show production costs rising, the club's leadership looked at the possibility of sponsoring a beer festival. The Fairfield University Soccer field was chosen as the site. With imported brew, and German music, the event was greeted in 1972 by throngs of people from throughout the Eastern states. The first Bavarian Beer

Festival netted $29,000. Subsequent festivals created a lucrative fund for use in meeting community requests for help including creating a vision examination clinic at Bridgeport Hospital, adding devices for the x-ray department at St. Vincent's Medical Center, updating the dental services for indigents at Park City Hospital and providing an arts and crafts building at the new Camp Hemlocks in Hebron. Significant contributions through the years have also been made to CLERF. The festival continued for 11 years. At that time operating costs forced the leadership to search for other fundraisers.

The Bridgeport Lions have for several years, sponsored a competition among high school seniors called a "Speak Up" oration contest. This project helps sustain the Lions image in the community.

The club points with pride to the leadership it has provided to District 23-A beginning with Governor Judge W.W. Bent in 1925 and followed by District Governors William S. Hewlett, Charles F. Stupps, Col. Lott R. Breen, Joseph W. Ganim, Leo J. Redgate, Edward D. Hagerty, William J. Carroll, Phillip G. Flaker, Raymond M. Zaleski and David R. Whitehead.

Joseph W. Ganim was later elected to the Board of Directors of Lions Clubs International.

The Bridgeport Host Lions Club, during a close to 90-year history, is among Lions Clubs, one of the most outstanding.


## History of the Brookfield Lions Club

The Brookfield Lions Club, sponsored by the new Fairfield and Newtown Lions Clubs, received their charter on March 3, 1966.

For their community, the Brookfield Lions sponsored an "Ability Beyond Disability" group home, sponsored two Red Cross blood drives, and provide supervision for the Memorial Day Parade each year. The annual senior citizens picnic would not have become a reality each year if it were not for a group of dedicated Lions who saw and met a need. In the spirit of the Lions desire to eradicate preventable blindness, the Brookfield Lions both sponsor and participate in periodic eye screenings. Health clinics are held each year and these events are welcomed by all age groups in the community.

The Brookfield Lions maintain "Lions Park" in their town and assist the Parks and Recreation Department in their events by parking cars and providing cooking services.

This year the club will contribute in excess of $40,000 to Lions projects and community organizations. Principal causes include the Brookfield Emergency Fund, Camp Hemlocks, CRIS Radio, Fidelco, Hospice, the Brookfield Substance Abuse Coalition, scholarships for local high school graduates, and reading equipment for the Brookfield Library.

Additional contributions include CLERF, the Low Vision Center (both reading equipment and funds) and Macular Degeneration Research.

Major fundraisers for the club include an Annual Charity Ball (30th year) annual golf tournament (23rd year) New Year's Day "Run for Sight." (18th year), the "Father's Day Peace Run" (6th year), and auction (2nd year).

The Brookfield Lions Club is proud to have been the home club of PDG Bob Hoxie as well as the many club members that have served on the District Cabinet. They are also proud to have named 16 of their members as Melvin Jones Fellows and 30 as Knights of the Blind.

## History of the Cheshire Lions Club

The Cheshire Lions Club was chartered October 19, 1949, sponsored by the Southington Lions Club.

Since the mid 50's, the Cheshire Lions have sponsored a "Dinner Dance for the Blind." This was initially created as an occasion during which the visually impaired could gather for dinner, dancing, and a chance to co-mingle with each other as well as Lion members. Since its inception, the "Dinner Dance for the Blind" has grown from 50 to approximately 120 in attendance, not only from Cheshire but from surrounding towns as well. Many clubs sponsor their attendees, but the majority are guests of the Cheshire Lions.

Contributions to the community extend far beyond this annual event. The club sponsors youth baseball as well as a Boy Scout Troop and have sponsored a Leo Club at the Cheshire High School. The club purchased computer equipment for the Cheshire Public Library, benches for the Linear walk, and each year awards scholarships to college bound high school students.

A flag poll was erected at Bartlem Park in honor of World War II veteran and Past President of the Cheshire Lions Club, Judson W. Moore.

Current civic projects include the Peace Poster Contest, an ongoing eyeglass collection, blood drives, and eye screening exams.

On Veteran's Day in 2006, the Cheshire Lions conducted a town wide "Treats for Troops" project during which they collected over 80 boxes of food and personal items which in turn were sent to our troops in Iraq and Afghanistan.

The club has generously supported numerous community and Lions projects including CLERF, CRIS, LCIF, Low Vision, Camp Hemlocks, Hearing and Speech, Fidelco, and the Connecticut Institute for the Blind.

Fundraising projects have included craft shows, as well as annual flea market and wine tasting events.

The Cheshire Lions Club is proud to be the home club of Morton Reisenberg who served as District Governor in 1971 and Council Chairman during the following year. The club is also proud to have inducted PID Otto Strobino as an honorary member in 2003.

Perhaps the public's appreciation of the Cheshire Lions Club is best expressed by selections from a note signed by Janet N. England and Dr. Janet Rodell, both of whom attended the "Dinner Dance for the Blind."

*"...Your organization must be applauded for efforts to assist those here and beyond our borders who have vision handicaps. You are an ever present reminder to the public of our medical needs supplied by your gifts of time, talent and treasure but also by your projects which simply lift the spirit such as your dinner dance of 2007. May your efforts continue so all who hear your name will know of your good works."*

## Soldiers Send Thanks to Lions and the People of Cheshire

Editor. *The Cheshire Herald* - December 28, 2006

*I would like to thank the people of Cheshire and, particularly, the Lions Club for its hard work and generosity.*

*I have received close to 100 boxes of various sizes containing games, food, snacks, DVDs, clothing, phone cards, letters, and other items. The gifts were then broken down, and we distributed everything into 16 large packages.*

*Being the father of an infantry soldier and deploying forward myself, I realize the hardships that these men and women endure. Many do not understand that the foot soldier may literarily live in the field without bathrooms, showers, hot meals, or phone calls from home for months at a time. Your gifts were flown on choppers and small aircraft into the most austere locations in Afghanistan and will benefit the warriors who need these items most.*

*In the words of my son, Sgt. Joseph M. Farrington (United States Army), "Sometimes, you just want to kill yourself. Then you receive a letter from your mom or a gift from a stranger and everything is okay, at least for a while."*

*Thank you from my family. Thank you from the men and women fighting for your freedom and the peace and joy that you receive every day as Americans.*

*God will bless you.*

*P.S. As I was writing this, another seven packages arrived from Mr. Bob Vidla (Cheshire Lions Club)*

*MSgt Mark R. Farrington*
*Afghanistan*

Installation of Officers for 2003-2004: From the left, Lion Lillian Derganc, Second Vice President; Lorrie Canas, Secretary; PID Otto Strobino; Lion Colette Anderson, President; Lion Terri (Canas) Bousquet, Immediate Past President; and Lion Marge Jerin, Past President.

Lions at work during the Cheshire Lions Breakfast fundraiser.

## History of the Danbury Lions Club

The Danbury Lions Club was chartered September 8, 1927 and sponsored by the Bridgeport Lions. As they approach their 80th anniversary, the club's membership has risen to 106 individuals celebrating more than three quarters of a century filled with numerous accomplishments.

The first 25 years of community service focused on the construction and maintenance of Danbury's first playground. Much of the money was raised through theatrical performances sponsored by the club.

The 1930's focused on providing relief to those unemployed during the depression and an annual Thanksgiving basket program. The highlights of the 1930's were the 1932 visit by Helen Keller, and the 1935 visit to Danbury by International President Vincent Hascall.

In 1935, Bill Hoyt, first of four District Governors from the Danbury Club was elected. The other District Governors were Manny Merullo, Al Hazard, and Don Miloscia.

In the 1940's Civil Defense was the largest recipient of Lions generosity with over 3,000 hours donated in service to the Air Raid Warning Center.

The club also helped fund the first ambulance in Danbury.

During the 1950's the Danbury Lions began raising funds for their next project, the Lions Playground on Highland Ave. Funds were raised to build the playground, and maintain it for 15 years.

The 1970's saw another shift, Instead of long term projects, the club started providing funds for one time needs such as eye related equipment for the Danbury Hospital.

During the 1990's the club opened the Danbury CRIS studio, and installed a granite monument commemorating all the deceased Danbury Lions. The CRIS studio became the beneficiary of the annual Peter Winter Memorial Breakfast. The club supports the CRIS studio, coordinates the volunteers, and purchases and delivers CRIS radios to listeners in their area.

The club recently completed a $25,000 commitment to CLERF and also supports Fidelco, Connecticut Low Vision Centers, and LCIF.

Fundraising efforts include an annual raffle, and an annual golf tournament.

Since 1968 the club has awarded college scholarships to Danbury High School students. The current program provides six scholarships of $1,500 each.

The members of this club are involved in the Lions annual Peace Poster contest and also sponsor an annual Fire Prevention Poster contest with the Danbury Fire Department.

Funding for eye examinations and eyeglasses is available for both needy school children as well as adults.

The Danbury Lions stock a "cabinet" at the Danbury Low Vision Center providing, without cost, many items needed by clients. The club also runs a monthly Low Vision Support Group, and the members are invited to join the Lions luncheon held each year during the holiday season.

The Danbury Lions Club proudly practices the Lions motto, "We Serve"

## History of the Darien Lions Club

The Darien Lions Club was chartered February 17, 1949, sponsored by the Stamford Lions Club.

Since 1949, the Darien Lions have raised and donated more than three million dollars to critical projects in their town, in Connecticut and throughout the world.

CLERF and the Yale Eye Center have been prime recipients. In addition, "Challenger Park" is a handicapped accessible playground, and was built by the Darien Lions. Other recipients include Camp Hemlocks, Darien High School, Darien 60 plus club, Lance Armstrong Foundation, American Cancer Society, and the Connecticut Special Olympics.

Fundraising activities include a car raffle, super bowl raffle, eye research mailing, and the great annual "Shop Rite Fall Golf Classic."

The tradition of the Darien Lions Club is best expressed by the words of Helen Keller; "It is the caring we want more than money. The gift without the sympathy and interest of the giver is empty. If you care, if you can make the people of this great country care, the blind will indeed triumph over blindness."

## History of the Derby-Shelton Lions Club

The Derby Shelton Lions Club was chartered on March 30, 1950 with David Resnick serving as the club's charter president.

This club has served their community for over half a century with significant support for the eye clinic at the Griffin Hospital.

Outstanding students graduating from the Shelton High School have been among the recipients of Lions scholarships. One such scholarship was presented in memory of Lion Arthur Faroni.

The club has also supported the Derby Little League as well as the Ambulance Corp of Shelton

Fundraising events have included an annual golf tournament for eye research, a grapefruit and orange sale, raffle tickets, broom sales, and the sale of Eye Conservation Stamps.

The Derby-Shelton Lions Club has a mascot. Unfortunately in 1981, the mascot was stolen by the Naugatuck Lions Club. The terms acceptable for release of this valuable item were, "(1) Unconditional homage to the Naugatuck Club for a period of one year, i.e. 'don't try to rip us off!!'

(2) At least 10 raffle tickets must be purchased by the Derby Shelton Lions Club, and (3) The Derby Shelton Lions secretary must complete the Naugatuck M and A reports during the months of July and August 1981.

Raffle tickets are $1.00 each or a book of ten for $11.00, a special rate available only to the Derby Shelton Lions!"

These Lions are proud that the Derby Shelton Lions Club is the home club of PDG James Halligan.

When the Derby Shelton Lions provided a nine-year old child with a hearing aid, the response from a family friend perhaps speaks volumes about how this Lions Club has impacted their community:

"The unselfish humanitarian efforts of the Derby Shelton Lions Club are well known and those efforts have not only touched the lives of this grateful family but especially the life of a small profoundly hearing impaired child. Thank you for all you have done."

## History of the Devon Lions Club

Sponsored by the Stratford Lions Club, the Devon Lions Club was chartered April 30, 1942. Since that time the club has had numerous service projects.

Recently the club completed their 27th annual Christmas party for special needs children, a project that has grown to include the pre-school and 1st graders in the Milford school system, and the donation of gifts to terminally ill children. The club has also contributed to Devon's "Little Angels" at Yale New Haven Hospital and the Milford Hospital. The children's project was started by Lions Dick Dowin and Bruce Nichols.

Contributions received by the Devon Lions Club have been used for scholarships, as well as eye examinations and glasses for any child in the Milford School system whose parents are unable to meet this need.

There was recently a huge project involving over 3,000 student in the Milford School System that were given a complete eye exam by an ophthalmologist. This was most appreciated by the parents of the children and the school nurses, as the school did not have the equipment to perform this extraordinary service. Many children were not only found to need glasses, but were diagnosed with eye diseases that could have ultimately led to blindness if not treated.

As a token of appreciation, a fifth grade teacher is having her students assist the Devon Lions Club by collecting eyeglasses as a class project. This has helped the Devon Lions Club, which has over the years collected thousands of pairs of used eyeglasses for recycling.

During the Easter holiday, the Devon Lions Club sponsors an Easter egg hunt, and during the most recent event, over 75 children participated.

Annual contributions are allocated for Little League, Boy Scouts, CLERF, LCIF, Diabetes, Drug Awareness, Fidelco, District Pride, Camp Hemlocks, Low Vision, Speech and Hearing, CRIS and the post prom event for both high schools.

The club sponsors an eyescreening program, and has participated in screenings throughout the District as well as in New York's bordering towns.

To fund the work of the Devon Lions Club, there have been numerous fundraisers including oyster festivals, turkey basket raffles and the club's annual dance.

## History of the East Haven Lions Club

The East Haven Lions Club was chartered September 28, 2003 under the sponsorship of the Branford Lions Club.

On January 27, 2003, the then District Governor Marinus deJongh, was the guest speaker at the Branford Lions Club. Branford Lion Thomas Sudac talked with the Governor about his dream to organize a Lions Club in East Haven.

Lion Tom advised the Governor that East Haven resident and member of the Branford Lions Club Phil Van Deusen was interested in creating such a club.

By September 28th, 2003 their goal of 29 charter members had been achieved, and the members were inducted by the then immediate Past District Governor Marinus deJongh.

Since that date the club has increased its membership to 47, with many prospective members in the wings. The club has had several successful fundraisers, and have established themselves as a vital force in the East Haven community, as well as a contributor to the many Lions charities.

## History of the Easton Lions Club

Under the sponsorship of the Trumbull Lions, The Easton Lions Club was chartered April 19, 1967. Lion Robert Monk served as the club's charter president.

Easton is a residential community with no business district. It is with pride that the Easton Lion acknowledge the connection between Lionism and Helen Keller and the club's long support of eye research.

In 1925 Helen Keller addressed the Lions International Convention and challenged the Lions to become her "Knights of the Blind." Since then, Lions have played a major role in the fight against eye disease and in service to the blind. In 1936, following the death of her famous teacher, Anne Sullivan, Helen Keller needed a place where she could find privacy and solitude to continue her writing. She moved to Easton Connecticut and called her new home "Arcan Ridge."

"It was a colonial house surrounded by meadows, woods, brooks, and stone walls." Helen Keller wrote to a friend that "We have never loved a place more than Arcan Ridge." She remained at Arcan Ridge until her death in 1968. The house still stands in a beautiful setting on Redding Road in the town the Easton Lions call their own.

In pursuing the Easton Lions interest in giving something back to the town, the Easton Lions have become generous contributors to the major causes supported by Lions International. In recent years, in recognition of their service to the club, numerous Easton Lion members have been designated as Melvin Jones Fellows and as Knights of the Blind.

The Easton Lions annually donate to and participate in a variety of local causes such as the Easton Senior Center, Little League, girls softball, girls hockey, Easton PTA, Barlow Post prom party, Police Explorers, Easton Historical Society, carbon dioxide detectors for senior citizens, defibrillators for town police cars, bullet proof vests for the Easton Police, and a thermal imaging camera for the Easton Fire Department.

Each year the club participates in the Memorial Day parade, and since 1969 has sponsored the annual Halloween bonfire and costume parade. From 1988 until 2000, the Easton Lions awarded a $1,500 Community Service Scholarship for a graduating senior.

The Easton Lions annually contribute to LCIF, CLERF, Camp Hemlocks, Fidelco, Diabetes, and. CRIS. The club has also made a sizable commitment to the Macular Degeneration project. Since its inception, the Easton Lions have contributed in excess of $220,000 to their community and communities throughout the world through Lionism.

Major fundraising activities have included annual antique shows and golf tournaments.

## History of the Fairfield Lions Club

Both the Bridgeport and Stratford Lions Clubs shared in the sponsorship of the Fairfield Lions Club on October 20, 1936.

For over seven decades, the Fairfield Lions have served their community. During the holidays, the Fairfield Lions organized Christmas parties for children. Using a van purchased by the club, free glaucoma screenings were provided for the residents of Fairfield.

Contributions have been made to two Bridgeport hospitals for the purchase of laser equipment to treat eye disease.

To raise funds for charitable giving, the club has had numerous fundraising events including turkey shoots, raffles, spaghetti dinners, and pancake breakfast events.

## History of the Georgetown Lions Club

The Georgetown Lions Club under the sponsorship of the Ridgefield Lions received its charter on February 24, 1950, and engages the community through its fundraisers such as a carnival, "turkey shoot" and Georgetown Day.

This club is proud to reportedly be the only Lions Club in Connecticut to have its own phone number.

The Georgetown Lions Club also serves the community by managing the Gilbert and Bennett Ball Field.

## History of the Greenwich Lions Club

The Greenwich Lions Club was organized August 23, 1923. Eighty-three years later it is an active organization comprised of members dedicated to serving the needs of the Greenwich community and beyond.

Several of the club's early members have left a lasting impact on the community. The club's first president, Dr. John A. Clark, served as the medical advisor to the Town of Greenwich Police Department for several decades until his death in 1944. To honor the memory of Lion John, the club has, for the past 58 years, hosted an annual awards luncheon to present the "John A. Clark Award" to a member of the Greenwich Police Department. The honoree is chosen each year by the police chief to recognize his or her outstanding performance in the line of duty. This event is responsible for bringing together the town's Selectmen, members of Lion John's family as well as the family of Lions and members of the Greenwich Police Department.

In memory of Hardy R. Finch, another early member of the club and past Lion president, the club through its charitable funding affiliate, the Lions Foundation of Greenwich, founded and annually donates funds to the Town of Greenwich library to support the "Hardy Finch Large Print Library."

The town's municipal golf course is named for past Lion President Griffith E. Harris, who also served as the town's First Selectman. This golf course is the site of the club's annual fundraiser, the Selectman's Cup Golf Tournament run in concert with the Old Greenwich Lions Club.

In memory of Halford W. Park Jr., a Lion past president, the club established the "Hal Park Memorial Fund," which is a funding source for the Lions Club's Low Vision Center. The center was established several years ago as a collaborative effort of Greenwich Hospital Home Care, Greenwich Health Department of Ophthalmology and the Lions Clubs of Fairfield County, and provides counseling and visual aid devices to citizens of lower Fairfield County as well as bordering towns in Westchester County, N.Y.

The club's other fundraising projects include the annual Easter egg hunt, the largest egg hunt in Connecticut. The club also raises funds by selling grapefruit every November, and by operating a food booth at the United Way of Greenwich's annual fundraiser.

Other service projects include the annual scholarship awarded to a student interested in pursuing a nursing career, and assisting the Greenwich Social Services Department's Campership program, which awards scholarships to low-income children.

Initially and throughout its eighty-three year history, the club's members have had an impact not only within the club itself, but also within the Greenwich community at large.

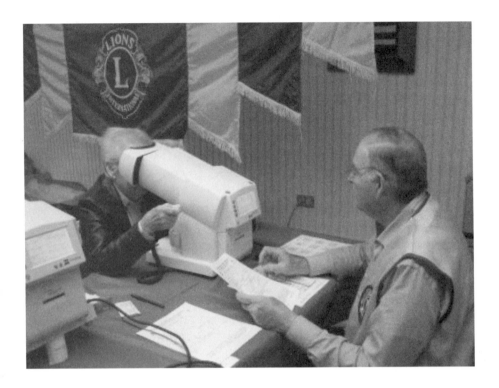

The Greenwich Lions Club hold a (LEHP) Lions Eye Health Care Program eye screening at their town's annual Heath Fair. The large attraction to the fair is the Flu Shot clinic. Shown here is the CT LEHP program's Humphrey FDT Visual Field Instrument, which is used to detect the early stages of Glaucoma.

## History of the Guilford Lions Club

The Guilford Lions Club was sponsored by the Hamden Lions Club and chartered April 26, 1950.

At the time of this writing, the Guilford Lions were looking forward to a great fundraising event, a Caribbean Cruise originating from New York. This is just one of many fundraisers sponsored by the Guilford Lions.

For eye research, the club holds a dinner annually and their Peach Shortcake Festival is the talk of the town. For car lovers the club's antique auto show is held each year in cooperation with the local antique auto club.

As part of their service to the community, the Guilford Lions have held glaucoma clinics and the club has given a great deal of support to the Guilford Recreation Department.

Contributions have been made to Camp Hemlocks, the Guilford Senior Citizens Group, Fidelco, Diabetes Awareness, SARAH, CRIS, American Cancer Society, The Guilford Food Bank, The VNA of Guilford, CLERF, and LCIF among others.

With over 50 years of service, the Guilford Lions remain a strong force in their community.

## History of the Hamden Lions Club

The Hamden Lions Club was chartered November 17, 1949 under the sponsorship of the New Haven Lions Club. Ralph Maisano served as the Charter President.

Through the years, the Hamden Lions Club has collected eyeglasses and hearing aides for third world nations. Year after year Lions Day and then Sight Savers Day have found the Hamden Lions meeting the public and collecting funds. The club has also distributed canisters throughout Hamden, and have conducted antique appraisals, tag sales, bus trips, as well as auctions.

As a service to their community, the Hamden Lions have held periodic glaucoma screenings.

The club has provided ongoing support for the Lions Low Vision Center, CLERF, CRIS Radio, and Camp Hemlocks Training Center for Children with Disabilities. Support has also been given to Fidelco, Diabetes Awareness, Drug Awareness, Hamden Youth Sports and the After Prom Program.

Each year the Hamden Lions provide scholarships for graduating high school seniors with a desire to pursue a college education.

The Hamden Lions prime mission is to serve the residents of Hamden as well as the world community, in hope of making a better life for all.

## History of the Madison Lions Club

The Madison Lions Club received its charter from Lions Clubs International in February. 1956 and held it's first meeting in May of that year. There were twenty-six charter members of this club, which was sponsored by the neighboring Guilford Lions Club. There had been a previous Lions Club in Madison dating back to 1929, but it was disbanded during World War II when most of its members were involved in the war effort.

In 1961, five years after it's founding, the Madison Lions Club had the rare honor of having one of their charter members, Joseph Darling installed as District Governor of District 23-A. This honor was repeated 41 years later when another Madison Lion, Marinus deJongh, was elected District Governor.

The Madison Lions Club is the youngest of the four service clubs in Madison. It competes with Rotary, Exchange, and Jaycees for members.

In 1994, the club received a $61,000 bequest designated to feed the poor in Madison. Working with the Probate Court, the principle was invested and the proceeds realized distributed to the local social services agency that assembles and distributes over 90 food baskets to the needy at Easter, Thanksgiving, and Christmas of each year. The club's donation to this project makes up over 50% of the cost of these items.

Some of the club's major fund raising activities include the sale of Christmas cards, framed prints, and posters, a flea market on the Madison Green, and sale of tickets to a premier movie shown locally. The club conducts a town wide mail campaign to raise funds for eye research and the treatment of vision problems and works with a local restaurant that operates a carousel with proceeds going to area charities designated by the club.

Proceeds of funds are used to support a scholarship program in which eight 4-year scholarships and one science award are provided for students at the Daniel Hand High School in Madison.

The club donates to eight local youth programs, and supports eight vision related programs including Connecticut Lions Eye Research Foundation, Lions Low Vision Centers, and the FIDELCO Guide Dog Foundation.

Support is also given to 14 community projects including "Lifeline" units, Habitat for Humanity, a program that provides food baskets for the needy at holidays, local library support as well as projects recommended by the District Governor.

The mail campaign conducted by the Madison Lions Club each year is called "Be Thankful You Can See." The mailing features the eyes of a female high school senior who is appropriately called "Miss Be Thankful."

The Madison Lions Club is composed of individuals who are most innovative, creative, hard working, and most importantly totally involved in the community they love.

## History of the Meriden Lions Club

The Meriden Lions Club was chartered November 5, 1923 under the sponsorship of the Bridgeport Lions Club.

For more than eighty years the Meriden Lions have been at the forefront of the growth of the city they love and cherish. In the 1920's one of the club's first projects was producing a radio show to benefit the visiting nurses association. Following the Second World War the Meriden Lions conducted a scrap drive and raised significant funds. In 1948 the club constructed a public pool on the west side of town, and in 1952 created a wading pool at Hubbard Park.

There is Lions pride in one Meriden Lions project; that of the restoration of the "Red Bridge" in South Meriden, as well as the construction of a computer room for the Meriden Boys and Girls Club. During this period, a catering kitchen was built by the Meriden Lions for the Augusta Curtis Center.

The Meriden Lions are credited with the refurbishment of Castle Craig, which included construction of a flag poll as well as lighting of the flag and construction of new stairs. The club was also responsible for the construction of a water park and other civic acts which contributed to the well being of the City of Meriden.

The Meriden Lions have had numerous activities including a fall foliage trip for senior citizens, the annual Lions Club Golf Tournament as well as the great Lions auction broadcast live on Cox Cable in February.

The Meriden Lions Club participates in the annual Daffodil Festival and is the primary sponsor of the Meriden Soap Box Derby.

Each year on Palm Sunday, people from miles around attend the Palm Sunday brunch, which serves in excess of 800 people.

More recently, the Meriden Lions have become known for their annual "Duck" race at Brookside Park. In conjunction with the Duck race, the club runs a duck-coloring contest in the elementary schools as well as a fishing derby on the day of the "Duck" race.

Charitable donations include $25,000 for the construction of an addition to the Mid State Hospital. Other large donations were allocated to CLERF, Lions Low Vision Center, American Cancer Society and the American Diabetes Association.

The Meriden Lions are proud to be the home club of nine Past District Governors, namely Howard Saviteer, Spencer Hirst, Albert Sprafke, Edward Papandrea, Theodore Samaris, William Roberts, William D. Phillips Jr., Rene Tompkinson, and Peter Gostyla.

The Meriden Lions are passionate about having a good time while helping others. They have always had a strong presence in the community as well as the Lions organization. If a job needs to be done, the Meriden Lions is the club to ask!

## History of the Middlebury Lions Club

The Middlebury Lions Club was chartered on February 27, 1952 under the sponsorship of the Southbury Lions.

Through the years, the club has provided lights for the Little League field and has given support to the town ambulance service as well. The Boy Scouts, Girl Scouts and the Saint Vincent DePaul Shelter, and various Lions charities have all been recipients of substantial donations from this very altruistic organization. The club is especially proud of contributions given to their local library for the purchase of large print books.

To raise funds, the club has held spaghetti dinners, a 1950's dance, as well as tag sales. In years past, the club entertained the public with their famous annual minstrel show.

The Middlebury Lions are proud to have been given the opportunity to serve both their community and Lions Clubs International for over fifty years.

## History of the Milford Lions Club

The Milford Lions Club was chartered July 24, 1951. Annual fundraising efforts include a ziti dinner, a wine tasting event, and bottle and can collections.

During the past year, the club collected and recycled 7500 pairs of used eyeglasses and more than 110 used hearing aids. The club is also recycling cell phones for emergency use by battered women and elderly individuals, truly a great public service.

The Milford Lions Club has received numerous awards for its charitable endeavors. Monies raised by the club support the work of local organizations such as the Beth El homeless shelter, Boys and Girls Village, the Milford Senior Wish Society, and Milford "Kids Count."

The Milford Lions Club also lends support to the Low Vision Center, CRIS Radio, The United Way of Milford, the Milford Library, CLERF, Diabetes Awareness, Camp Hemlock, Journey for Sight, and Fidelco.

This club has also been involved in purchasing Christmas gifts for residents of the Pond Point Rest Home who no longer had family members.

In conjunction with the Orange Lions, the Milford Lions sponsored a Leo Club at the Foundation High School. This Leos Club has more than 40 members and is reportedly the only Leos Club in the world comprised of students with special needs.

The Mildford and Orange Lions Clubs work collaboratively each year providing multi phased eye screenings at the Orange County Fair. Recently, more than 200 individuals were screened and presented with free information regarding eye health.

Although this club was placed on status quo in 1995, they did a remarkable turn around, and reorganized in 1996 with 20 new members. This Lions Club has performed splendidly since that date serving their local community as well as Lion charities.

## History of the Monroe Lions Club

The Monroe Lions Club was chartered in March, 1952 under the sponsorship of the Bridgeport and Trumbull Lions Clubs. There were a total of 35 charter members, and John Ryan served as the club's first President.

Almost immediately the club became a household name in their community with a dinner dance at the Harmony Grange Hall. This huge social gathering during their very first year resulted in profits that allowed the club to present a generous donation to the Little League Association.

During that first year the club received the gift of land donated by Vincent Bartosic to allow the Lions to build a house.

Through the years the club has been involved in several lucrative fundraisers including a horse show, a "Clothing for Appalachia" drive, Lions Day collections, and donut and pumpkin sales. There were several innovative fundraising events including a big band dance, Valentines Day dinners, a "Cruise to Bermuda" raffle, golf tournaments, and their famous "Funnel Cakes" fundraisers at the firemen's carnival.

During the town's 175th anniversary, the Monroe Lions operated a concession stand selling only hot dogs, and apparently word traveled rapidly that these were in fact the greatest hot dogs ever produced. During the day the club ran out of food several times, but after an exhausting day, the resulting profits were most gratifying.

Services to the community has included the delivery of Christmas baskets, scholarships for graduating seniors, and holiday wreaths for the town hall and library.

On a regular basis, the Monroe Lions holds blood drives for the Red Cross, and this humanitarian act in itself is an indication of their sense of community.

The Monroe Lions constructed benches and picnic tables for the new children's playground at Wolfe Park. This serves as a daily reminder to the town's residents that the Monroe Lions continue to serve their community each and every day.

In 1973 the members of the Monroe Lions Club organized a "handicapped" Boy Scout troop for the town. They concentrated their efforts on this project as well as a joint project with the Monroe Police Department. The Monroe Lions raised funds for their "windshield etching" project, just one more service to the people of the town they love.

The innovative ideas of the membership has allowed this club to serve their community with excellence, and at the same time generously contribute to International, as well as Multiple District and District Lions charities.

## History of the Naugatuck Lions Club

The Naugatuck Lions Club was chartered December 12, 1960 and sponsored by the Derby/Shelton Lions Club. Mario Schiaroli served as the Charter President. One of three $500 scholarships awarded to high school seniors is in honor of Mario Schiaroli who was a Lion member for 53 years.

The Naugatuck senior elder housing was in need of a piano for their activities room, and the Naugatuck Lions were there to meet this need. When children in Naugatuck are in need of eyeglasses and their parents are unable to meet the cost, this Lions Club always stands ready to meet the need, as well as the cost of the eye examination.

Individuals, who have hearing problems, can't always afford to meet the cost of a hearing aid. The Naugatuck Lions are often asked to consider meeting this cost as well.

The citizens of this town are often reminded of the services provided by the Naugatuck Lions when they read notices on the "Lions Club Town Bulletin Stand" located in the lobby of the town hall.

During a fifteen-year period, the members of this club have collected in excess of 8,300 pairs of used eyeglasses.

The American Red Cross is thankful that the Naugatuck Lions have taken the initiative to sponsor two blood drives each year. Two flags have been donated by the Naugatuck Lions, one for the World War I monument and the second for a meeting room in the town.

Fund raising activities include an annual "Be Thankful You Can See" mailing, gum ball machine proceeds, an annual ziti dinner, Lions Day collections, and an annual poinsettia sale. Donations are also received from various corporations and these funds are used for the scholarships fund.

The Naugatuck Lions are proud to be the home club of PDG Dominic J. Minicucci, who served as District Governor in 1955.

## History of the New Canaan Lions Club

The New Canaan Lions Club was sponsored by the Stamford Lions Club and chartered on March 15, 1929.

On a weekly basis, the New Canaan Lions volunteer for "Meals on Wheels" delivering meals to area shut-ins. The Club also participates in the annual "Village Sidewalk Sales," the "Clean Your Mile" campaign and is active within the community collecting eyeglasses and promoting the Philosophy of Lionism.

The New Canaan Lions Club has sponsored many basketball shootouts in connection with the New Canaan YMCA. This was a great fundraiser, which was coordinated by Lion Ron Fournier both a Lions Club member and a YMCA officer.

In the 1990's a raffle was the club's major fundraiser. Such items as a Harley Davidson motorcycle, cars, and designer watches were raffled. During the past five years the club has run a Yankee ticket fundraiser, and this has brought a great response from the community.

Through the years the club has contributed towards scholarships, awards to business education students, Little League, the Pegasus riding project for handicapped children, Camp Hemlocks, and the New Canaan Library. Along with neighboring Lions Clubs, the New Canaan Lions had pledged $10,000 to Norwalk Hospital toward the purchase of a Zeiss Fundus camera and an Argon laser photocoagulator. $5,000 was contributed for a Lions recreation room at the YMCA and contributions were made to the Visiting Nurses Association, the New Haven Polio Center, the Horizons Program for the Handicapped, as well as CLERF.

Civic projects were many. One of the first was creating a skating pond in Mead Park. Much of the labor was done by the Lions but it cost the club over $1,000 for dredging and maintenance.

The club paid $1,500 to hire the town's first recreation director in 1938. In 1946, $1,000 was donated for dredging millpond and later at this site the club constructed the "Lions Den" with a fireplace for skaters. At a later date the club installed lighting so that skaters could find enjoyment during the evening hours.

The New Canaan Lions Club is honored to have been the home club of Past District Governors Wilbur Dixon and Charles Naylor.

## History of the New Fairfield Candlewood Lions Club

The New Fairfield Candlewood Lions Club was chartered April 11, 1995, and was sponsored by the Yalesville/Wallingford Lions Clubs. Hillery Bassriel served as the Charter President.

It is noted that the then Lt. Governor of the State of Connecticut, M. Jodi Rell was among the charter members of this club and she was sponsored by PCC Robert Gyle. New Fairfield Selectman Richard T. Grant was also a charter member of the club.

During the first year, this organization found immediate acceptance into the community. In July 1995, they held the first New Fairfield pancake breakfast and later that year started the tradition of a town wide Christmas celebration and tree lighting ceremony. The New Fairfield Candlewood Lions donated over $4,000 of lighting and underground wiring to the town and convinced the Parks and

Recreation Commission to continue this project. The club also donated a large screen television set and sound system to the town's new Senior Center.

During the year 1996, this organization along with a local newspaper, sponsored a "Citizen of the Year" award.

Other highlights in the short history of this club include the establishment of an annual "Chili Contest" and a wine tasting event, a new tradition that continues to this day.

The club has presented New Fairfield High students with cash awards based on their community involvement.

Since 1995, the New Fairfield Candlewood Lions have participated in District, Multiple District and Lions Clubs International activities, and have each year acknowledge individuals by naming them as "Melvin Jones Fellows" or "Knights of the Blind."

A tradition within the club is honoring their president by each year having that individual attend the USA/Canada Lions Leadership Forum.

This club, which was created under the leadership of PCC Robert Gyle, has grown to over 60 members. In the fall of 2006, its charter member M. Jodi Rell was elected Governor of the State of Connecticut, and for only the second time in Connecticut's history, a woman has served in this position and has caused many Lions and others to describe the Candlewood Lions Club as the "Governor's Club."

Connecticut's Governor M. Jodi Rell came to help celebrate her Lions
Club's 10th Anniversary.  Shown from left to right are PDG Art
Davies, PDG W. Keith Wuerthner, Governor M. Jodi Rell and PCC
Bob Gyle.

## History of the New Fairfield Lions Club

The New Fairfield Lions Club sponsored by the Danbury Lions Club was chartered on December 21, 1951. They have the distinction of being the first service organization to be formed in New Fairfield.

Since its inception, the club has developed numerous service projects, which take place throughout the year. These projects include annual events such as Fourth of July parade, Easter egg hunt, Breakfast with Santa, the senior citizen's end of summer picnic and holiday luncheon, spring clean up of the Girl Scout camp, holiday decorations in the town center, the collection of eye glasses, and eye screenings. In addition the club's foundation account is used to support programs such as local athletic leagues, drug awareness programs, the New Fairfield Public School wish list, "Ability beyond Disability," "Dreams Come True," Regional Hospice, as well as donations to the fuel bank and food bank.

Annually the club provides scholarships to local high school and vocational school graduates with contributions to date totaling in excess of $150,000.

The New Fairfield Lions Club also provides annual support to LCIF, CLERF, Camp Hemlocks. Fidelco, Low Vision Center, Speech and Hearing and Diabetes Awareness.

In the early 1950's, the New Fairfield Lions Club founded the local Little League baseball program, which has grown from 30 children to the current enrollment in excess of 500 boys and girls each season. The club is also the sponsor of two Boy Scout troops and a Cub Scout Pack, and continues to provide financial support.

In 1994 the club designed and built a gazebo on Memorial Field. Upon completion, the gazebo was donated to the Town of New Fairfield, and is used throughout the year for various community events.

Service projects are supported by multiple fundraising events including an annual summer carnival, antique car show, vacation raffle, the sale of entertainment books and holiday coloring books, Sight Saver Day, and bus trips to sporting events, the casino and the horse track.

Numerous members of this club have served in various leadership positions for both the District and Multiple District. The club has given their support to two District Governors who also served as Council Chairmen, namely Robert Gyle III and Robert Redenz.

The club has served the citizens of New Fairfield for over half a century and has become an intricate part of the fabric of this community.

## History of the New Haven Lions Club

The New Haven Lions Club was chartered February 9, 1922 under the sponsorship of the Bridgeport Lions Club. There were 25 charter members in this, the second Lions Club to be formed in New England.

The club's secretary, PDG Jim Bennett reports that charitable contributions have averaged $18,000 per year for the past twenty years and estimates total donations from the club's inception to be about $700,000.

A consistent supporter of all District projects, the New Haven Lions have always contributed their fair share whenever special needs have arisen. The club, for example, pledged $15,000 to CLERF's 1984 Boardman Building renovation, another $10,000 to the Macular Degeneration Research initiative, and most recently, a $5,000 contribution for the UConn Vascular Eye Center project.

Service activities have included the collection of eyeglasses, bell ringing for the Salvation Army, holiday food collections, blood drive sponsorships, eye screenings, a Leo sponsorship and the club's very unique "One to One" program. This last activity was formalized in 1975. With a wide variety of trips and activities, one Lion is matched with one blind individual and involved in four to six events each year.

Fundraising activities have evolved from bridge parties to car raffles, celebrity concerts, holiday card sales, and a wine tasting and raffle. The club's largest fundraiser is their annual golf tournament.

Over the years, five members of this club have served as District Governor, namely, Walter Kenney, Bill Buckingham, Ted Hyatt, Bob Pilot and Jim Bennett. Major George Hewlett in 1922 served as New England's first ever "Chief Administrator."

This is a club which believes in honoring members for their contributions. To date, the New Haven Lions proudly boast twenty-four

Melvin Jones Fellows, sixteen Knights of the Blind, five Ambassadors of Sight, three Good Shepherd Fellows, and one life member.

Charles M. Bakewell, the club's second President, was probably the most famous member. Lion Charles studied at the University of California, Harvard, as well as universities in Europe. He was a professor of Philosophy at Yale for forty-eight years, a member of the State Senate, served a term in Congress, and was a Lions International Director. He died in 1957 at the age of 90.

Over the years the Bennett family has been extremely active in Lionism. Al Bennett joined the club in 1957, and in 1975 sponsored son Alan as a Lion member. In 1980 Alan sponsored brother Jim who was elected as District Governor in 1998. Jim sponsored his spouse to be Joan as a new member in 1992 and she in turn sponsored her mother-in law Jean Bennett in 1996. Finally in 2000 Jim sponsored brother Peter to club membership.

The Bennett family combined has made significant contributions helping the club assist its local, state and world communities.

2001 photo shows the New Haven Lions "Six Bennett Family Members". From left to right are Peter, Alan, Al, Jean, Jim and Joan.

## History of the Newtown Lions Club

The Newtown Lions Club was chartered on November 30, 1946, sponsored by the Danbury Lions.

George R. Trull served as the charter president. His name lives on as the Newtown Lions present the annual "Trull" award to an outstanding member of the Newtown High School junior class.

The club has sponsored a Leo Club at the Newtown High School and continues to provide an advisor to assist the Leos with their activities. Annually the Newtown Lions present the "Leo of the Year" award to the most active and productive Leo.

The Newtown Lions contribute to camperships for children with diabetes and cancer, and the Lions camp for handicapped children. Annual contributions are made to CLERF as well as the Macular Degeneration Research Center at Yale University, and the Connecticut Lions Low Vision Centers.

Recent projects have included sending packages of food and personal care items to active duty military personnel deployed in Iraq, Afghanistan and Kuwait.

The Lions provide for the continuing needs for the "Abilities Beyond Disabilities" house in Newtown, and they also raised funds for two new playgrounds at Treadwell Park.

During the past six years, the Newtown Lions have repaired and refurbished homes in Newtown under the "AmeriCares Home Front" program. The club also provides financial assistance to "Kevins Community Center" a newly established non-profit medical center for those unable to afford medical care.

The Newtown Lions provide funding for eye examinations and glasses for those in need, and helps fund meals on wheels, the Family Counseling Center, Newtown Youth Services, drug education programs, and local food and fuel banks.

Members of the Newtown Lions provide food baskets for those in need at Thanksgiving and during the holiday season.

The Newtown Lions annually sponsors the United States Air Force Band concert, which is provided at no cost to the public. The club members also participate in Newtown's annual "Relay for Life" which raises funds for the American Cancer Society.

The club recently completed leading a town wide project to replace seats at the Edmond Town Hall Theatre.

In addition to serving their community, the Newtown Lions Club offers several social activities to its members and their families. Lions and their significant others are invited to the holiday dinner meeting in December, a Valentine's Dinner/Dance in February and the "Pass the Gavel" meeting in June during which time the officers of the club are installed.

The club also holds a progressive dinner, attends a Bridgeport Bluefish baseball game and enjoys local theater productions with friends and family.

After the completion of the annual Memorial Day duck race fundraiser, a family picnic is held to celebrate another successful race.

The Newtown Lions have shared the joy of serving with members of their families and continue to be a vital force in meeting the needs of their community and communities throughout the world.

Newtown Lions member Gordon Williams serves as the town's 2004 Labor Day Parade Marshall. He is seated in the back seat with his wife Lina of the 2004 Newtown Lions Car Raffle Prize, a classic red Ford Mustag convertible. Lion Gordon is one of the club's outstanding members; Past Club President, past Cabinet member, Melvin Jones Fellow and Knight of the Blind.

The Newtown Lions celebrated their Anniversary in November 2005. They honored 14 of their Past Presidents. Shown seated from the left are William Honan, Jon Christensen, George Mattegat and Frank DeLucia. In the middle are Joe Grasso, Keith Dupree, Charles Lewis and Paul Arneth. In the back row are Robert Schmidle, Gordon Williams, Jerome Meyer, Les Burroughs, Bill Denlinger and Robert Rice.

## History of the North Bridgeport Lions Club

The Bridgeport/ North Bridgeport Lions Club, 125 members strong, was chartered on February 7, 1966, with the Bridgeport Host Lions Club serving as their sponsor.

Many of us can recall the world famous bellhop who stepped out of store windows all over the world issuing a "Call For Phillip Morris." That bellhop was none other than Bridgeport/North Bridgeport Lions Club charter member Al Altieri who toured with Bob Hope entertaining our troops during the Second World War.

Of the original 125 plus charter members, Lions Robert Dortenzio and William Minty continue to be active members today.

The history of the Bridgeport/North Bridgeport Lions Club began with Joseph Ganim, a member of the Bridgeport Host Club, and an International Director. Having an interest in becoming International Lions President, Ganim sought to enhance his image by establishing additional Lions Clubs in Bridgeport. He succeeded in this effort with the establishment of four clubs: North Bridgeport, Host Bridgeport, East Bridgeport and West Bridgeport. Although the clubs were all successful for a period of time, the longest lasting of these clubs was North Bridgeport and East Bridgeport. East Bridgeport later changed its name to Beardsley Bridgeport and for a short period met together with North Bridgeport. However, Beardsley Bridgeport later surrendered its charter, and its members become members of the Bridgeport Host Club, the oldest chartered Club in Connecticut, thus leaving North Bridgeport as the last of those clubs chartered under the Ganim effort.

The Bridgeport/North Bridgeport Lions Club has been extraordinarily effective in its support of Lionism since it's beginning. Although today their membership numbers have diminished, they continue to actively work for and support a number of worthy activities and projects. Lion Yvette Benedetto, in chairing several very successful Candy Sale fundraisers, has enabled North Bridgeport to continue these efforts.

Lion Janice Faye and Lion Bob Dortenzio, working under the able direction of Lion Pat Pallotto of the Bridgeport Host Club, have served a number of District Governors in the production of the "District Pride." Lions Bill Minty, Nick Framularo and Richard Krodel are also proud to have served on the cabinets of a number of District Governors.

All Lion members of the Bridgeport/North Bridgeport Lions Club can be proud of the efforts that they have made for Lionism.

Five members of this organization have been honored by the Club as Melvin Jones Fellows.

With a rich and exciting history, and an undying spirit, the future looks bright for this extraordinary organization.


## History of the North Haven Lions Club

The North Haven Lions Club was chartered on March 28, 1952 with the Branford Lions Club as their sponsor. For more than half a century this club has made substantial contributions. CLERF alone has been the recipient of over $20,000. In 2004 the club sponsored the "Walk for Eye Research" and subsequently contributed $8,000 to the Yale Eye Research Center.

This club has contributed annually to all Multiple District and International Lions charities.

Locally the club has provided funds for eye examinations and glasses for students whose families could not meet the cost, and has met the cost of hearing aids for students as well.

For the past several years, the North Haven Lions have conducted eye screenings for the community, and these have proven to be quite successful.

During the past three decades, the club has purchased over 1500 turkeys, which were included in the Thanksgiving and Christmas food baskets for those in need in the North Haven Community.

Within North Haven the club has several drop off points for used eyeglasses and to date they have collected over 7,000 pairs of glasses for their "Gift of Sight" program.

The North Haven Lions are proud to be the home club of PDG William W. Grosberg as well as others who have served on the District Cabinet.

## History of the Norwalk Lions Club

The Norwalk Lions Club was chartered July 10, 1946, sponsored by the Stamford, Springdale, and New Canaan Lions Clubs. Robert Gillespie served as the club's charter president.

Club activities include glaucoma and hearing clinics, and assisting the Salvation Army. The Norwalk Lions each year "ring the bell" for this organization. In addition the club supplies the Norwalk Public Library with large print and talking books. Each year the Lions Charity Golf Tournament is the talk of the town, and the club raises funds for their several charities.

The Norwalk Lions are proud to have installed a listening system in the Imax Theatre at the Norwalk Aquarium and opened the first hearing aid bank in Lower Fairfield County. Each year the Norwalk Lions provide entertainment at the Senior Homes. The club sponsors antique fairs and during the Memorial Day parade, distribute thousands of American flags.

The Norwalk Lions contributed $25,000 to the Norwalk Hospital for a ceiling mounted operating room microscope. The members have also collected thousands of eyeglasses for use in third world nations.

Each year the Norwalk Lions award a scholarship to a graduating disabled high school senior.

Over the years the Norwalk Lions Club has conducted several types of fundraising events. In addition to their golf tournament, they have operated the "Lions food booth" at the Oyster festival, and have conducted an annual pancake breakfast.

The Norwalk Lions are proud to be the home club of PDG's Philip Jakob, William Hewlett and Theodore Beauregard.

The members of this club are pleased to be part of their community of over 80,000 people with a rich history dating back to the Revolutionary War when the British burned the city. The members applauded the opportunity to celebrate the city's 350th anniversary and the members took part in both the activities and the huge parade honoring the city.

## History of the Old Greenwich Lions Club

The Old Greenwich Lions Club was chartered on May 18, 1933 under the sponsorship of the Greenwich Lions Club. At least four or five times a year, the club meets jointly with the Greenwich Lions in an effort to foster cooperation as well as to combine their efforts on a major fund raiser, the annual golf tournament.

This club also holds a grapefruit sale, a pancake "fry," and a "Charitable Trust" mailing, all of which are significant sources of income.

Funds raised are used to support Connecticut and International Lions programs, as well as the community. Annually, the club's contributions total is between $25,000 and $30,000 a year.

Through the years, the Old Greenwich Lions Club has served as a source of talent used to fill several cabinet positions.

As this club approaches its 75th anniversary year, it stands proud to be a major part of the fabric of their community.


## History of the Orange Lions Club

The Orange Lions Club was sponsored by the Milford Lions and received their charter April 23, 1952.

The club began a "Community Grants" program in 2003. Applications are sought from community organizations, and grants ranging from $200 to $1,500 are provided to groups that utilize funds to improve the community. Organizations that have received such grants include the Orange Senior Center, Orange Youth Services, the Orange Historical Society, and the Orange War Memorial committee.

The Orange Lions have provided numerous service activities. Vision acuity and glaucoma screening exams are provided at the annual Orange County Fair. Each year the Orange Lions sponsor a luncheon party for senior citizens in Orange. Since 1989 these Lions could be found at the Community Center providing a Thanksgiving dinner on the Sunday before Thanksgiving for members of the community who did not have family of their own. For those who are homebound, the Orange Lions on that same day, deliver complete dinners to the recipient's home, a great public service.

One of the Lions major events since 1961 has been the Easter Egg Hunt held on the grounds of the Community Center. During the Memorial Day Parade, the Orange Lions distribute miniature U.S. flags to the children along the parade route, and also feature a float including a Lion in costume.

The Lions have accepted donated used eye glasses since 1978, and to date have collected in excess of 10,000 pairs.

Each year, two outstanding graduating seniors of Amity High School receive a $1,000 scholarship.

In March 2000. The Orange Lions, in conjunction with the Milford Lions, sponsored a Leo Club at the Foundation High School in Milford. Since it's founding, it has proven to be highly successful. It is noted that this is reportedly the only Leo Club in North America whose total membership is composed of special needs children.

Annually the club contributes to the American Diabetes Association, Camp Hemlocks, CLERF, CRIS, Fidelco, LCIF, Low Vision, Speech and Hearing, and the Youth Outreach program. The Lions also contribute to the Case Memorial Library for the purpose of purchasing large print books and books on tape for the visually impaired. It is said that the Orange Library has one of the finest collections of large print books in a municipal library in Connecticut, no small feat for a town of 13,000.

Fundraising activities include a Golf Shoot Out, wine tasting events, fundraisers at shopping malls, Sight Saver Day, selling refreshments at Orange Community Center summer concerts, and a dinner event featuring about twelve restaurants from the Orange area.

The Orange Club looks forward to continued growth and success in the years ahead as it provides service to both local and world communities.

## History of the Oxford Lions Club

The Oxford Lions Club, under the sponsorship of the Southbury Lions, received its charter on March 15, 1951.

During its early days in the 1960's, the club developed "Kirk's Pond" as a recreational facility for the community. With the town hall being constructed adjacent to this area at a later date, the pond today serves as the town's center. A monument at the pond commemorates the Lions' contribution to the town of Oxford.

After years of planning, fundraising, and ultimately construction, the club dedicated a pavilion in 2002 at Jackson's Cove Town Park on Lake Zoar along the Housatonic River. The pavilion provides a shelter for summer events.

Today the club continues to work with the Oxford Parks and Recreation Department planning for additional improvements at the park including kitchen and toilet facilities.

For students, the club each year, awards scholarships to graduating high school students and also participates in the International Peace Poster. The club also provides support for the DARE program, Fidelco, Camp Hemlocks and CLERF.

Fundraising activities have included an extremely successful 2004 raffle for a 1973 Corvette. This involved the volunteer efforts of every Lion and was the club's largest fundraiser in its fifty plus year history. Future Corvette raffles are currently in the planning stage.

In 2005, the Oxford Lions held their first wine tasting fundraiser, and raised over $2,000 during their annual Christmas poinsettia sales project.

One member, Joseph Persico, was recently honored as an "Advocate for the Blind."

## History of the Prospect Lions Club

The Prospect Lions have been involved in numerous projects since their inception. Fundraising has been both innovative and profitable with activities from a "Poker Run" to a 50-50 raffle, a Ziti Dinner and of course their most profitable fund raising event, the annual golf tournament.

The "Poker Run" is held in August and originates from Hotchkiss Field located in Prospect on Route 69. It is an exciting event, which includes five stops throughout Litchfield and New Haven counties. The cost is $20 for each motorcycle and $10 for each passenger, and of course included in the price are hot dogs, homburgs and great music.

The Timothy J. Keeley Scholarship Fund is important to the members of the Prospect Lions Club, and that is why the club invests much time and effort into the "Ziti Dinner" held at the St. Anthony's Church Hall.

The club's annual golf tournament is held in September at Highland Greens in Prospect and there is always an all out effort to make the event a great success.

With funds raised, the Prospect Lions proudly support their community as well as District, Multiple District and International Lions causes.

## History of the Ridgefield Lions Club

The Ridgefield Lions Club received its charter on April 19,1929. During their almost 80 years of service, the Ridgefield Lions have continuously served their community.

In 1997, the club members created a rather unique project when they introduced the "Native American Arts Festival," which has remained one of their most popular events.

Since it's beginnings, the Ridgefield Lions have delivered holiday food baskets to those in need during the Thanksgiving and holiday seasons. As many as 90 families have been the recipients of these timely and welcome gifts.

The club members participate in the Visiting Nurse Association's annual Health Day, and continue to select a worthy student each year for a Lion's scholarship.

Other services associated with the early days of this club include bus trips for school children to the Bronx Zoo and the New York Museum of Natural History, glaucoma screening clinics, vision and hearing clinics, and sponsorship of Scout units.

In recent years, the club has actively participated in the annual Peace Poster contest.

Lion Anna Lossius has the distinction of being the first woman to serve as President of the Ridgefield Lions Club. The Ridgefield Lions are proud that seventeen of its members have been named as Melvin Jones Fellows, six as Knights of the Blind, and one Ambassador of Sight.

Fundraising projects include the clubs annual golf tournament and raffle, which together result in generating income totaling more than $20,000.

## History of the Seymour Lions Club

The Seymour Lions Club, sponsored by the West Hartford Lions, was chartered August 27, 1952. During their more than half century of service, the members have been sensitive to the needs of others. Christmas gifts have been given to patients at a local convalescent hospital and the club has sponsored Christmas parties at two senior housing complexes.

A long-standing project has been one of making phone calls on Halloween night to school children. If the child is at home at the time of the call, a silver dollar is awarded by the club. This project was featured in the Lions Clubs International magazine indicating that this was considered as an outstanding Lions project.

During the past thirty years, the Seymour Lions have been collecting used eyeglasses totaling in excess of 5,000 pairs.

The club also provides funding for examinations and glasses for school children whose parents are unable to meet this need.

Each year the Seymour Lions award two scholarships for graduates of Seymour High School.

The Seymour Lions Club recently received first prize in the town's annual Christmas parade.

Fundraisers are numerous including antique car shows.

The Seymour Lions Club is proud that one of their members, Rose Marie Spatafore served as District Governor during the Lions year 2007-2008 and was the first woman to hold that position in the District. She previously served as both CST and VDG and was the recipient of two International President's Certificates of Appreciation.

## History of the Southbury Lions Club

The Southbury Lions Club was sponsored by the Bethel Lions Club in December 1948, beginning a proud tradition of volunteer services in their community.

The Southbury Lions raise funds for scholarships, Camp Hemlocks, fuel banks, the Connecticut Lions Eye Research Foundation and other district and state projects.

The club also sponsors an annual Halloween party at one of the town's elementary schools.

This club's history tells us that they provide the Southbury Lions Club Ambulance as a free service to the town.

Money is raised through their annual golf tournament, barbecues, and ham and bean suppers. In more recent years, the Southbury Lions have sold Christmas trees.

For over half a century, the Southbury Lions Club has been a vital force within their community.


## History of the Stamford-North Stamford Lions Club

The Stamford-North Stamford Lions Club under the sponsorship of the Stamford Lions Club was chartered November 11, 1965.

This organization proves that helping others can most certainly be fun. For example, the members every few months sort through hundreds of pairs of eyeglasses during what they term as "A Grand Sorting Party." One or two of the members will make huge pots of chili and clam chowder, and during the party these Lions will sort between 10 and 15 boxes of glasses and hearing aids for recycling.

Some of the members joke that in the North Stamford Lions Club, few things dramatically change. The club has been meeting at Anthony's Restaurant for over a decade, and for over a decade desert has never been a surprise, as it is always the same ice cream roll. Recently after many years of the same ice cream roll, the restaurant started serving the members a slightly different ice cream roll. This was an extraordinary moment and the members were absolutely thrilled to witness what they described as a pleasant change after 10 years.

As fund raising events, the club holds fall and spring pancake breakfasts with Halloween, St. Patrick's Day, Spring, and Super-Bowl themes. They have held pasta and comedy night fundraising events for the past 4 years along with a silent auction.

During Stamford's "Big Balloon Parade Blow-Up Event" the club sells hot chocolate, candy, cookies and other assorted items.

In the past the club sold potted plants a week before Mother's Day but recently do to extreme competition the project was discontinued.

This Lions Club has generously donated funds to Hurricane Katrina victims through a southern Lions Club. In addition the club supports a local theater group called "Curtain Call" as well as "Smart Kids with Learning Disabilities."

During the most recent period the club donated funds to CLERF, LCIF, the District Pride, Fidelco, and Camp Hemlocks as well as funds to purchase "Assistive Listening Devices" for the Stamford School System.

As for the future, the members will be working to help raise funds for baseball and softball equipment for children in the Dominican Republic.

The members of the Stamford-North Stamford Lions Club have enjoyed more than forty years of serving their community and communities throughout the world, and look forward to a very bright future.

## History of the Stratford Lions Club

It was in November 1929 that the Stratford Lions Club began its journey of service.

Their projects include an annual scholarship, which is funded by a trust fund that they developed. This fund ensures that scholarships will continue, even if the club ceases to exist.

The club's history tells us that they helped build the Roosevelt Forest in town, and that they provide assistance to many of the other charities in their community.

They have provided support to the town's Shakespeare Theater and supported the Red Coat Executive Band.

As they look forward to their 80th year of service, this club is proud of their past and excited about the years to follow.

## History of the Trumbull Center Lions Club

On January 26, 1986, the Trumbull Center Lions Club, 38 members strong, received their charter from Lions Clubs International. The club's first president was Dr. Chester A. Sobelowski who three years later would become their District Governor.

The club immediately set out to make a difference for their town.

The members solicited the citizens for funds and raised $75,000 to build the Trumbull Town Hall Gazebo. In 1989 it was completed and dedicated to the Town of Trumbull.

The bocci courts at Indian Ledge Park were in need of repair, and in 1998 in honor of Lion Harry V. Lickey, were once again reopened.

This club has supported the "Winterfest" as well as health fairs and blood drives. Among the club's service activities, these Lions proudly participate in a health fair where the public is invited to have their eyes and ears examined along with blood pressure.

During the annual Hospice "Tree of Light" the Lions purchase a light for each deceased member. As they gather together to view the magnificent tree, they pray in silence for those who have given their all in service to their community and communities around the world.

Annually awards are presented to three students in each of the six elementary schools for outstanding achievement. The Trumbull Center Lions are very aware that they are honoring tomorrow's leaders, and that this is a most important annual activity.

The Trumbull Center Lions support the school's annual drug program by supplying book covers and T-shirts.

Each year the members contribute to the charities endorsed by the District Governor including LCIF, CLERF, CRIS, Low Vision Center, Diabetes, and Hearing and Speech. The club also regularly contributes to the Red Cross and Fidelco.

Fundraisers include light bulb sales, art auctions, "Breakfast with Santa," an annual carnival and wine tasting as well as a most lucrative walk-a-thon.

Although a relatively young club, the Trumbull Center Lions Club is both active and innovative, and a credit to their community. The club is proud that two of their members were elected as District Governors. In addition to Dr. Chester Sobelowski, Gene Poulos not only served as District Governor but also was extremely active in numerous multiple district activities.

## History of the Trumbull Lions Club

The Trumbull Lions Club was chartered on November 20, 1950 under the sponsorship of the Fairfield Lions Club.

Camp Hemlocks, a summer camp for handicapped children, one of the most significant services offered in Connecticut, was both conceived and implemented by the Trumbull Lions Club. But the contributions of this Lions Club far exceed their involvement with Camp Hemlocks. The Trumbull Lions created the Emergency Medical Service in Trumbull, and this was the first such facility in the United States.

During the Christmas, Thanksgiving and Easter holidays, food baskets are provided for those in need in their town.

The DARE program has been implemented in local schools, and the club awards scholarships annually, as well as high school good citizenship awards. The club also holds a dinner for all of the fall athletes annually. This event is known to the Trumbull High School as "Sports Night."

The Lions of Trumbull erected a town bulletin board and donated EMS Defibrillators to the Trumbull Police Department.

The Trumbull Lions have supported CLERF, Campaign Sight First, Connecticut Institute for the Blind, Lions Low Vision Center, New Eyes for the Needy, Eye Glass Recycling Program, Stern Village, LCIF, Fidelco, Macular Degeneration, Oak Hill School for the Blind, the District Pride Newsletter, the Salvation Army, and the Thomas Merton Soup Kitchen.

The Trumbull Lions have been a vital service club in the Trumbull community for over 50 years. The International Lions motto, "We Serve," has been the driving force in raising funds for numerous town-oriented projects.

## History of the Waterbury Lions Club

The Waterbury Lions Club was chartered October 18, 1923. It was at that time that thirty-five business and professional men in Waterbury joined together in a service-oriented club called "Lions."

As early as 1927, the Waterbury Lions Club published a book in Braille. Between 1927 and 1934 the club sponsored numerous children at summer camps, and conducted local activities directly benefiting underprivileged children.

In 1934 the Waterbury Lions Club created what was to become the "Lions Club Health Foundation of Waterbury." This foundation has been the club's primary vehicle for raising and disbursing funds for its charitable activities.

In October 1938 the club leased a campsite on Bantam Lake in the town of Morris. The camp for underprivileged children was named for Layton Rose, the clubs second president and its most ardent supporter of the cause of the underprivileged child. Since 1938 Camp Layton Rose grew from a single building to a modern rustic complex of five buildings including a main dining and recreation building, dormitories, a crafts building, a staff residence, and appropriate recreational facilities. Commencing in 1975, and continuing until 1993, the camp operated in cooperation with the Waterbury Association for Retarded Citizens. In 1993 the camp was made available to New Opportunities Inc., Waterbury's inner city agency, for the operation of its mini camp and other summer programs. Recently the camp was given to New Opportunities Inc.

Over the years, the club and the Foundation raised $500,000 and used the funds for the improvement of Camp Layton Rose and for providing over 6,000 children and adults with a summer camping experience.

In addition, the club has continued to support the sight, hearing, and other Lions service projects, and has assisted numerous individuals with sight and hearing problems. The club has contributed thousands of dollars to CLERF. Waterbury Lion, PID Harold A. Ashley, was the first President of the Connecticut Lions Eye Research Foundation, and the club has, through the years contributed thousands of dollars in support of the foundation. The Waterbury Lions are currently committed to contributing thousands of dollars to the foundation for the treatment of macular degeneration.

The Waterbury Lions Club is proud to have been the home club of Past District Governors J. Sidney Wakely, Harold A. Ashley and Michael Granatuck.

Through the years, the Waterbury Lions Club has honored thirteen members as Knights of the Blind, six as Melvin Jones Fellows, and three as Ambassadors of Sight.

The Waterbury Lions Club is proud of its past achievements and eagerly looks forward to future opportunities to serve their community.

## History of the West Haven Lions Club

The West Haven Lions Club, with 33 charter members, was organized on April 25, 1951 under the sponsorship of the New Haven Lions Club.

From the beginning, this club has been quite active. During the 50's, funds were raised for community projects by sponsoring boat trips, and holding "Ladies Nights." Even broom sales were successful. Their very first sale grossed over $500. In the early 50's after sponsoring a musical show, the club made their first purchase of a device to test eyes, which was donated to the local school system. They went on to purchase equipment for the high school driver training program as well as specialized diagnostic equipment for the local board of education.

Through additional fundraisers, the club was able to provide state flood relief and purchase glasses for those in need.

During the 60's, the club expanded their "Be Thankful You Can See" fundraiser with an expanded mailing list. The additional funds allowed them to expand their community service with acts of altruism such as purchasing a wheel chair for a 7-year-old child whose family could not afford this costly purchase.

Through the years the club has continually collected and donated used eyeglasses. In the 70's they displayed their colors with a magnificent float created for the city's "Golden Jubilee." The members marched in the parade to remind the towns' people of the importance of this very vital service organization.

In the late 80's, their very successful major project was the "Savin Rock Festival" under the sponsorship of the local Chamber of Commerce, with booths of all descriptions, rides, crafts and of course the club's annual "beer booth," a most popular event. Contributions to the community continued including support of the Diabetes Association, the Community House, Little League, Eye Research, Boy Scouts, LCIF, Camp Hemlock, and the purchase of large print books for the local library.

During the early 90's the West Haven Lions answered the call of a 40-year-old woman who was diagnosed with Multiple Sclerosis This individual, the mother of two children had been confined to a wheel chair for over five years. She was the first person in Connecticut to receive a specially trained service dog. The dog required training, and the West Haven Lions said, "Yes, we will help in meeting the cost of the required training." As a result, this individual achieved a high degree of independence and freedom.

As the club entered the 21st century, they created new fundraisers, which resulted in income beyond all expectations, with contributions to both old and new charities, all in the interest of continuous service to their community.

## History of the Western Greenwich Lions Club

On November 21, 1996, the Western Greenwich Lions Club was chartered through the sponsorship of the Greenwich Lions Club.

The Western Greenwich Lions raise funds selling grapefruit during the winter months as well as sponsoring an annual wine tasting event within their community.

Although slightly more than a decade in age, the Western Greenwich Lions Club looks forward to a bright future.

## History of the Wolcott Lions Club

The Wolcott Lions Club was sponsored by the Waterbury Lions and received its charter April 23, 1952. Carl Mattson served as the club's charter president.

During their first three years as a Lions Club, major fund drives were conducted for cancer, the March of Dimes, and flood relief for the greater Waterbury flood.

During this period the Wolcott Lions Book Fund was created for the purpose of purchasing books for the local school's libraries.

In the 1960's and 1970's the club sponsored an oratorical contest to both challenge and reward high school students. More recently, the club sponsored local teachers to attend the Quest program, and also sponsored the DARE Halloween dance for middle school students. The Wolcott Lions are proud to annually present four $1,500 scholarships.

This club has sponsored medical services from purchasing polio vaccine serum in 1957 to a flu shot clinic for senior citizens more recently. Equipment such as wheel chairs and eye testing equipment have been provided to local schools. Over the years the Wolcott Lions have donated emergency equipment to the Wolcott Police and the volunteer ambulance service, culminating with significant funding for the new ambulance headquarters, which was dedicated in June 1991. The Wolcott Lions host five blood drives each year and have been the recipient of the "American Red Cross Lions Cup" awarded each year since its inception for being the Lions Club in Connecticut that has delivered the most pints of blood.

The Wolcott Lions support numerous community activities including scouting, funding a girl scout camp, purchasing uniforms for high school teams, donation of a football scoreboard and cosponsoring the Wolcott Special Games.

Each year the Wolcott Lions sponsor a picnic for the elderly referred to as "Project Elderly."

A new event called the "Winter Wonderland" features a horse drawn wagon or sleigh rides, and a visit by Santa Claus. While the event is totally free to the community, the Lions ask for toys and food items, which are then distributed as part of "Toys for Tots" and "Food for the Needy" programs a short time later.

In 1979 the Wolcott Lions created the "Wolcott Country Fair" which became the club's major fundraiser replacing over thirty years of light bulb sales. The Fair brings over 30,000 people annually to the town over a three-day period. The townspeople also look forward to the Lions hosting a ziti supper fundraiser if a fire puts a family out of their home or if an illness strikes.

The members of this Lions Club truly feel the joy of helping others. They feel as a club of over 100 members that they are extremely fortunate to be part of a community that cares.

## History of the Woodbridge Lions Club

The Woodbridge Lions Club was chartered on May 24, 1951 under the sponsorship of the New Haven Lions Club.

From the beginning, the Woodbridge Lions have served the needs of their community. The club sponsored a girls softball team, organized Easter egg hunts for children, and donated radio equipment to their police department.

The Amity High School was the recipient of lighting demonstration equipment, and the Beecher Road Elementary School was thankful to the Lions for purchasing a diving board for their pool. Each year the Woodbridge Lions also award scholarships to promising students about to enter college.

In the month of October, the children of Woodbridge look forward to the annual Halloween party sponsored by the Woodbridge Lions.

During the bi-centennial celebration in 1976, the Woodbridge Lions constructed and staffed the booths at the Woodbridge Day Fair, and created a float, which was the talk of the town during the Woodbridge parade.

Lion Coleman Kramer saw a need for a health screening program in Woodbridge, and thus with the full cooperation of the membership, this program became a reality.

Lions' charities are always remembered by the Woodbidge Lions including CLERF, Camp Hemlocks, and Fidelco, among others.

Fundraising during the early years involved the selling of light bulbs and brooms, and this evolved into the "Cake and Cookie Sale" where each Lion had his territory, thus covering every house in Woodbridge. It was in 1983 that the club held its first auction, and this very successful event was under the chairmanship of Lions Len Plotnick and Mike Epstein.

Since that time, the Woodbridge Lions initiated an annual fund raising via mail event chaired by Lion Dave Gibson, and this has proven to be quite successful.

In 1984, under the guidance of Lion Alex Satmary and co chairs Lions Ed Cohen and Harry Tuttle, the first Lions Charity Golf Tournament was held, and for the next four years proved to be highly successful. During the first tournament, there was a momentous occasion; one of the players actually won the $1,000 hole-in-one contest. During subsequent golf tournaments, the club purchased insurance, and of course, no one since has won the hole-in-one contest.

Today the club's membership is composed of 17 men and women. Interestingly, there is a family of Lions in the club, namely, Club President Lion Bob Fries, Lion Secretary Beverly Fries and their daughter Lion Dr. Joyann Fries.

Lion member Dr. Phyllis Liu has utilized the eyeglass collection program in a unique way. Dr. Liu has personally delivered hundreds of pairs of eyeglasses and lenses to China for use by the Chinese people.

Although small in numbers, the Woodbridge Lions Club has served their community and communities around the world for over half a century.

## History of the Yalesville-Wallingford Lions Club

The Yalesville-Wallingford Lions Club was sponsored by the Meriden Lions and chartered on December 18, 1967.

Within recent history, the son of a member of this Lions organization received a devastating eye injury, however with emergency intervention provided by the staff of the Yale Eye Center, the eye was saved and eyesight ultimately restored. Having personally witnessed the miraculous work of the Yale medical staff, the members of the Yalesville-Wallingford Lions Club have been most generous in their funding of the Connecticut Lions Eye Research Foundation, and thus the Yale Eye Center.

The efforts of this club have always focused on the original challenge received from Helen Keller, that Lions be her "Knights of the Blind." The club has recycled used eyeglasses, and during the past year alone, collected over 3,000 pairs.

The club throughout the year meets the cost of eye examinations and eyeglasses for those in their community with insufficient funds.

This Lions Club has provided funding for their local library to purchase large print editions of newspapers and periodicals. They have also provided the library with funding to purchase a reading aid for patrons with Macular Degeneration.

The members have provided funding for improvements at a local park as well as streetscape improvements that give Wallingford its local charm. Funds have also been provided for the local volunteer fire department.

These Lions are proud of one of their most rewarding projects, that of providing food baskets for needy families during the Thanksgiving holiday. This past year the club provided 15 baskets complete with a frozen turkey and all the "fixings." In future years the club hopes to expand the scope of this project and provide additional families with holiday baskets.

The secondary focus of the club has always been the youth of their community. Each year for the past five years, the club has sponsored a Peace Poster contest working with the children of the town's Middle School. The local winner receives a monetary prize from the club before the wining poster is forwarded to the next level.

The Lions have helped to sponsor many high school aged students to be goodwill ambassadors to other countries and has hosted foreign students and their chaperones visiting our country.

Aid to young students is provided in the form of scholarships for those planning to continue their education.

Each year two scholarships are awarded, each in the amount of $1,000.

A tribute to their community for over forty years, the Yalesville-Wallingford Lions Club enjoys serving those who need the hand and the heart of a Lion.

## History of the Communications Disorder Center

For over 25 consecutive years, the Lions of District 23-A have generously supported the Communications Disorders Center at Yale-New Haven Hospital.

The support has been in the form of cash donations to purchase necessary equipment to benefit infant and adult patients. In the words of the center's director, Steven Leder, Ph.D., "The enduring loyalty and kindness of the Connecticut Lions is truly a meaningful investment in the Communications Disorder Center."

It all began in 1979, when word was received that Yale New Haven Hospital saw the need for a Brain Stem Evoked Response Machine (BSER) for the Department of Otolaryngology. The Lions Clubs of District 23-A were considering the possibility of helping to fund such a device. During this process PDG Michael Granatuck received a letter from the mother of a 15-month-old child who had her hearing tested at Yale-New Haven Hospital using such a device on loan from another hospital. She said that she was able to see first hand the importance of such a device.

Her daughter Kristen was born with multiple birth defects, the most serious affecting her vision and hearing. Although they knew at birth that the child was blind, hearing tests given to her shortly after birth and again at one year were inconclusive. To Kristen, any chance at a normal life rested on whether or not she could hear.

The BSER gave the family the answer that the child could function well enough to actually hear normal conversation. The father related to PDG Michael that if such a machine had not been available to her, the family would still be wondering about the extent of her hearing potential. In the mother's words, "I am certain that I could write much more and still never begin to tell you the joy and relief my husband and I felt when the BSER confirmed Kristen's ability to hear. I know there must be other parents in Connecticut and elsewhere who would benefit from Yale-New Haven having this equipment. I feel that it would be a very worthwhile project for the Lions Clubs involvement."

Twenty-five years later, in excess of $250,000 in equipment has been donated to the hospital's hearing clinic. As a result of these contributions, physicians and audiologists have identified and treated thousands of children and adults with hearing impairments.

More recently, the Speech and Hearing Committee established a hearing aid bank to provide hearing aids to needy children and adults. This low cost project is made possible through the collection of used hearing aids and special discounts from a manufacturer of hearing aids. The hearing aid bank is centered at the Communications Disorders Clinic located at Southern Connecticut University in New Haven. With the assistance of Clinical Director Kevin McNamara and students in audiology, hearing aids are tested and maintained for eventual use.

Every District Governor from District 23-A, starting with the District Governor Michael Granatuk in 1979, has determined how the Yale Speech and Hearing program would be served during their year as Governor. Each has left his mark in the history of this district.

In 2005, PDG Michael Granatuck planned a celebration at Yale New Haven Hospital to mark the 25th anniversary of Lions involvement in providing funds to aid in the purchase of the newest equipment for the Department of Communications Disorders. There is much pride in this district for their accomplishments through the years.

# Chapter 4 - History of the Lionism in District 23-B

## History of the Avon Lions Club

The Avon Lions Club was organized June 18, 1951 under the sponsorship of the West Hartford Lions Club.

This organization has participated in several hands on community projects including painting homes for elderly residents, building handicap ramps for the disabled, painting and restoring offices to benefit the disabled, and clearing a hiking and nature trail for the town and one of the Avon schools. The club also assisted with environmental clean-up projects along the Farmington River. Each month the members serve coffee at a local nursing home.

The club's largest recent donation project was the raising of over $40,000 to breed, raise, and train two Fidelco Guide Dogs. In addition, the club has given funds to over 45 local organizations, several District projects, and numerous International endeavors.

To fund these many projects the club has held many fund raisers over the years including auctions and tag sales, flea markets, pancake breakfast events, pasta suppers, harvest breakfasts, and hot dog and hamburg sales at the local Firemen's Carnival.

Each year the Avon Lions honors an outstanding member of the community with a "Citizen of the Year" or a "Public Servant" award. The club has honored twelve "Citizens of the Year" for their dedicated volunteer work to benefit the town, and given nineteen public servant awards to groups and individuals who have excelled in their jobs as town employees, or who have served on town boards and commissions or the Police or Fire Departments.

The Avon Lions have contributed 56 years of service to their town, their state and Lions Clubs International. They look forward to the years ahead serving the Avon community as well as assuming responsibility for new District and International initiatives.

## History of the Barkhamsted Lions Club

The Barkhamsted Lions Club was organized on October 20, 1966 under the sponsorship of the Winsted Lions Club, and received its charter in January 1967.

This club is totally involved in their community including youth programs, charitable organizations, health programs, as well as the various aspects of town life and educational programs. They are also fully involved with world wide humanitarian concerns through Lions Clubs International.

Since its inception, the Barkhamsted club has raised and contributed in excess of $50,000 to support community activities including the annual July 4th parade, scholarship funds, the "Open Door" Soup Kitchen, CLERF, the Barkhamsted Historical Society, and youth baseball. This club generously contributed to the Barkhamsted Sports Field upgrade, and funded a water cooler, sound system, a snellen eye chart, a controlled reader and tape recorders to the Barkhamsted School. In addition they purchased picnic tables for Stancliff Cove, and supported the exchange student program and numerous other community projects.

What motivates the members of this club is getting together to help those who need their assistance. They are diligently working to increase their membership, as the needs of their community are many, and increasing every day, and so much more could be done with more members involved in fundraising and service projects.

With this feeling of community, their future will no doubt be a bright one.

## History of the Berlin Lions Club

The Berlin Lions Club was organized October 27, 1941, sponsored by the New Britain Lions Club.

Veterans returning from the war wanted to have a safe swimming place for their children. In 1947, the club borrowed money and purchased land. They built the town's first community swimming pool which was named the "Lions Memorial Pool" in honor of those service men and women who gave their lives for our nation.

The Berlin Fair was created to pay for the construction and continued maintenance and operation of the pool. Community projects of the Berlin Lions include the maintenance and operation of the swimming pool, and working with local civic and church organizations including DARE. These Lions are also very involved preparing dinners for local senior citizens.

The club provides food baskets at Thanksgiving and Christmas and they are involved with the Soap Box Derby and challenger Baseball.

Club contributions have been used to fund payments for eye examinations and eyeglasses for those unable to meet this need. Funds are also used for youth projects, scholarships, LCIF, CLERF, CRIS, Fidelco, Oak Hill School for the Blind, The American School for the Deaf, as well as the American Red Cross and the Connecticut Lions Low Vision Centers.

The members are proud to be part of an organization that serves as the home club of District Governor Robert A. Weiss and Past District Governors Nunzio Rosso, Theodore Boryczki and George Ondrick.

The Berlin Lions have always fostered a strong commitment to the community and have actively supported a wide range of projects.

## History of the Bethlehem Lions Club

The Bethlehem Lions Club was organized May 30, 1972, sponsored by the Woodbury Lions Club.

The beginnings of this club's fundraising activities can be traced to the Bethlehem Fair where the members sold Belgian Waffles. Other fundraisers soon followed including the annual "Harvest Dinner." The Valentine's Day Dance soon became the annual "Sweethearts Ball," and it was at this event that the club used their home-built food trailer. The food trailer is also a very popular meeting place for those attending the Bethlehem Christmas Bazaar in early December.

When the food trailer was first completed, club members tested it during the opening day of the Bethlehem Little League. Hot dogs, hamburgers and French fries were cooked for the children and their families. Members described the event, as "It was great seeing a bunch of kids having a great time." This is a donations only project allowing families with limited income to pay what they wish for a delicious meal in the midst of a great social event.

The Bethlehem Lions Club contributes to the entire community, from youth to the elderly. The Lions Club is credited with installing the clock in the new town hall, and built and paid for the gazebo on the town green.

The club also sponsors the Bethlehem Elementary School D.A.R.E. program and awards scholarships to Nonnewaug High School students. The club also helps support the local "Visual Impairment and Blindness Services," supports the Lions Eye Institute at the Albany Medical Center and collects eyeglasses and hearing aids.

Perhaps what is unique about this club is the overall feeling of closeness that the members feel for each other. In the words of Lion Bob Overton, "I love this club and everyone in it!"

## History of the Bloomfield Lions Club

The Bloomfield Lions Club was organized on March 5, 1942 with the Hartford Host Lions Club serving as its sponsor. Fundraisers over the years have varied from comic book and sports card shows to a weekly flea market at the Copaco shopping center at a store donated by Lion Herman Bercowetz. The club has held Mother's Day pancake breakfast events and has sold soda and water at concerts, as well as Christmas wreaths and pecans.

In recent years, the Bloomfield Lions have sponsored an annual awards banquet, honoring Bloomfield citizens who have contributed to their community.

Past President and long time Lion Frank Kulig has tirelessly worked at the club's fund raisers. In addition, he and his wife Julianna have continued over the years providing musical entertainment at Alexandria Manor Nursing Home during the Christmas holiday, while other members of the club served cake and distributed gifts.

The club has held eye screenings for seniors and met the cost of eye examinations and eyeglasses for those in need.

The Bloomfield Lions are proud to be the home club of PDG and PCC Sydney T. Schulman and PDG Ronald Wolpoe. PCC Sydney, as of this writing, was serving as President of the Connecticut Lions Eye Research Foundation. PDG Ron is credited with creating the Connecticut Singles Lions Club, a new concept internationally. PDG Ron served as that club's first president.

This club was also honored to have had PCC Tom Hubbs serve as President of the Connecticut Lions Eye Research Foundation.

Other members of the Bloomfield Lions Club who have served their District include Lions Bill Maloney, Leslie Perry, Howard Hunter, Pat Sullivan, and Cynthia and Herman Bercowetz.

## History of the Bristol Lions Club

The Bristol Lions Club was organized March 23, 1926 under the sponsorship of the New Britain Lions Club. Dr. William Hanrahan served as charter president.

The Bristol Lions have collected over 330,000 pairs of usable eyeglasses for those in third world countries. For the citizens of Bristol, however, the Bristol Lions meet the needs of those who cannot afford eye examinations and glasses. The club also made it possible for one blind Bristol resident to receive treatment and surgery in Boston with the result being the actual restoration of sight. The club also financed A 12 year old child's trip to Washington, D.C. for laser treatments for an eye disorder. For one blind Bristol child, the club has paid for several years of music lessons, as the child's parents were without sufficient funds.

This club, in cooperation with the Bristol Health Department, donated four Titmus Eye Testing machines for school use.

The hearing impaired of Bristol have also been recipients of assistance from the Bristol Lions. The club donated two sets of telecaptioners for hearing impaired families.

The seniors of Bristol give thanks to the Bristol Lions for the medical examination table donated to the Senior Center as well as making glaucoma screenings available.

For the safety of the local fire department, the Bristol Lions donated a Thermal Imaging Helmet, which has proven to be invaluable.

This club has participated in numerous District, state, and International Lions sponsored programs. Substantial funds are donated to CLERF, the Oak Hill School for the Blind, the Gallery of the Senses at Wadsworth Athenaeum, the American School for the Deaf, and the Lions Low Vision Center. In addition Fidelco has benefited from the Bristol Lions Clubs generosity.

One very special gift to the city of Bristol was the Ice Skating rink at a cost of $8,000.

During the holiday season, the Bristol Lions can be found ringing bells next to Salvation Army kettles, helping that organization raise funds. At other times this group of citizens is sponsoring the annual United Way Pancake Breakfast.

Fund raising events have included tag sales, pasta dinners, a Valentine's Dinner Dance in conjunction with the Bristol Eastern High School, an annual pancake breakfast on Palm Sunday, and the Fred Soliani Memorial Golf Tournament. It should be noted that Lion Fred Soliani, a life member of the Bristol Lions Club, was a tireless worker who contributed consistently to each activity of his club and community.

Through the years there has been a continuous and enviable record of achievement in terms of service to the community, the state, and Lions Clubs International. The Bristol Lions, the club with a "heart" is loved and respected by the citizens of Bristol.

The Bristol Lions celebrate winning Best Community
Float at the town's  Annual Mum Festival Parade.

On October 8, 1990 Lion Cecil Turton of the Burlington
Lions Club is presented the Melvin Jones Fellowship
recognition from then District Governor Dan Uitti.

## History of the Burlington Lions Club

The Unionville Lions sponsored the Burlington Lions Club, which was organized March 12, 1968.

These Lions are committed to the youth of their community as is evidenced by their sponsorship of youth basketball, Little League, Scouting, DARE, and other programs for young people.

The Basketball League is a very intensive project. Registrations take place during October and November. Registration fees are charged for insurance, equipment, and any other costs incurred by the basketball program. Games are played in all of the Region 10 school's gymnasiums every year from November to March. Uniforms, basketballs, score books, first aid kits and equipment are furnished to every team coach in the program by the Lions, and collected during the annual basketball party, so that they can be used during the following year. During the basketball party, food is provided for over 400 children and their families by the Burlington Lions.

As part of its mission, the Burlington Lions provide financial support to several local organizations including the Burlington Library, volunteer fire department, Police Explorers, and the high school's "Project Graduation." The club also sponsors scholarships each year for members of the graduating class of the Lewis S. Mills Regional High School.

Additionally the club is sensitive to the needs of organizations that support eye conservation and those that work with the blind, specifically Fidelco, CLERF, American Diabetes Association, and CRIS Radio. Support has also been provided for hearing conservation, a playscape at the Burlington Recreational center, BESB, Quest, the American Heart Association, the Burlington Historical Society, and DARE. The club also donated a snow blower to the Burlington Library.

To finance these projects, the Burlington Lions sponsor an annual carnival each Memorial Day weekend. The club's "Turkey Shoot" is held annually prior to Thanksgiving. "Tavern Day" is held each autumn, and it is here that the Burlington Lions sell the best hot dogs this side of Burlington as well as delicious flavorful ice cream for young and old alike.

The Burlington Lions, in an effort to provide the service of hope, actively sell items manufactured by blind citizens, thereby providing a market for these products.

Additional funds are raised through the club's annual flower sale and their very popular pancake breakfast.

In keeping with the organization's motto, "We Serve," the Burlington Lions strive to help those in need, wherever the need exists.

## History of the Canaan Northwest Lions Club

The Canaan Northwest Lions Club was organized June 12, 1992 with the Unionville Lions Club serving as their sponsor. Formerly the Canaan Lionesss Club, 29 new members were inducted during their charter night.

Elizabeth Kowalski served as the charter president.

This club has sponsored a variety of fund raising events, with the most popular ones involving food. There have been numerous dinners where the members served succulent ham, corned beef and cabbage, chicken and polenta, steak barbecues, spaghetti dinners, and of course their outstanding pancake breakfast events.

Funds raised were used to assist members of the community providing gift baskets to those in need during the Thanksgiving and Christmas holidays, and to help support the local fuel bank. Senior citizens have been assisted in several ways, and the cost of eye examinations and glasses for seniors and children has been met by the club when the cost for these individuals was prohibitive.

Contributions have also been made to the local fire department, ambulance service, and the food bank.

Picnics and Christmas parties have been hosted by this Lions Club for residents of Wangum Village and Beckley House, and birthday parties have been organized for residents of Geer Nursing and Rehabilitation Center.

For graduating high school seniors, two scholarships are granted each year.

In 1993, the Canaan Northwest Lions Club and the Canaan Lions Club combined their resources to establish the "Kara Zinke" fund used for families in the community who have experienced emergency or catastrophic situations. Kara was a young lady whose death was unexpected, and the fund was established in her memory. It is noted that Kara's mother and aunt are members of the Canaan Northwest Lions Club.

This is a small Lions Club in the Northwest corner of the state, and the members are proud that one of their own, Marilyn Minacci served as their District Governor in 2002.

## History of the Canton Lions Club

The Canton Lions Club was organized November 23, 1951 with the Unionville Lions Club serving as their sponsor. According to the club's historian,

"No moss grows on the Canton Lions" and it is quite evident that this is an accurate statement.

Many of the club's fundraisers include "lots of cooking." Lions can be seen flipping burgers and dogs at many town wide events. The club is celebrating its 14th year of pancake breakfast events, the first in the spring and the second in conjunction with "Sam Collins Day" a town wide fall celebration of the town's founding. The Canton Lion's grills are a place where old friends meet to enjoy great food.

The Canton Lions Club's holiday poinsettia sale has both businesses and individuals lining up for top quality poinsettias and Christmas cactuses.

The club's birdseed sale in the fall has also been a great fundraiser, but more importantly the club realized years ago that having the members in the public eye helps both fund raising and membership. The club's free children's Fishing Derby is but one such example. The club stocks a local pond and provides both food and prizes for young anglers, with lots of fun for the adults afterwards. The Canton Lions annually park cars for the Canton Volunteer Fire Department's lobster fest. The club has also built wheelchair ramps and even a gazebo.

According to the Canton Lions, "In all possible ways, we DO serve."

## History of the Colebrook Lions Club

Sponsored by the Winsted Lions, the Colebrook Lions Club was organized June 30, 1980. It all began when a group of like-minded neighbors in one of Connecticut's smallest communities came together with the desire to serve their community.

Soon after its inception, a personal connection to diabetes and vision impairment led the club to embrace an organization dedicated to providing employment to the visually impaired, The Board of Education and Services to the Blind. At its peak, the Colebrook Lions sold more than $15,000 of goods manufactured by this group each year, more than any other club in the state.

Early club activities included sponsorship of the "Town Square" dances and Turkey Shoots - the later being fund raisers that involved selling pie shaped areas of a dart board with frozen turkeys going to the winners.

Other projects included the selling of lobsters, spaghetti, pancakes, fried dough, hamburgers, hot dogs, and pulled pork sandwiches to raise money for local causes. The club also sponsored the "Colebrook Challenge," a road race later renamed the "Maple Syrup Run." A long running fundraiser that remains popular to this day is the clubs annual poinsettia sale during which members are able to sell more than 600 plants.

Today the Colebrook Club, comprised of more than 30 members, contributes to a wide variety of local causes, and awards scholarships each year to outstanding graduating high school seniors. The club also sponsors the annual Red Cross blood drive and actively supports the town's emergency medical technicians.

Youth baseball and softball sportsmanship awards are presented annually in memory of member Russell Green. The club also sponsors a haunted house tour, skating parties and Easter egg hunts for children of all ages. The club is responsible for a local art competition as part of the LCI Peace Poster Contest and sponsor youths wishing to participate in Lions Day at the United Nations.

More than 25 years after it's founding, the Colebrook Lions Club remains committed to serving the community.

## History of the Connecticut Singles Lions Club

The Connecticut Singles Lions Club was organized June 3, 2001. Under the sponsorship of the Windsor Locks Lions Club, it was one of the "new concept" clubs that did not depend upon a specific geographical area for its existence. The club sought to bring together single adults who wished to serve the community and to assist Lions Clubs with insufficient membership to carry on some of their activities. They were proud of being "roving volunteers."

It was PDG Ronald Wolpoe, a member of the Bloomfield Lions Club, who was the force behind organizing this club. Upon its creation, Lion Ron transferred to the Connecticut Singles Club and served as its Charter President, as well as Guiding Lion. It is noted that Lion Ron went on to become District Governor during the 2003-2004 Lions year.

The Connecticut Singles Lions Club has sponsored fund raising single dances, which were very successful, raising sufficient funds to generously contribute to Fidelco, The American School for the Deaf, CLERF, and LCIF.

Service activities have included assisting other Lions Clubs with eye screenings, and helping to refurbish and renovate the original Jonathan's Dream Playground for the Handicapped and Non Handicapped Children of West Hartford.

## History of the East Granby Lions Club

The East Granby Lions Club was sponsored by the Granby Lions Club and was organized on April 28, 1960.

Through the continued support of the community, the Granby Lions Club has been able to award scholarships to graduating high school seniors and support scouting, little league and other youth activities within East Granby, as well as charities throughout Connecticut and beyond.

For almost five decades, the club has supported the local food pantry, medical supply closet, flu shot clinics, and sponsored Red Cross blood drives. Eye examinations and glasses are provided for needy residents, and thousands of pairs of used eyeglasses are collected and recycled through the Lions eyeglass-recycling program.

Contributions are provided annually to Lions charities including Journey for Sight, CLERF, Macular Degeneration, CRIS Radio, FIDELCO, LCIF, Hearing Conservation, and Diabetes.

The East Granby Lions Club also provides "scholar athletic" awards as well as scholastic grants, and is responsible for the "Citizen of the Year" award and the Memorial Day Parade. Contributions are also given to the Cultural Council and the Library Association.

Since the club's inception the members have served thousands of dinners, sold shrubbery and candy and held dozens of flea markets.

In 2004, the East Granby Lions had the good fortune to have a bright orange 1932 modified Ford pickup Truck donated with the stipulation that proceeds from its sale be used to establish a scholarship program for local high school graduates with aspirations of going into trades such as auto mechanic, hair dressing, plumbing, and electrical. The club raised sufficient funds from the raffle of the vehicle to provide a $5,000.00 award to a 2005 graduate, and create a baseline fund for future awards.

In October 2006, the club raffled a 1978 Chevrolet Corvette T-Top (automatic transmission) as their main 2006/2007 fundraiser. This effort was successful in providing the funding for the club's educational scholarships. The income from the project will also fund a number of other charitable projects for youths during the following Lion's year, including scouting and youth sports activities.

The club has qualified as a 501(c)(3) charitable organization known as the "East Granby Lions Charities, Inc." and this it is hoped will encourage additional contribution from the general public.


## History of the East Hartford Lions Club

The East Hartford Lions Club was organized January 16, 1950, having been sponsored by the Hartford Host Lions. Leon Winslow served as the charter president.

The club's contributions to the community over the past 50 plus years carry a monetary value of over a quarter of a million dollars. The services performed are many and most significant.

The East Hartford Lions sponsored the first Little League teams, organized a musical organization within the community and participated with a quartette of their own. These Lions have also donated musical instruments to the school system on a regular basis.

The club's first commitment to vision became a reality with the donation of several eye-testing machines to the East Hartford High School. In addition the club has an eyeglass and treatment project that has provided the funding of eye examinations and glasses for over three hundred individuals. For blind students, the Lions provided Braille tape machines and other services.

This organization observed that the East Hartford High School was in need of a basketball scoreboard, and proceeded to raise sufficient funds. With the desire to honor local students for their athletic achievements, the club initiated the annual East Hartford Lions Sports Banquet, and a scholarship in honor of Lion Russ Richards was also established for a graduating East Hartford High School senior who exemplifies the qualities of scholarship and community service.

Direct services were provided for the community when the club members provided food baskets for those in need during the holiday season. To assist the patients of the Visiting Nurses Association, hospital beds were purchased and donated.

Support of Lions projects has always been a priority. The Quest Skills for Life program has been instituted at the East Hartford Middle School, and LCIF contributions have resulted in the naming of 16 individuals as Melvin Jones Fellows. The club has been recognized for its support of Lions Clubs International "Sight First" campaign and has continually supported the Connecticut Lions Eye Research Foundation.

The East Hartford Lions are proud to be the home club of PDG George Precourt.

Fund raising activities have included a wine tasting event along with a silent auction. The club has sold beverages during events at the Uconn football games at Rentchler Field, and this has become a major fundraiser.

Pancake breakfast events, a Christmas Flower Sale, staffing the food concession at the Pratt and Whitney Air Show, a carnival held jointly with the Manchester Lions Club, a Holiday Bazaar Crafts Sale, and a "Shootout for Diabetes" are but a few of the many efforts by this club to raise funds to serve their community and communities throughout the world.

## History of the East Windsor Lions Club

The East Windsor Lions Club was organized on June 29, 1953 under the sponsorship of the Enfield Lions Club, and has been an intricate part of their community ever since. Their fundraising ability has allowed them to make substantial contributions to their community as well as the community of Lions.

This club has contributed $1,000 annually for scholarships, as well as providing funds for the payment of eye examinations and eyeglasses for those in need. Contributions have been made to Girls State and Boys State, the East Windsor Booster Club, the "Close up" foundation, the "Five Corner Food Shelf," the American School for the Deaf, the East Windsor Nursing Association, CLERF and LCIF.

The club has sponsored many youth activities over the years including Little League, basketball, girls Little League, soccer, and high school student trips to Washington, D.C.

Service activities have included co-sponsoring a health fair with glaucoma screenings, and the annual delivery of cookies and hams to about 200 senior citizens. The club has continually been involved in the Lions Youth Exchange program. Interestingly, one child of a Lion member has been sent to a foreign country each year and many young people from other countries have been hosted by club members.

Civic projects have included purchasing equipment for the high school gym including glass backboards and score boards, letter jackets for the high school athletes, and funds for the high school band. An extraordinary contribution was made in 1978 when the club purchased the first ambulance for the East Windsor Ambulance Association.

During the 1987/1988 period, $5,000 was contributed for a new addition to the South Windsor Library, and as a result a new service, the "Lions Corner" was created and the East Windsor Lions have provided annual funding for large print reading material and books on tape for the sight impaired community.

Other contributions to the community include the installation and maintenance of park benches in several locations. Picnic tables were built and put in placed for the Park Hill residents and for residents at the Warehouse Point housing for the elderly.

Through the years, club fundraisers have included an annual scholarship variety show, an annual spring auction, an annual turkey shoot, fuel raffles and armchair horse racing. Later in their history they held turkey shoots, "farmers breakfast" events, a golf tournament and a dance, the latter two jointly with the South Windsor Lions Club.

The club reflects on members who have passed away, and plants a tree in their memory. Trees have been planted at the grammar school, the park on Reservoir Avenue and at the Broad Brook Fire House.

An outstanding club with accomplishments too numerous to list. A proud past with expectations of a very bright future.

## History of the Enfield Lions Club

The Enfield Lions Club was organized on March 31,1942 under the sponsorship of the Hartford Host Lions Club. As this organization approaches its 65th anniversary, the members look back with pride. The club's fall foliage tours for nursing home residents in their town as well as Christmas parties in each of the three nursing homes brought happiness to the most vulnerable population. The foliage trip continued for several years and was ultimately replaced by bringing bingo parties to the nursing homes, awarding cash prizes.

The youth of Enfield were beneficiaries of scholarships awarded by the Enfield Lions, as well as sponsorship of one softball and two baseball teams. Contributions to the Senior Center also allow for expanded activities for the town's seniors.

The Enfield Lions along with eight other Lions Clubs sponsored a "Special Ed" Christmas party, which was highly successful.

This club has always participated in the Sight Saver Day collection.

Other fundraising activities include an annual pancake breakfast, and tag sales in the late 80's. In 1993 the club raised funds for Campaign Sight First by participating in the "Four Town" fair and joining the "Journey for Sight." Until 2002, the club raised most of their funds at their annual Doll House and Miniature Show, however due to increased costs and diminished attendance, the activity was discontinued.

This was the home club of PDG Ron Jones who was always a strong force in the club. PDG Ron however passed away in 2004.

In 2005, the Enfield Lions joined forces with the East Windsor Lions and held an auction to raise funds for the Low Vision Center. Together they raised $14,000.

More recently, the Enfield Lions instituted a second pancake breakfast in the fall and they also sell bagels and donuts at craft shows at the Enfield Senior Center.

The club members are currently searching for what they term as "A blockbuster" fund raising event and are confident that this will become a reality in the very near future.

## History of the Farmington Lions Club

The idea of creating the Farmington Lions Club began during the 1984-85 Lions year while George Lomnitzer served as District Governor. Due to opposition, the idea lay dormant until 1995. The then District Governor Allan Dodge began the task of formally organizing the club, however it didn't come to fruition until the year 2000. The club was officially organized on June 1, 2000 under the sponsorship of the New Britain Lions Club.

Christopher Grip was named as the charter president with PDG W. Keith Wuerthner serving as the club's Guiding Lion.

Fund raising projects conducted by the club included the sale of holiday wreaths, participating in Lions Day activities, and a miniature golf tournament with the proceeds targeted for the Lions Low Vision Center, Fidelco, and the East Farms Volunteer Fire Department. The club also raised funds for the Foodshare program to help those in need.

Service projects included assisting at the Red Cross Bloodmobile sign-in desk as well as the canteen at the Red Cross Farmington headquarters.

In an attempt to attract potential members, the club held two "Get to Know the Farmington Lions Club" public information sessions. One of the sessions was attended by a newspaper reporter who wrote an article about the club that resulted in a four-page spread in the subsequent edition.

This was a great effort by the Farmington Lions Club, however with dwindling membership, the club's directors voted to relinquish their charter effective December 31, 2002.

## History of the Glastonbury Lions Club

The Glastonbury Lions Club was organized March 27, 1951 under the sponsorship of the Newington Lions Club.

The charitable efforts of this club have emphasized services to youths.

Sizable contributions have been made to charities such as the American School for the Deaf, Friends of Glastonbury youth, Glastonbury Little League, scholarships for graduating high school seniors, the Children's Home of Cromwell and the Village for Families and Children.

Along with generosity to children, the club is sensitive to the vision impaired and ultimately conquering preventable blindness. Generous contributions have been given to the Connecticut Lions Eye Research Foundation, The Connecticut Radio Information System, Fidelco Guide Dog Foundation, and the Lions Low Vision Center. Additional contributions have been made to the YMCA, St. Pauls Church, FISH, and the Arthritis Foundation Society, Northeast Chapter.

To finance their generosity, funds are raised primarily from the club's pancake breakfast events, and of course their annual golf tournament.

It can be said that for over half a century, the Glastonbury Lions Club has been sensitive to the needs of their community.

## History of the Granby Lions Club

The Granby Lions Club was organized March 20, 1953 under the sponsorship of the Unionville Lions.

To the Granby Lions, community is everything. These members welcomed the opportunity to participate in the organization of the Little League in Granby and the continued sponsorship of a team.

To the people of this town, the Granby Ambulance Association is most important, and the Lions have purchased numerous items to assist in the operation.

The club supports the town library, and in support of the schools, there are the annual scholarship grants to Granby Memorial High School students presently totaling $6,000 a year.

For many years, the Granby Lions sponsored the Labor Day picnic and provided the only public swimming area in the community. In addition the club was responsible for the construction of a pavilion and rest rooms at Salmon Brook Park.

Understanding the medical needs of a community such as Granby, the Lions were responsible for the purchase of a senior citizen van as well as a heart defibrillator for the police department. Another ongoing medical need is eye care for those without sufficient funds, and therefore the Granby Lions provide for eye exams and glasses for this group of individuals. For special needs children, each year, the Granby Lions host a Christmas party.

The Granby Lions have supported CLERF as well as the Low Vision Center in New Britain.

Fundraising activities have included a shrub sale, golf tournament, birdseed sale, and Christmas tree sale. In the past the members have operated food booths at local events and sponsored a turkey shoot.

The members of the Granby Lions Club are a group of diversified individuals, businessmen, engineers, professionals and retired individuals with a common goal; to serve their community. They feel that they are the ones who have gained the most from membership in the Lions organization

## History of the Greater Hartford West Indian Lions Club

The Greater Hartford West Indian Lions Club was organized June 29, 2001, with the Bloomfield Lions Club serving as their sponsor. It was created primarily due to the growing West Indian population in the Hartford region. PCC Sydney and Lion Elba Cruz Schulman were the club's Guiding Lions during the first two years.

Since its creation this Lions Club has been quite active within the West Indian community, performing civic activities such as holding health fairs for the general public at the West Indian Social Club and for police officers and their families at the Hartford Police Department. Services offered included eye, chiropractic, and blood pressure screenings. Counseling services were available regarding nutrition as well as AIDS and sexually transmitted diseases. During the NAACP Convention in Hartford, the members conducted eye screenings. The club has also met the cost of eyeglasses for those without the necessary funds.

As a result of fund raising activities, the club has been able to contribute to local and national charities such as the African-Caribbean American Parents of Children with Disabilities, Sickle Cell Association, the American Diabetes Association and to various Lions charities.

This is an active club participating in all regional and statewide Lions activities, and some of the members recently attended the Lions Clubs International Convention.

Members have collaborated with the Hartford Multi-National Lions and the Bloomfield Lions in arranging for the 2005 Holiday Party at the West Indian Social Club in Hartford.

This is a rather young club that has increased its membership during every year of its existence, and continues to provide vital services within the West Indian Community.

## History of the Hartford County Fidelco Lions Club

The Hartford County Fidelco Lions Club held their charter night on June 5, 2003. The ceremony appropriately was held at the Fidelco Training Center. Twenty-one members along with over 100 guests came together to celebrate their founding.

The club held its "Night for Sight" during which time members and friends collected eyeglasses on Halloween. Turkeys were purchased for "Food Share" and the club, having sponsored a family, asked for a "wish list" and proceeded to provide the family with everything they desired. The family consisted of grandparents who were raising their ten-year-old grandson. They were having financial difficulties as the grandmother was forced to leave her job due to a progressive eye disease.

The club has contributed to Foodshare's summer food drive, the Lions Low Vision Center, CLERF, and the Channel 3 Country Camp. Donations of games, towels, gardening tools, and toiletries were also sent to the Vacation Camp for the Blind in New York.

The Hartford County Fidelco Lions held a fund raising activity in conjunction with "Pooches and Pumpkins," a Colchester Lions event held on the Colchester Green. The club's booth offered grooming, ear cleaning, and nail clipping to the many dogs in attendance. Doggie bandanas were also given to all of the four-legged customers.

The members held a "flapjack" breakfast at Fidelco, and the Colchester Lions donated their food trailer to cook the flapjacks and sausages. They also participated in the Buckland Mall's "An Evening of Giving."

The club has a "Pennies for People" fund, and contributed the money collected to the veterinary fund established to meet the needs of pets displaced following the devastating hurricanes in the south.

A unique activity of this club is sharing stories and thoughts as to why the members partner with Fidelco. One such story concerned the story of a kitten that woke her master in the middle of the night. The owners were somewhat irritated until they realized that the kitten sensed that the Fidelco Foster puppies needed to go out, and could not wait another minute. The kitten was just performing a humanitarian deed! All was forgiven.

## History of the Hartford County Motorcycle Lions Club

The Hartford County Motorcycle Lions Club was organized on May 13, 2003. With 24 charter members, Lion Karen Gerhauser served as the club's first president.

This unique organization has a motorcycle run each year with the proceeds contributed to eye related projects. The club's philosophy is rather unique. Regardless of the reason for the motorcycle run, it is most important for the members to ride their bikes enjoying the weather while raising funds for those in need.

In the not to distant past, the club members participated in a hurricane relief project designed to provide supplies to the hurricane battered states of Mississippi and Florida. This project was made possible through the efforts of Guiding Lion Glenn Boglisch.

The club members have been involved in several eye screenings and created unique receptacles for used eyeglasses, which have been placed in the motorcycle shops in their area.

Although there are currently only 11 members in the club, with their enthusiasm and unique approach, this organization will undoubtedly grow over time.

## History of the Hartford Evening Lions Club

The Hartford Evening Lions Club was organized May 29, 1974. Sponsored by the Hartford Host Lions Club, Jose Flores served as the charter president.

The Hartford Evening Lions have provided support to Lions and to Hispanic community organizations in the Hartford area. The club has demonstrated dedication, leadership and commitment to the Latino community and the Hartford area in general.

Service to the community is demonstrated by their many service projects including the distribution of food baskets and clothing, providing toys at Christmas and on Three Kings Day, and organizing health fairs with Hartford Hospital. The club organized glaucoma screenings, and held diabetes testing and educational workshops. They also held blood pressure screenings as well as eye screenings at the Latino Expo. Together the members worked with the La Casa de Puerto

Rico to assist in relief efforts (Radio and TV marathons) to gather food, money, and medical supplies for the victims of earthquakes in Mexico, Hurricane Hugo, and flooding in Honduras, Columbia, Puerto Rico, Venezuela, and the Dominican Republic. The club also organized fundraising activities for the Katrina and the Florida relief efforts.

As a result of other numerous fundraising events, the club was able to contribute to Fidelco, Diabetes, American School for the Deaf, CLERF, CRIS, Lions Low Vision Center, and LCIF.

This club has also established a scholarship fund, which has allowed them to award three scholarships each year during the past thirty-two years to Hispanic high school seniors.

On January 26, 2005, the Hartford Evening Lions Club sponsored a Leo Club at the Thomas Quirk Middle School, the first Leo Club to be established in the Hartford School system.

The Hartford Evening Lions Club is very proud to have named thirteen members of their club as Melvin Jones Fellows and is honored to be the home club of PDG Francesco Medina, who served as District Governor 2005-2006.

## History of the Hartford Hispanic Seniors

The Hartford Hispanic Seniors Lions Club was organized June 23, 1999 with 28 charter members. This was the very first Lions Club in the Multiple District to be chartered by and for seniors. It was also the first club chartered as a Spanish-speaking club. Under the sponsorship of the Hartford Multi-National Lions Club, the organizers of the club were Lions Elba Cruz Schulman and Norberto Bello.

The charter day ceremonies were conducted in Spanish by then District Governor Sydney T. Schulman and Eduardo Rivera was elected charter President.

This club has continually supported CLERF and other Lion's programs and has donated funds to the Senior Center to benefit their activities.

A defining event for the club occurred in 2003, when several members traveled to Puerto Rico where they visited other Lions Clubs and shared information concerning Lion's activities. They returned to Hartford with great enthusiasm and new ideas and hopes for the future.

The club looks forward to building their membership so as to allow for the implementation of new and exciting activities.

In January 2002, Rondale Williams won the Hartford Host Lions Club sponsored Peace Poster Contest. The winner's entry was then entered at the District, then state level contest. The top state winner is then submitted to the Lions Clubs International Peace Poster Contest, which awards its finalists at the United Nations each year in March. Hardford Host President Steve Thal and Lion Mary Clare Quirk, who chaired the committee present Rondale with the contest prise for the club level.

## History of the Hartford Host Lions Club

The Hartford Host Lions Club was organized May 18, 1922 becoming the third oldest club in the Multiple District. One of their charter members, Robert Kellogg composed the famous song, "Don't You Hear Those Lions Roar." It was first performed by the Pittsburgh Quartet at the Lions convention in 1924. To this day, this song continues to be part of the four-point opening at club meetings.

The club has sponsored holiday parties for the students at Oak Hill School for the past forty-nine years, and established a "Lions Park" located on the school's grounds in Hartford. This project was created to honor the passing of active members of the Hartford Host Lions Club. Dr. William Pehl was the first member so recognized for his tireless efforts on behalf of persons with vision loss.

Dr. William Pehl, a well known Hartford Optometrist and club member, was instrumental in establishing a Low Vision center within the State of Connecticut Board of Education and Services for the Blind (BESB). A plaque has been placed outside the Low Vision room recognizing Dr. Pehl for his dedication and pioneering efforts. Dr. Pehl is credited with the ultimate establishment of Low Vision Centers and the Lions Gallery for the sightless at Wadsworth Atheneum in Hartford.

Dr. Ashok Mehta, LCI President, sent his congratulations and a certificate of achievement to the Hartford Host Lions Club for their entry in the 2005-2006 "Best Practices" contest. The club was selected for one of the 39 third place prizes.

A collaborative effort was made with the A.I. Prince Vocational School in Hartford in 2006 whereby seniors in the woodworking class volunteered to construct seven eyeglass collection boxes to be distributed throughout Hartford.

The Hartford Host Lions Club awards three scholarships each year through the generosity of Lion Paul and Beatrice Lowenberg.

Many service projects have been completed over the years including support of the Fox Manor Retirement Community, and transportation of campers to Camp Harkness. The club supports the Low Vision Center, and provides eyeglasses for students in Hartford's public schools. For several years the club has participated in the annual Peace Poster contest, and awarded annual scholarships to deserving students. Funds have been used to support the Channel 3 Country Day

Camp, Walk America, the Hartford Neighborhood centers, Brotherhood Homes, West Hartford Day Center, LCIF, CLERF, and eye screenings.

To support their numerous service projects, fund raising has included annual variety shows and annual pancake breakfast events, Journey for Sight, a cheese sale, a food booth at the Italian Festival, gum ball machines, the sale of entertainment books as well as auctions and antique fairs.

Our hats are off to the Hartford Host Lions Club for over eight decades of making the words "service" and "Lions" synonymous.

## History of the Hartford Multi-National Lions Club

The Hartford Multi-National Lions Club was organized on May 29, 1991 under the sponsorship of the Hartford Evening Lions Club.

Originally organized as the Hartford Lioness Club, it was certified on May 22, 1976 and was the first Lioness Club in District 23-B. Organized as a group of Hispanic women, the club broadened its membership efforts to include women of many ethnic backgrounds from the greater Hartford area.

The Hartford Lioness Club held a series of fundraisers including bake sales, raffles, auctions, and fun trips to Atlantic City as well as publishing an international gourmet cookbook. Funds were donated to the Girl Scouts and much needed medical equipment as well as television sets were donated to the Golden Age Senior Center. Financial assistance was given to hurricane victims in the Dominican Republic and disabled children in Puerto Rico. Information was received that two children from Puerto Rico were orphaned while on vacation in Florida. Upon learning of the children's plight, transportation funds were provided so that the children could return to Puerto Rico.

The Hartford Lioness also participated in the Three Kings Festival, and the Red Cross annual marathon. Together the club members collected over 1,000 food items for the Greater Hartford Commission on Hunger.

The Harford Lioness Club became the Hartford Multi-National Lions Club in 1991 with Aurelia Hicks serving as the Charter President. The club continued to create additional fundraising activities including the St. Valentines Day Dance, a fashion show and pancake breakfast events. Their contributions continued to be directed to the social services needs of their community. Funds were donated for homes for battered women such as My Sister's Place and South Park Inn. Recognizing the AIDS problem within greater Hartford, funds were provided for an organization called the "Touch of Love," an organization for helping children with AIDS. The City of Hartford's Child Development Clinic and the city's schools' reading groups have also benefited from their donations.

Service projects include offering free eye examinations and glasses for those in need, assisting "Latinos Against AIDS" in their fundraising events and providing refreshments at the annual March of Dimes Walkathon. During the Thanksgiving holiday, the club has provided free turkeys to families in need.

Contributions to District 23-B projects have included The American School for the Deaf, Fidelco, CLERF, LCIF, and the Lions Low Vision Center.

In 1996 Elba Cruz Schulman, Maria Gonzalez, Lourdes Sanchez, Gladys Rodriguez and Gladys Diaz celebrated twenty years of continuous service to their community and to Lions Clubs International.

## History of the Hartland Lions Club

The Hartland Lions Club was chartered on June 13, 1978, sponsored by the Barkhamsted Lions with Art Andreasen serving as the Guiding Lion. There were 24 charter members with Lion Walt Swanson serving as the club's first president.

At the date of this writing, the president of the club was Gerry Baril who has the distinction of being the one remaining active charter member.

The club is proud that four of their members have been named as Melvin Jones Fellows and two as "Knights of the Blind."

One of the club's first fund raising projects was their annual wood raffle. It required many hours of hard work by a dedicated core group of members who dropped the trees, cut them into 4' lengths, hauled and stacked the wood at various sites in town prior to the raffle being held.

For 25 years, the club has supported the East Hartland Volunteer Fire Department by running a food booth at their annual carnival. It began with the cooking and selling of sweet corn, steamed clams, clam chowder and eventually evolved into the making and selling of fried dough. This has become such a popular item that people come to the carnival from all over specifically for the Hartland Lions fried dough. Between 1,500 and 2,000 are sold in the 4 nights of the carnival. About 90% of the members and spouses support this effort by working the booth. All profits go directly to the fire department as repayment for allowing the club to meet in its facility.

Food seems to be an ongoing theme of the Hartland Lions who annually serve a roast beef dinner to senior citizens in October, a soup and sandwich supper in January and a Mother's Day pancake breakfast in May.

One of the most unique Hartland Lions projects is the annual "Pumpkin Launch" held every October. A huge ancient sling-shot shoots pumpkins through the air at targets which results in fun and excitement for all.

Refreshments are also sold at this entertaining event, which draws people from surrounding towns for an afternoon of fun.

Patriotism is important to Hartland's 2,050 residents who annually buy about 125 American flags sold by the Lions at the Memorial Day parade in May.

The latest fundraiser to make Hartland Lions unique is Hartland – the "Moose Capital of Connecticut" t-shirts which are sold at Riverton General Store and at Granby's "Lost Acres Orchard" Farm Store.

The Hartland Lions are a picture of Americana similar to that, which has been viewed through the eyes of Norman Rockwell.

They not only represent service to the community but a trip back to yesteryear allowing us to sit back, close our eyes and enjoy nostalgic memories.

## History of the Harwinton Lions Club

During the spring of 1961, Hurlbut Clark invited several of Harwinton's business and professional men to his home to consider forming a Lions Club under the sponsorship of the Litchfield Lions Club.

On January 30, 1962, the club was organized with Hurlbut becoming the club's first president. His was an idea whose time had come, as at that time there was not a single nonpolitical or non secular service club in town to help support the many worthy causes.

Once organized, the Lions went right to work raising funds by conducting annual house tours, pancake breakfast events, a food booth at the Harwinton Fair, and by organizing and sponsoring the very successful Home shows held at the Torrington Armory.

Small crowds at the Memorial Day parades prompted a veteran, Edward Thierry, to ask the Lions for their help in initiating and organizing a better program. Today, large gatherings can be found on the Center Green for participation in these services.

The Historical Society asked for the Lions help in meeting the cost of moving the old First District School a considerable distance along the highway to a new sight. Once this was accomplished, the Historical Society completed the restoration of the property, just another example of Lions working together with others to benefit their town.

The Harwinton Lions purchased the first ambulance to replace an old Cadillac hearse that had been servicing the town. Two Lions, Frank Rondano and Lloyd Shanley flew to the factory in Indiana to drive the new vehicle home to Harwinton.

Other projects include the building of a pavilion for the town's recreation area, the distribution of holiday baskets, as well as supporting the scouts, youth sports, eye research, college scholarships, among others.

More recently, the Harwinton Lions accepted the challenge of two new fund-raisers. The Golf Tournament held at Fairview Farms is committed to raising sufficient funds to sponsor a Fidelco guide dog. They also sponsored their third "Concert for Sight" a highly successful indoor concert held at the Harwinton fairground in July 2006.

The club is proud to have named nine members, including two charter members, as Melvin Jones Fellows.

Special celebrations were held for the 25th and 40th anniversaries, and there will undoubtedly be many celebrations yet to come as the Harwinton Lions move forward and continue to serve.

## History of the Kent Lions Club

The Kent Lions Club was organized February 3, 1978, with the New Milford Lions Club providing their sponsorship.

The members of this club have opened their hearts and at the same time their homes during the Christmas season during the past three years, inviting 50 individuals from their town to enjoy a holiday celebration.

Over the years the Kent Lions have donated funds to support a wide variety of activities and organizations. Each year the club awards two scholarships to promising graduating high school students. They have also generously supported the high school's nationally ranked robotics team of which they are extremely proud.

A unique civic activity each year is the sponsoring of the entire fifth grade of the Kent Center School during their annual journey to Gettysburg.

Every year the club presents the "Most Improved Award" at the Kent Center School graduation. This has become a great incentive for local students.

The altruism of this organization expands to the disabled in the community as well. A wheelchair bound child was in need of a ramp to facilitate exiting and entering her home. The Kent Lions took charge, and soon the ramp became a reality. The child's father was so impressed, he asked to become part of this organization, and soon thereafter was inducted as a member of the greatest service organization in the world, Lions Clubs International.

Most of the funds raised by the Kent Lions Club are a result of their semi annual lobster sale as well as their concession stand at the Connecticut Antique Machinery Shows held each year in May and again in September.

The Kent Lions relationship with surrounding clubs is quite evident. The Kent Lions hosted a neighboring club at their local "Club

Getaway" in the spring of 2006, and played a spirited Kent vs. Sharon softball game. Later that day all were treated to a sumptuous dinner compliments of "Club Getaway."

The Kent Lions Club has prospered during their almost 30 year life. Although Kent is a relatively small town, this club's membership has rarely dropped below 70 members. In comparison with other clubs this is a remarkable record.

## History of the Litchfield Lions Club

The Litchfield Lions Club was organized January 30, 1950 under the sponsorship of the Torrington Lions Club.

Within the Town of Litchfield, it is well known that when someone in town becomes ill, has no insurance and has no place to turn, they can count on the Litchfield Lions to hold a special fund raiser to meet the emergency need.

For over 50 years, the presence of the Litchfield Lions Club has meant scholarships for promising high school seniors, and the semi annual scholarship breakfast fundraiser is well supported.

The Litchfield Lions sponsor an annual road race and this event attracts more than 1200 runners.

Fundraisers to support the club's many community projects have included an annual "Mystery Ride" and the participation of the townspeople has been gratifying.

Funds raised by the club have not only been used for scholarships but for Lions causes including CLERF, LCIF and District 23-B Hearing projects. Support is given as well to the American Red Cross and numerous humanitarian projects.

A community flag poll bears the name of the Litchfield Lions Club, just a sampling of civic projects funded by this Lions Club, and symbolic of the community presence of a dedicated organization.

## History of the Manchester Lions Club

The Manchester Lions Club was organized June 28, 1949, sponsored by the West Hartford Lions Club.

During their over half century of service, the Manchester Club has served their community with a variety of service projects. These included the Annual "Fenix Memorial" bowling tournament, established in 1996 to benefit Fidelco. To date this activity alone has raised well over $100,000 for Fidelco, providing sufficient funds to train five guide dogs.

Their annual Comedy Show, which was established in 1995, benefits "Christmas in April" a community home improvement project. To date, over $15,000 has been raised for this vital project.

In 1990 the club established the Manchester Lions Club Scholarship program to provide financial assistance to Manchester High School students planning to further their education. In 1997 the name of the scholarship was changed to honor their last charter member. It is now known as the Manchester Lions Club George F. DeCormier Memorial Scholarship. To date, over $15,000 has been raised to sustain this program.

The club provides local eye screenings. Eye examinations, glasses, and hearing aids are provided for town resident without sufficient funds. Annually financial support is provided for CLERF, The Lions Low Vision Center, and the American School for the Deaf, among other charities.

The annual "Fishing Derby" has been held in April since 1976 in an effort to provide for an outdoor family activity. It is noted that many of the original trophy winners have returned with children of their own.

Since 2004, the club has operated a lemonade stand at the "Cruisin On Main Street" antique car show. Other programs sponsored by the club include Little League Baseball, and a holiday food program.

The Manchester Lions Club has become a vital force in the community, and their members proudly support the International motto, "We Serve."

## History of the Marlborough Lions Club

The Marlborough Lions Club was organized October 28, 1952, and was sponsored by the Glastonbury Lions Club. Bob Farley served as the club's Charter President.

Community involvement of the members began almost immediately. The Marlborough Lions sponsored a youth baseball and basketball program in 1954, and held numerous fund raising events to meet the team's ongoing expenses.

The Marlborough Boys Baseball League was created in 1970 by the Marlborough Lions and later renamed the Marlborough Youth Athletic League. The Marlborough Lions installed fencing and a backstop for the baseball field.

In 1980 the league was expanded to include baseball, softball and basketball.

Today, many of the club's members are ex-presidents, officers and coaches of both the Marlborough Athletic League and the Marlborough Soccer Club, and the soccer field bears the name of the club's Charter President, Bob Farley who donated the land to the town for that purpose.

Through more than fifty years, the Marlborough Lions have left their mark in numerous ways. They built a wishing well near the town tavern. Although this was one of the original fundraisers, today the wishing well still stands but the original intent has long been forgotten.

The name of the Marlborough Lions is associated with everything from wind shelters to skating rinks; baseball diamonds to basketball courts; food drives to fuel banks, and eye examinations and glasses for those who cannot meet the cost.

Most significantly, these Lions have held true to the Lions motto, "We Serve."

## History of the New Britain Lions Club

The New Britain Lions Club was organized July 11, 1922, one of the original five clubs in Connecticut established between 1921 and 1922.

From its inception, a priority for the club has been helping to meet the needs of children, although the club has touched the entire community of New Britain. The President of the United States, Herbert Hoover, in 1930 sent the following telegram to the club:

"There is hardly an institution or community effort where the New Britain Lions Club has not been involved, including the library, both museums, the YMCA, New Britain Symphony, food banks, Salvation Army, Scouts, sports, The American School for the Deaf, community festivals, and literally scores of others."

There were several members through the years who displayed extraordinary leadership ability. The New Britain Lions Club has been home to a total of ten District Governors.

Among those who left their mark, PDG Thomas Leonard was one of the founders of CLERF. PDG Howard Wry, who began the annual eyeglass collection, promoted flood relief following Hurricane Diane in 1955, initiated the New Britain Lions Emergency Food Bank in 1981, and organized the New Britain Lions Charity Golf Tournament also in 1981. Lion Howard was also responsible for the Lions Leadership Seminar, which was ultimately expanded to serve clubs throughout the state. It is noted that when Lion Howard passed away in 1984, the flag over city hall was lowered to half-staff.

W. Keith Wuerthner, as one of his projects as District Governor, initiated the Fidelco van replacement program. PDG Alan Daninhirsch, for many years has been responsible for the success of the Connecticut Lions Teenage Dances at our International Conventions and the club's most recent District Governor, Lion Stephen N. Polezonis, assumed the position in July 2007.

Lion Otto Strobino served as District Governor in 1981, and also served as the President of the Connecticut Lions Eye Research Foundation. In 1983 Lion Otto was the force behind having the Main Street Bridge in New Britain named the "Lions Memorial Bridge" and this may be the only bridge in the United States so named.

Lion Otto initiated the planting of the Lions Memorial Forest at the University of Connecticut, was the driving force in producing the first Connecticut Lions History in 1984, and was project manager of the current Connecticut Lions History prior to his death in March 2007.

He became an International Director in 1990 and served as Financial Chairman during his tenure on the board. He was also responsible for establishing the New Britain Lions Community Eye Clinic, which has provided free services since 2000 and serves over 300 people a year. This is one of the New Britain Lions Club's major service project.

The New Britain Lions Club has set the example of excellence in Lionism. It has served the people of New Britain and has served Lionism in its finest tradition.

## History of the New Hartford Lions Club

The New Hartford Lions Club was organized September 17, 1970 under the sponsorship of the Barkhamsted Lions Club.

Since the club's inception, the community has been the beneficiary of funds and services provided by the New Hartford Lions. Support has been given to the Lions Low Vision Center, Fidelco, LCIF, the New Hartford and Bakersville Libraries, the Oliver Wolcott Technical School, the Historical Society, the Pleasant Valley Food Bank, the fire department and ambulance service, as well as the Recreation Department for the purpose of financing summer concerts. In addition, scholarships have been provided to graduating students at the Regional #7 High School.

To raise funds for their projects, the New Hartford Lions currently have three annual fundraisers; two giant flea markets, one held in June and the other in September as well as an antique show, held in March.

The New Hartford Lions are proud of their achievements, and eagerly look forward to future opportunities to serve their community.

## History of the New Milford Lions Club

The year was 1929. It was the age of jazz. On March 4th, President of the United States Herbert Hoover, riding the crest of the economic boom of the roaring 20's, prophesized in his inaugural address, that the day would come when poverty would be eradicated in America. Six months later in October, the Stock Market crashed, plunging the United States and the world into the Great Depression.

On April 18, 1929, a group of local young men organized a Lions Club in New Milford. Paul Barton served as the Charter President.

During the 1930's the Lions paid for summer camp for children, and in 1931 they sponsored the Cub Scouts, only the second such group ever organized in the United States. Since 1931, the local Boy Scout Troop has been under the continuous sponsorship of the club.

In the early years the club purchased playground equipment for schools, as well as park benches, which were placed on the town green. In 1945 the Lions established a skating rink at Young's Field.

In 1959, during the club's 30th anniversary, the guest of honor and principal speaker was the founder of the International Association of Lions Clubs, Melvin Jones. This was certainly a moment in their history that they shall never forget!

The Lions Club Memorial Scholarship was established in 1965 and to date has awarded over $150,000 in scholarships to graduates of New Milford High School.

In the 1970's the Lions Club purchased an ambulance for the New Milford Ambulance Association. Donations to the New Milford Hospital have exceeded $20,000 and local, District and International Lions projects have received over $50,000 in support. The club has also met the cost of eye examinations and glasses for children whose families were without sufficient funds.

Annual contributions have been given to Fidelco since 1983, as well as the Heart and Cancer fund, the United Way and a host of other worthwhile charities. In addition, equipment has been donated to the Visiting Nurses Association.

On the occasion of their 40th anniversary, the club built and equipped the pavilion at Lynn Deming Park. Continuing the tradition, the project for the club's 50th anniversary was the completion of the pavilion and facility at Young's field.

For over 25 years the seniors of New Milford have celebrated a holiday dinner and Christmas party courtesy of the Lions. Since 1997 a summer picnic for seniors has also been held.

The club's fund raising efforts have included raffles, as well as a beer fest in the 70's. It has hosted corned beef dinners, spaghetti suppers, and pancake breakfast events.

A remarkable history and a promising future for the New Milford Lions Club.

## History of the Newington Lions Club

Organized January 26,1942 and sponsored by the New Britain Lions Club, the Newington Lions Club is the towns oldest service organization.

To the Newington Lions, visibility in the community is very much a priority. Club members have appeared on television, volunteering for Connecticut Public Television during its fundraising campaign. Easter flower sales, plant sales at the Berlin Lions Fair, Lions Day collections as well as tag sales will find the Newington Lions banner proudly displayed. Thanksgiving and Christmas finds the members distributing food baskets to those in need, and Santa Claus has even helped with a public "Breakfast with Santa" event.

Towns people gather together for the Lions "Wednesday Night Bingo" which has been a popular event for several years. Each Memorial Day the members will be found proudly marching in the annual Memorial Day parade.

Each year the Newington Lions participate in the "Life Be In It" event with their own food booth. Profits subsequently are donated to the Parks and Recreation Department.

Another popular event with great visibility is the club's annual Antique Show, as is the concert series in the gazebo at Mill Pond Park.

Recently the Newington Lions sponsored a social for thirty French students at the American School for the Deaf. Other projects include the annual awarding of scholarships to Newington High School students.

An active community organization, the Newington Lions Club has donated two park benches to the local Parks and Recreation Department, contributed to the Student Assistance Loan Program in Newington, and donated a showcase to the Joseph P. Doyle Community Center. The club also donated a gazebo to the town in honor of Lion Harry Mandell and his wife, Edyth.

The Newington Lions also provide hands on services such as painting two houses in a town wide service project, and provided painting service at the Senior and Disabled Center. The Lions also donated yard cleaning services as one of the auction items sold at the Senior Center auction, and has a year round collection of used eye glasses.

For their membership drive, the Newington Lions held a wine and cheese party, and it reportedly was quite successful.

For over 60 years "The Newington Lions Club" has been a household name in this town, and will undoubtedly continue to be for years to come.


## History of the Norfolk Lions Club

Sponsored by the Sharon Lions, the Norfolk Lions Club was organized January 30, 1951 as an entity through which a volunteer ambulance service could be established and maintained. Today the main focus of the club continues to be the need to provide emergency medical services to Norfolk and surrounding towns.

The original 25 members managed to get the service started by using an old black Cadillac hearse. The members were able to raise sufficient funds to build an ambulance barn that continues in use today.

It was the club's dream to raise the thousands of dollars necessary to purchase a new fully equipped ambulance, and this soon became a reality. It is noted that since that original purchase, there have been two additional vehicle replacements.

The Norfolk Lions Club also offers training for ambulance volunteers. The ambulance squad currently has over 50 volunteers including fully trained EMT's and drivers.

The Lions also sponsor the "Explorers" a group of dedicated teenagers who attend meetings and classes studying to become emergency medical technicians. They train with the ambulance volunteers and at times respond to calls with them.

In addition to their primary project, the club annually supports Lion charities including CLERF, Lions Low Vision Centers, Diabetes Awareness, Fidelco, and Macular Degeneration.

On a local level, the Norfolk Lions provide funds for eye examination for children whose families are unable to meet this need. They also support "Project Graduation" and provide scholarships each year totaling $2,000. Each year at least two high school students are chosen by the school to spend a day at the U.N., sponsored by the Norfolk Lions.

On Memorial Day the club's members distribute flags to all parade participants as well as those who are viewing the parade.

The club's primary fundraiser is its annual appeal letter. Norfolk residents are extremely proud of the Lions ambulance service and support it generously. Other fundraisers are the annual tag sale, spaghetti supper, pancake breakfast, a mum sale, apple sale, and a valentine day sale.

The amounts raised are at times small, but their importance lies in the fact that the townspeople get to know the Lions organization and subsequently support the club's efforts. Because of the cooperative efforts, the members of this community feel that the ambulance service belongs to the entire town.


## History of the Plainville Lions Club

The Plainville Lions Club was organized May 15, 1941 under the sponsorship of the New Britain Lions Club.

Service projects performed by the Plainville Lions through the years are but an indication of their dedication to their community. The club has collected groceries for the town's food pantry. During the holiday season, Christmas cards were signed by members of the club, and along with 20 pounds of fruitcakes, sent to a nursing home.

Each year there is a picnic for the senior citizens of their town, and each and every year the Plainville Lions are found cooking and serving hot dogs and hamburgers during the picnic.

In the spring, the Plainville Lions are found packing Easter baskets with apples and presenting the baskets to families throughout Plainville.

The Lions constructed a bathhouse for the town park, and poured a concrete floor at the park's pavilion. They planted a dogwood tree at the senior center, and were responsible for building four benches at the library's mini park. With the help of a local nursery, the club landscaped the area with seed, shrubs and trees.

Sheds were constructed at the Paderewski and Norton Parks, and the club funded the original swimming pool constructed at Norton Park.

The Plainville Lions have provided scholarships for high school seniors since 1951.

The sight impaired have been the beneficiaries of contributions of large print books to Plainville Public Library, and the children have been helped by the Plainville Lions donations of show cases and furniture for the newly renovated children's room at the library.

Each year there is a concert series in support of Norton Park and this event is supported by the Plainville Lions.

Lions charities are annually supported by the Plainville Lions including CLERF, Fidelco, and the Lions Low Vision Center, and during each and every year, the Lions can be found collecting used eye glasses that will be recycled and utilized where needed.

Among the current fund raising events, the Plainville Lions annually sponsor an event at the New Britain Rock Cats baseball park. Fundraising events during past years have included an annual golf tournament, quarterly paper drives, fruitcake sales, annual pancake "festivals" and the selling of fried dough at the town fair.

The club members are proud to have awarded two of their members with the "Ambassador of Sight" award, and are also proud to be the home club of Past District Governors Anthony Caparrelli, George Cooper and Robert Irving.

## History of the Plymouth Lions Club

In 1987, the President of the Terryville Lioness Club, Barbara Gilbert and several of the members began talking about becoming Lions. This resulted in the Plymouth Lions Club being organized on August 11,1987 under the sponsorship of the East Windsor Lions Club.

This organization reportedly was the first Lioness Club in the Multiple District to become a Lions Club as well as the first in New England and the second in the United States.

Since its inception, the club has been involved in numerous community projects. Examples are planting flowers at fire stations, collecting eyeglasses and hearing aids, sponsoring walk-a-thons for diabetes, sponsoring the pumpkin festival, and providing workers with refreshments following the Litchfield tornado in 1989. The members together assisted a family whose home had been destroyed by fire. They also arranged for children to attend the Diabetes camp. The Plymouth Lions have also assisted the Terryville Lions Club with many of their projects.

The club has participated in Lions Day, collecting funds for CLERF. During "Plymouth Village Days," the members have operated the baked potato booth for several years, while selling articles made by blind individuals. They also operated the "Corn on the Cob" booth at the Terryville Country Fair, and also sold pecans, walnuts, fruit and spices.

Other fundraising activities are "Pampered Chef" events, and jewelry and candle parties. The club has sold Lions cook books, and used the proceeds to help fund the Low Vision Center, CLERF, The American school for the Deaf as well as LCIF.

The Plymouth Lions Club works very closely with the Terryville Lions Club, and meets jointly with them on a regular basis. They consider themselves as a "branch" of the Terryville Lions Club.

## History of the Rocky Hill Lions Club

Sponsored by the Newington Lions, the Rocky Hill Lions Club was organized on February 28, 1949. The club annually raises and disburses about $8,000, supporting all District and International programs including LCIF, CLERF, The Lions Low Vision Center, and CRIS Radio. Contributions are also made to Fidelco, and the American School for the Deaf. On a local level, scholarships totaling $2,400 to $3,600 annually are awarded to Rocky Hill High School seniors as well as college students.

Support is also provided for various local teams, and the club annually funds Boy's State. We are told that Santa Claus helps the club distribute pencils to local elementary school children during the Christmas holiday.

The Rocky Hill Lions have purchased low vision equipment as well as CD's for the Cora Belden Library, in memory of deceased Lion Bert Angelo.

Each year there is an alcohol free party called "Project Graduation" for graduating high school seniors, and this club has been an annual supporter of the event.

There has been a long-standing tradition for this club. Each year an American flag is presented to the town during the Memorial Day activities, and these flags are flown at various town locations. In addition, the club has another long standing tradition, that of planting a tree in town for each deceased Lion.

Fundraisers include an annual carnival and raffle. The raffle is the club's largest fundraiser with prizes totaling $5,000.

This organization also meets the cost of eye examinations and glasses for those without necessary funds and collects used eyeglasses and hearing aids for processing and distribution.

The Rocky Hill Lions Club has proudly named eight members as Melvin Jones Fellows and four as Knights of the Blind.

The Rocky Hill Lions Club is proud of their traditions, which are well received in the town they love.

## History of the Salisbury Lions Club

The Salisbury Lions Club was chartered on April 24, 1995 under the sponsorship of the Canaan Northwest Lions Club.

Although a relatively young organization, the Salisbury Lions are very much involved in their community, and can be found selling programs at the Lime Rock track during the annual Labor Day race. This activity coupled with their annual raffle raises funds for the club's scholarship program. Since 1996, the club has awarded scholarships totaling in excess of $28,000.

Place mat ads are sold for the annual pancake breakfast. The breakfast is a joint effort with the local volunteer ambulance service, and funds raised are used for community projects. In addition the club provides food gift certificates for the Salisbury Family service agency three times a year during the Easter, Thanksgiving and the Christmas holidays.

Each year the club participates in the Lions Clubs International Peace Poster contest as well as the Journey for Sight, and faithfully contributes to CRIS, CLERF, LCIF, Fidelco, the Lions Hearing program, Lions Low Vision, and the CLERF Macular Degeneration program.

Anually, the Salisbury Lions Club joins other organization for the Litchfield County Awards Breakfast, and it is noted that Lion Secretary Kathy Hawley has been selected twice to chair this annual event.

## History of the Sharon Lions Club

Under the sponsorship of the New Milford Lions, the Sharon Lions Club was organized on April 30, 1941 with Clarence Eggleston serving as the charter president. The last charter member, Lion Floyd Laird, passed away April 3, 1995 at 103 years old.

Over the years, the club has supported several local activities. They hold the charter for the town's Little League team, and have supported the team through the years buying their equipment and uniforms.

The club also supports the Sharon Boy Scout troop, and paid for two scouts to attend a weeklong camp. It was here that the scouts learned many of life's skills. During the past five years the Sharon Lions have invited the scouts and their families to a special event where merit badges are awarded.

The club's primary effort is in raising funds for scholarships, which have been awarded during the past thirty years. In the eighties and early nineties the club raised most of their scholarship funds by parking cars at the Lime Rock Race Track. With funds raised they were able to award up to five scholarships a year. In 1992 they dropped the racetrack project in favor of a golf tournament as their major fundraiser. The tournament has been extremely successful raising over $100,000 since its inception. The club is now able to award in excess of ten scholarships a year.

The Sharon Lions are also proud to contribute to Lions projects including LCIF.

This is an organization where the members are extremely proud of the accomplishments of their members. They talk of Lion Dr. Curt Gudernatch who joined the club in 1942 and rarely missed a meeting. Lion Paul Wanser was one of the original pilots of the Army Air Force and fought in World War 1. The members recall one cold February meeting night when the scheduled speaker failed to arrive, and Lion Paul volunteered to speak about his World War 1 experiences as a fighter pilot in France. For the few members who braved the cold evening, it was a night to remember, as his stories were fascinating.

The members of this Lions Club are bonded together. They hope for a strong future for their club, and continue to be vital partners in the well being of their community.

## History of the Simsbury Lions Club

The Simsbury Lions Club was organized June 15, 1965 under the sponsorship of both the Bloomfield and West Hartford Lions Clubs. Bernard "Red" Francis served as the club's charter president.

The club's major service projects include eye screenings, the annual Peace Poster contest at the Henry James Jr. High School, and the collection of used eyeglasses for distribution to developing nations. The club funds one "Souper Tuesday" luncheon for local senior citizens each year and provides staff throughout the year.

The Simsbury Lions Club recycles ink cartridges and cell phones to benefit the Lions Low Vision Center, and provides eye examinations to needy residents.

With the cooperation of neighboring Lions Clubs, the Simsbury Lions sponsor an annual special needs children's Christmas party. When the ABC House and the YMCA hold their phonathons, members of the Simsbury Lions Club stand ready to assist.

Each year the Simsbury Lions organize and participate in "Jack Bannan's Farmington Valley Turkey Trot" collecting frozen turkeys and non perishables for "Food Share" in Windsor, CT.

Contributions are made to worthy humanitarian causes, and the club assists local organizations and groups that might benefit from the club's assistance. Organizations receiving such assistance include CLERF, LCIF, Fidelco, Lions Low Vision Center, American School for the Deaf, the Farmington Valley VNA and YMCA, Meals on Wheels, Special Olympics, and the Simsbury Volunteer Ambulance. In addition each year the club grants scholarships to graduating Simsbury High seniors.

During their early days, the largest fundraisers were the annual beerfest, which was a tremendous success for about twenty years and gave the club visibility in the community. The club has held many fund raisers for decades but the Pecan Sale ranks as one of the most profitable thanks to the dedication of one member, Lion Lew Tolan, the project's longtime chairman.

Current fundraising events include the pecan sale, the annual pancake breakfast with the Knights of Columbus, and Parking vehicles for Flamig Farm's Haunted Hayride. The club holds wine and cheese socials at a local art gallery, and runs a golf shoot-out at Simsbury

Farm to benefit sight related causes. As of 2007, the club will be holding an annual golf tournament along with another Lions Club to raise funds to replace Automated Electronic Defibrillators in the community.

Several club members have served at the District Level and PDG Marianne Bannan also served as New England Lions Council President in 2002-2003.

The Simsbury Lions Club is proud to have become the first Campaign SightFirst II Model Club in District 23-B, and the top fundraising club for 2005-2006 in the District.

## History of the South Windsor Lions Club

The South Windsor Lions Club was organized June 8, 1961, sponsored by the East Windsor Lions, with Frank Ahern serving as Charter President.

The South Windsor Lions Club has had many interesting and varied projects and fund raisers over the years. Their largest fundraiser has been a golf tournament, which has been held every year during the past eighteen years. The club has also held pancake breakfast events, craft shows, auctions and flower sales.

Proceeds have been shared with the town's food and fuel bank, a scholarship fund, and numerous Lions charities. One of the club's most gratifying projects is their monthly bingo, which is held at the South Windsor Nursing Center.

Several members have served on the District cabinet, and many have been honored as Melvin Jones Fellows.

In 1981, the South Windsor Lions sponsored a new Lioness club in South Windsor. The club was active for several years before disbanding, and at that time several of the members became part of the South Windsor Lions Club.

In 1996 the South Windsor Lions sponsored a Leo Club at the Middle School. Their membership quickly grew to 106 members in their peak year. Here we have kids helping kids with proceeds from their fundraisers donated to children's charities.

During the past 42 years, the South Windsor Lions have become an important and meaningful part of their community.

The Easter Bunny made a rare appearance at the 2003 South Windsor Lions Club Annual Palm Sunday Breakfast.   In District 23-B, eight Lions Clubs hold a Palm Sunday Breakfast and challenge the District Governor, Vice District Governor and Vice District Governor Candidates to attempt to visit all eight on that morning.

## History of the Southington Lions Club

The Southington Lions Club was organized February 5, 1942 and sponsored by the Meriden Lions Club. Milton E. Chaffee served as the club's Charter President.

The Southington Lions have involved themselves personally and financially in assisting the sight and hearing impaired through eye examinations and glasses as well as payment for surgical procedures. They have also conducted glaucoma screenings, and sold items made by blind individuals.

This club has made substantial contributions to CLERF, as well as the Red Cross, and LCIF, and they sponsored the training of a Fidelco Guide Dog. The Southington Lions purchased eye equipment for Bradley Memorial Hospital and the club has contributed bulletproof vests to the Southington Police Department as well as equipment for the Southington Fire Department.

The Southington Lions have collected food for the local food bank and purchased a van for the "Help Us Grow" organization. Tennis courts were constructed and the club initiated development of the town's Veterans Memorial Park. More recent projects include a major installation of a basketball court at the YMCA-Slopers Day Camp

Fund raising activities include pancake breakfast events including the sale of apple crepes, ziti dinners, turkey shoots, Sight Saver Day collections, as well as the Sight Seal campaign. The club sold raffle tickets, advertising space in programs, light bulbs, candles and Christmas trees, and of course, they held their annual charity auction. Projects were enlivened by Lion Al Busset dressed as the Lion and as Santa, and John Kania and Mike Busico as auctioneers.

The Southington Lions Club is proud to be the home club of PDGs Ed Smith and Bill Jerin.

## History of the Suffield Lions Club

The Suffield Lions Club was organized on April 29, 1955 with the Granby and the Agawam, Massachusetts Lions Clubs jointly providing sponsorship.

Services performed for the community include annually organizing a Christmas party for special education children. This project has been ongoing for the past eighteen years, and serves as an altruistic example of service to the community.

For graduating seniors, the Suffield Lions annually award two scholarships. The club sponsors a health fair each year and in one of the churches in Suffield, the Lions have placed a collection box for eyeglasses and cell phones. The cell phones are donated to the senior center so that local seniors can carry a phone for emergency use. The eyeglasses are processed for recycling.

The club has, over the years, provided for eye examinations and glasses as well as hearing aids for those in need.

The Suffield Lions annually contribute to CLERF, The American School for the Deaf, Fidelco, and the Red Acres Farm Hearing Dog Center, among other charities.

Services to the community have included painting and caulking windows for an elderly woman.

Fundraising events include the annual pancake breakfast event "On the Green" and the annual fuel raffle and Thanksgiving Turkey raffle.

The Suffield Lions continue to maintain a relationship with one of their sponsoring clubs. Each year the club meets with the Agawam Lions Club (Massechusettes) to exchange ideas and enjoy each others company.

## History of the Terryville Lions Club

The Terryville Lions Club was organized on June 27, 1941, under the sponsorship of the Bristol Lions Club.

In 1949, several members of the club decided to reorganize the Terryville Fair, which had gone out of existence some years earlier. One of the prime movers of this project was J. Francis Ryan, who had been involved in the earlier fair. Naming it the Terryville Country Fair, the first event was held in September of that year. The Terryville Fair has grown to become the clubs largest fund-raiser involving all club members and many community volunteers.

Over the years, the club has been involved in pre-school vision screenings and health fairs. This Lions Club also supports Little League and Babe Ruth League baseball as well as youth soccer.

Each year, the club sends two students to the American Legion Boys State and Girls State conferences, and provides two high school scholarships. A meaningful event at the beginning of August each year finds the board of directors at Camp Mattatuck in Plymouth for dinner with the Boy Scouts after which a check is presented to support their programs.

A proud moment came in the mid 1960's when the club purchased the town's first ambulance. Today there is an ambulance corp. with two ambulances housed in a new two-story facility. Though largely town supported, the Terryville Lions continue to make annual contributions.

This club has made itself known throughout the District and state. Five years after being organized, Terryville member, Merrill G. Scott became District Governor. Dick Foote was elected District Governor in 1993, and numerous men and women have served on the District cabinet in various position.

A recent accomplishment of the Terryville Lions Club has been the formation of the Terryville High School Leo Club. Chartered in 2004 with 54 members, the club grew to over 70 members the following year. This club has become indispensable to the Lions at the Mother's Day Breakfast, Christmas Basket projects, and the Terryville Fair.

The Terryville Lions work very closely with the Plymouth Lions Club, which had its origins as the Terryville Lioness Club. The

Plymouth Lions have provided significant assistance to the Terryville Lions in carrying out the club's projects and are faithful in attendance at meetings as well as District affairs.

With a 65-year history, the club has numerous elderly members whom they refer to as their "Elder Statesmen." One member, Lion George Skilton is currently 94 years old, and continues to be a very active member.

## History of the Terryville Country Fair

The Terryville Country Fair, sponsored by the Terryville Lions Club, was first held in September 1949. This event replaced an earlier Terryville Fair, held under the aegis of the Plymouth Agricultural Society. Someone in the Terryville Lions Club, probably J.Francis Ryan, a charter member, suggested that they take on a country fair as a major fundraising project. Lion Fran was a longtime member of the Association of Connecticut Fairs, and more than likely was part of that earlier fair.

Excitement was building all over town as the date of the fair approached. Townspeople drove up to Town Hill to catch a glimpse of what was going on, while trucks hauling carnival rides rattled through town and up Town Hill or Scott Road to the fairgrounds. Tents were set up, carnival "joints" were lined up in rows, and horse and cattle rings were marked off.

When the great day arrived, just about everyone in town showed up. Food was plentiful, and music could be heard from the grandstand and the merry-go-round. In the open spaces, people could meet their friends and neighbors on the midway.

In 1952, and again in 1956, the fair was completely rained out. The 1956 chairman, Josiah Wood and the rest of the members of the Lions Club met to discuss whether or not the club should continue sponsoring the fair. Undaunted, "Jo" Wood persuaded the creditors to wait awhile so that arrangements could be made to pay outstanding bills. This, more than anything, is what kept the Terryville Fair running.

Operating on leased land, the club decided to purchase a one acre plot in the middle of the fairgrounds in an effort to secure ownership of a hand dug well that had been part of the old Higgins farm. An old garage was moved from downtown to cover the well. The water is not for human consumption, but is used for animals. The fairground now has two artesian wells and a city water line.

Early on, long wooden tables and upright chicken wire screens were made for the display tents. Many of these are still in use. These had to be laboriously set up inside the tents, which arrived about five or six days before the fair, and were taken down the day afterward. Of course, everything had to be removed from the tents on Sunday night before anyone could go home.

The tables had to be dismantled, nails had to be removed, and all of these had to be stacked on a rack-body truck to be transported downtown to C.Dana Purrington's barn. This process took several hours. This was most difficult, as the Lions had worked all week setting up, parking cars, and working the gate. Pity the poor wife of the Fair Chairman for that year. She would have to put on a party for all the Lions late on Sunday night, usually after midnight, and in her own home. The "after fair" party is now held at the fairgrounds a week later.

Table storage became less of a problem in 1959 when a second permanent building was erected. This structure, of frame and plywood construction, was brought in pieces to the fairgrounds and bolted together. With all the tables, legs, and screen frames in place in the building, the late night trips downtown were no longer necessary.

The "storage" building also served as the Lions' Administration Building during the fair; used by the Fair Secretary and Treasurer, and was their "rest" area. With the addition of further permanent buildings, storage became even less of a problem, and the Administration Building became the Lions' "base of operations" for many years, with a kitchen as well as storage area.

The land was purchased in 1975, and a large section of woodland was cleared for parking. More permanent buildings were added, and the club purchased their own mechanized equipment. Many organizations rent the fairgrounds for outings and other events and with two of their latest acquisitions, winter storage of automobiles and boats has become a good money making activity.

Expansion of program is also a factor in keeping the Terryville Fair the great attraction that it is. Some years ago, it was suggested that the club could improve their "bottom line" by remaining open later on Saturday. The attraction would be a special fireworks display. This has proven to be quite successful. For their 50th Anniversary, they attempted to add entertainment with name recognition. For that fair, they were able to book the Marshall Tucker Band, and this drew a great crowd as attested to by an aerial photograph taken during their performance.

The Fair Committee has also approved the addition of several new features; a woodchopper's contest, a second bandstand, a children's peddle tractor contest, and a Bingo game. Also, within the last three years, they added an antique tractor pull and display, and a lawn tractor race. Robinson's Racing Pigs have long been a favorite attraction.

As is typical with a Major Connecticut Fair, the club provides a place for local and regional farms and crafts people to display their wares, and for old friends to meet; to enjoy great food and fun, and to watch horses and cattle, sheep, goats and poultry in shows and contests.

## History of the Torrington Lions Club

The Torrington Lions Club was organized November 30, 1925 under the sponsorship if the Waterbury Lions Club. Although the organization has been involved in numerous fundraisers, those of long standing include the annual golf tournament, "Wheels of Wonder," and a food booth at the Goshen Fair. Since its inception this club has contributed in excess of $300,000 to Lions projects as well as regional and local communities.

A very significant event occurred in 2001 when the club set out to raise $20,000 for a Fidelco guide dog. Not only did they meet their goal, the club was the first in Connecticut to raise that amount within one year. As a result of their efforts, two members of the Torrington Lions Club were named as recipients of the Fidelco "Loyal Shepherd Fellow Award," and in 2004 the club rewarded another long time member with the club's first "Ambassador of Sight" award while another member became the club's first "Knight of the Blind."

Interestingly, the club, since the mid 80's had several significant occurrences. The club membership began to decline as older members either passed on or decided to leave the organization. Club membership dipped as low as 20, and there was a discussion regarding terminating their charter. Several of the members were very vocal and refused to allow the demise of a club with such a rich history. The members worked together rebuilding the club and today they brag about a membership in excess of 50 members.

Let this serve as an example to other clubs, that with significant effort, anything is possible.

In 1997, the club named six of their long time members as Melvin Jones Fellows, and another three members were added to this elite group three years latter.

More than 75 years have passed since the word "Lion" became a household name in Torrington, and that tradition will certainly continue for decades to come.

## History of the Trinity College Lions Club

The Trinity College Lions Club was organized February 9, 2000 under the sponsorship of both the Simsbury and the Windsor Locks Lions Clubs. They have the distinction of being the first campus club chartered in New England.

Membership is possibly the clubs biggest challenge. Each year Trinity College Lions Club members graduate and subsequently leave the club, although many transfer to other Lions Clubs once they determine where they will be living during the months and years to follow. It is estimated that there is a complete turnover of student members every three or four years. The club has been fortunate to have one or more college administrators among its members, which has given the club some much-needed stability.

This Lions Club has managed to contribute each year to Fidelco, CRIS, CLERF, LCIF, and the Lions Low Vision Center.

The club's major service project has been the campus bone marrow drive, occasionally in conjunction with local blood drives. With the cooperation of Hartford's inner city middle schools, there has been significant participation in the Lions Peace Poster contest, and receptacles have been placed in strategic locations for collecting eyeglasses for recycling.

Fundraising activities by the club include the sale of mums in the fall at the Berlin Fair, and occasional food sales during football tailgating parties.

In an effort to raise funds specifically for Campaign SightFirst II, the members have sold bracelets in and around the campus area.

Although the members have found that the greatest hurdle in overall planning for campus activities is the length of the college year, they have been successful in meeting their own intermediate goals.

It is interesting to note that the club sponsors an on campus wine and cheese party only for Lions and their guests. Funds raised are applied toward the member's International dues, thus assisting students whose income is limited during their college years.

This campus club creation has been and continues to be successful.

## History of the Unionville Lions Club

The Unionville Lions Club was organized on November 29th 1941 under the sponsorship of the Hartford Host Lions Club. It was at that time that seventeen local businessmen interested in serving their community chose to be part of the greatest service organization in the world.

The club received its charter on January 2nd, 1942. One of their early civic projects was sending each serviceman in the Asian and European theatres during the Second World War, a bi-fold leather wallet with a $5.00 bill inside.

The club's meetings were held on a piece of land that the Girls Club had used for camping trips. It is said that the this area made them "happy," and thus the area became known as "Camp Happy Hill." Following the war, in 1947, the then club president Howard Pulver led the club in purchasing the sixteen acres of Camp Happy Hill for $2,800.

One of the club's largest projects was the construction of the Lions Memorial Swimming Pool completed in 1948. In recent years the pool and surrounding land was given to the town of Unionville and the area is now known as "Lions Park."

To list all the accomplishments of the club during the past 66 years would fill volumes. The Unionville Lions Club then and now believe in the motto "We Serve," and every day of the week members are working to raise money to help those less fortunate in their community.

The club is very well known in the district for their major fund raising activity, "Cans and Bottles." This daily project is currently raising over $25,000 per year enabling the club to better serve their community and communities throughout the world.

## History of the Washington Lions Club

The Washington Lions Club was sponsored by the New Milford Lions Club and organized May 31, 1941.

The Town of Washington is thankful that their Lions Club created the Washington Ambulance Association February 4, 1942, only eight months after the club itself was founded. The first ambulance was an old Packard Hearse which was all the club could afford at the time. Today however they have the "best" ambulance available.

This club has also sponsored a First Aid program, installed lights at the town's skating rink, and built a pavilion for the town.

To fund these projects, the Washington Lions have held bingo games at the town hall, a minstrel show, and planted thousands of small evergreen trees to be sold years later as Christmas trees. Annually the club has held a summer auction, which has been very successful.

As fundraisers, the club sponsors two annual "Lobster Sales" and a cow chip raffle among others.

The members are currently working to raise $20,000 for raising and training a Fidelco guide dog.

## History of the Watertown Lions Club

The Watertown Lions Club was organized October 25, 1949 under the sponsorship of the Waterbury Lions Club. Their many fundraising projects assist the community throughout the year. These events include a food booth at the town's fall festival, a bowling tournament, a Christmas tree sale, a golf tournament in May, and a lobster sale on Fathers Day weekend. The club also participates in a number of District and Multiple District events such as the "Shoot Out" for diabetes and Lions Sight Saver Day.

The Watertown Lions Club shows its commitment to area youth by providing eyeglasses to needy school children, sponsorship and support of the Gordon C. Swift Middle School Leo Club, Watertown High School Scholarships, and the Al Dodge Outstanding Youth Citizen Award, named in memory of Past District Governor Alan Dodge. A fishing derby is also held on a well-stocked private pond for "Special Citizens" in April.

The Watertown Lions also provide Easter baskets on Good Friday to many of the town's needy families.

The service activities of the Watertown Lions Club are enhanced by a group of retired Lions under the name of the LOFPC. Contrary to popular belief, the group is officially called the "Lions Old Fellows Professional Craftsmen." This group raises funds and provides many free and low cost services to residents of Watertown-Oakville. Painting the stage at the Watertown High School, and dismantling and reconstructing the Old Nova Scotia Hill School are but a sample of the projects.

Assistance is provided to the elderly in a number of areas. A free breakfast is provided to the seniors at the Watertown Senior Center each fall and the "Life-Line" alert system is provided to a number of elderly citizens in town.

The most memorable project of the club was providing assistance to a woman who was facing blindness as a result of a rare retina degenerative disease. The club assisted her by meeting costs that were not covered by her insurance, as she underwent experimental eye surgery in Cleveland. Several other Lions Clubs in Connecticut also provided assistance.

Following more than a year of treatment, the club received the good news that she no longer needed to use a white cane, and with her returning sight, could achieve independence and returned to work.

The Watertown Lions Club is proud to say, WE SERVE!

## History of the Watertown Lions "Cow Chip" Raffle

The Watertown Lions Club has a rather unique raffle. They're not giving away a car or baskets of fruit or a trip to Aruba. You might say that there is a strange "aroma" associated with their contest as it is called the "Cow Chip Raffle."

The Watertown Lions Club found help in developing the Cow Chip Raffle from nearby Lions Clubs that have run this event in the past.

A local farm provides a cow on the morning of the raffle to support this event. When asked how long the selection process takes, Lions Club President Craig admitted that he has heard that "this can be as quick as twenty minutes, or as long as several hours." Craig also added that the farm provides a "backup cow" ... in the event something does not work out.

Here is how it works: First, mow the field. Design the field with 1-foot squares and erect a fence around it. Use a lime marker to draw the 1-foot grid on the entire 100 by 100 field to create 1,000 squares. LET THE COW LOOSE, and wait for nature to take its course. Of course, you must try to witness the FIRST DROP; and immediately rush out and lead the cow off the field. Other witnesses might get excited if the cow keeps "dropping".... therefore you don't want any other squares to get HIT.

Judging the winner is another wonderful chore. First, you must decide which square has the largest quantity. By this time, flies begin to arrive and become witnesses as well. You must then observe which squares were SOLD. There are very specific rules on how to determine the winner, by "who is closer." The rules make it impossible for there to be a TIE.

Of course, the club must sell the chances. If your prize is $2,000, then you know that you must sell at least 400 $10 chances to make a profit.

When applying for a permit there must be a time frame within which the tickets may be sold. It is necessary therefore to work feverishly to sell the required number of tickets.

The Watertown Lions Club was conservative and set up the program so that they would not lose if only 400 of the 1,000 tickets were sold.

It has been reported that Alice the cow, is willing to participate in the club's 2008 event.

The most important instruction for this raffle is WATCH WHERE YOU WALK!!!

Here is the press release offer by the Watertown Lions Club:

*The Watertown Lions Club is selling raffle tickets for their first annual Cow Chip Raffle. Tickets can be purchased at the local Fire Department, any Lions Club member or President Craig Lamphier. First Prize is $1,000, as determined by a local bovine specialist. Proceeds will benefit a number of projects. The Lions*

*Club has begun a new Softball Field construction project at Veteran's Park on Nova Scotia Hill Road, which this raffle will help fund. The drawing will take place at Veteran's park at 11:00 am on Saturday, April 19th. Young's Farm is providing a cow on the morning of April 19th to support this event.*

## History of the West Hartford Lions Club

The West Hartford Lions Club was organized on March 26, 1946, and on May 28th of that year Wallace Hale, the first President of the club was presented with the club's charter by District Governor Harold Ashley. During that evening 59 charter members were inducted into Connecticut's newest Lions Club.

From its earliest days, the West Hartford Lions Club has always placed a high priority on fundraising. The lifting, pushing and pulling that went into the first fundraiser, an auction, were signs of events to follow. Over the next 60 years, West Hartford's Lions would donate thousands of hours to raise hundreds of thousands of dollars for the club's charitable activities. Horse shows, opera productions, bridge nights, light bulb sales, pancake breakfast events and theatre parties were among the club's earliest fundraisers.

To raise funds today, the West Hartford Lions Club conducts an annual pecan and cashew sale, and continues the tradition of the annual pancake breakfast. The club also presents an annual "Scramble" event, and a draw down lottery and dinner party.

Local residents unable to pay for eyeglasses and eye examinations have always been able to turn to the West Hartford Lions Club. The American School for the Deaf has been an annual recipient of funds from the club, but additionally the West Hartford Lions donated the school's first van and erected a flag pole in front of a dormitory.

The club sponsors youth basketball, football and hockey teams. In addition the club presents a scholarship annually to a deserving high school graduate. In honor of its fiftieth anniversary, this club accepted the challenge of raising sufficient funds to train one guide dog. Soon thereafter the West Hartford Lions presented a check in the amount of $18,000 to the Fidelco Guide Dog Foundation.

Beyond their community, the West Hartford Lions enthusiastically support Lions charitable programs including LCIF, CLERF, Lions Low Vision Centers, and Hearing conservation.

The West Hartford Lions are committed to the world of Lionism. The club sponsored the formation of Lions Clubs in Manchester, Avon, Elmwood, Simsbury (co-sponsored with Bloomfield) and Vernon. Two West Hartford Lions, George Staib and Edward Dillon have served as District Governors. Numerous Lions have served on the District cabinet over the years and many have been honored as Melvin Jones Fellows, Knights of the Blind, and Ambassadors of Sight.

The enthusiasm of the West Hartford Lions Club today remains as strong as it was more than 60 years ago

## History of the Wethersfield Lions Club

The Wethersfield Lions Club was organized November 29, 1949 and was sponsored by the Newington Lions Club.

These Lions are active in their community collecting eyeglasses, assisting at blood drives as well as co-sponsoring an awards dinner for the high school soccer team. The club also has food drives and eyeglasses are collected year round.

The Wethersfield Lions contribute to the Low Vision Center, LCIF, and the Wethersfield Camp fund. In addition the club supports the town's scholarship fund, Fidelco, American School for the Deaf, the Oak Hill School for the Blind, and the Wethersfield Camp fund. The Connecticut Lions Eye Research Foundation alone has been the recipient of $17,000 to date.

To make all of this possible, fundraising activities have included tag sales and through the years, eye seal sales as well. Annually there is a town wide fund drive as well as successful golf tournaments.

## History of the Windsor Lions Club

The Windsor Lions Club was organized December 15, 1949 under the sponsorship of the neighboring Bloomfield Lions Club. This was the beginning of a long tradition of proud service to the community in the spirit of Lionism.

The Windsor Lions established themselves as leaders and innovators in the community. The club's first projects included digging a wading pool by hand, constructing concrete park benches, and creating a message board, which is still in use today. The 60's introduced the "Shad Derby Festival" in their town, and the Windsor Lions were among the policy makers for this event.

The following decade brought the Mother's Day Arts and Crafts Festival, which is now celebrating its 30th anniversary. Through the years this event has become one of the biggest and best arts and crafts festivals in New England with over 100 crafters enrolling each year. Fifteen years later the Lions added a second crafts festival held in the fall of each year. Combined with the Easter flower sales, these combined events provide the club's core operating funds.

Special needs including a kidney transplant for one resident, a high tech wheel chair for a paraplegic child, and the donation of a glaucoma tonometer for the District's eye screening program, were financed by the club.

Present day focus has been directed at providing eyeglasses for needy school children and senior citizens. These services have been made possible through memorial endowments of generous Windsor citizens. Over 200 individuals have been fitted with eyeglasses at a cost of over $40,000 during the past eight years alone. Many of the children referred by their elementary school nurse, receive eye care right through to graduation.

This record of service also includes support of State and International programs. The members are proud that the Windsor Lions Club was the home club of Lion Angelo Salvatore. Lion Angelo served as a club President, District Governor, and President of the Connecticut Lions Eye Research Foundation. As a fitting memorial to Lion "Ange" one of his projects, a Braille trail at Northwest Park, was refurbished in 2003 and dedicated to his memory.

In the spirit of the town's 375-year heritage, the Windsor Lions Club has repeatedly answered the call to help the less fortunate. With Windsor's needs always in focus, numerous youth, aged, blind, deaf and disabled individuals including accident victims have been served by this outstanding Connecticut Lions Club.

## History of the Windsor Locks Lions Club

The Windsor Locks Lions Club was organized on June 6, 1942.

Community service has been highlighted with scholarships, and educational and sports awards along with the sponsorship of a Cub Scout and Boy Scout Troop. The club has awarded camperships as well as serving as sponsors of Little League and softball league teams. Holiday food baskets have been distributed and the club has been involved in World Service Day activities, environmental programs, as well as providing for eye examinations and glasses for those unable to meet this need. The club has also sponsored eye screenings and these have been most successful.

In 1987, the Windsor Locks Lions Club held its first "Journey for Sight" along the Windsor Locks Canal. Two years later, this project was shared with District 23-B and continues today as an annual District event. The walk which takes place along the banks of the Connecticut River has raised as much as $30,000 in one day for sight related programs and projects.

As they have since 1944, the Windsor Locks Lions proudly own and operate the town's only ambulance service. The Lions Ambulance Corps continues to meet every challenge, including coverage for Bradley International Airport. The Corps, now a paid service, continues to set the standard of excellence for emergency care, with paramedics, EMT's and full time staff to meet the needs of Windsor Locks residents.

Many of the members have been involved in District and Multiple District activities. The club has produced six District Governors, namely, Richard O'Leary, 1968, Clifford Randall, 1980, Scott Storms, 1989, Ronald Storms, 1995, Normand Messier, 2000, and Carolyn Messier, 2004. Lion Scott Storms also served as International Director during the 2001-2003 period.

This Lions Club proudly supports LCIF, the Lions Low Vision Center, CLERF, Fidelco, CRIS, and The American School for the Deaf, and contributes to hurricane and tornado disaster relief as well. The club also plans to strongly support Campaign Sight First II.

During the 1980's, the Windsor Locks Lions Club set a goal to become one of the largest Lions Clubs in the state. During the ensuing period, the club has grown from 75 to 160 members.

Windsor Locks Lions have always stepped forward and led the way with compassion in service to others.

## History of the Winsted Lions Club

The Winsted Lions Club was organized on March 16,1960 under the sponsorship of the Torrington Lions Club. There were 35 charter members with James E. Condon serving as the club's first president.

Through the years the Winsted Lions have served both the youth of the town as well as the disabled and elderly. Many of their deeds were hands-on, for example the club built a ramp for disabled members of the community, provided packages of personal items to homeless shelters, and coats and hats for the towns people during the winter months. Cancer patients have been the recipients of kerchiefs made by club members, and blind and disabled individuals have been transported to job interviews or to a doctor's office.

The members organized a fishing derby for children at the Oak Hill School for the Blind. During the holidays, the Winsted Lions distribute food baskets so that others might enjoy the holiday season. Members of the club regularly volunteer at the food bank and soup kitchen, and visit senior citizens at Nursing homes and senior centers. On Memorial Day Winsted Lions place flags on the graves of the fallen. Those in need of low vision services are transported to the Low Vision Center by members of the club.

On an as needed basis, the club provides funds for eye exams, eye glasses and hearing aids.

The Winsted Lions have held a health fair, have volunteered their time for Special Olympics, and participated in Winsted's Laurel Queen festivities.

Fundraising events sponsored by the Winsted Lions include a family as well as a Mother's Day breakfast, a Bike-a-tron, casino trips, turkey shoots, Monday night bingo, raffles, bake sales, tag sales, Lions mint sales, and a walk for Juvenile Diabetes.

Contributions are made to Lions charities including LCIF, CLERF, and the Lions Low Vision Center, and the club financed two students so that they could attend the Lions Day activities at the United Nations.

This club faithfully supports community charities such as The American School for the Deaf, Scholarships for graduating seniors, the Winsted Police and Fire Departments, and the local ambulance service.

Several of the clubs members have been honored as Melvin Jones Fellows, Knights of the Blind and Ambassadors of Sight.

The Winsted Lions Club sponsored the Gilbert School Leo Club. One Lion, Blanche Sewell was the recipient of a Top Ten Extension Leo Club Service pin.

## History of the Woodbury Lions Club

The Woodbury Lions Club was organized April 8, 1936, sponsored by the New Milford and Torrington Lions Clubs. Earle W. Munson served as the charter president, and was instrumental in forming a club of businessmen from both Woodbury and Southbury. The club remained a joint Woodbury-Southbury organization until the mid 1940's when Southbury members started their own Lions Club.

The Woodbury Lions Club is devoted to public service. Its primary focus has involved scholarships for local high school students with plans for higher education. The first scholarship was awarded in 1946. This past year alone, ten scholarships were awarded to students at the Nannewaug High School.

Sight conservation has long been a major concern for the Woodbury Lions Club, and contributions have been made to the Yale Eye Research Center. The club also supports Fidelco, LCIF, and the Sight First programs.

Contributing to their town has been a priority, and they have been involved in the organization and development of the swimming area at Hollow Park as well as the construction of the pavilion.

The club also constructed the "Leroy Anderson" Band Stand located on the North Green, and they built and installed park benches in various areas of town. The benches are dedicated to deceased Lions and their families.

The Woodbury Lions also donate funds as well as a "Giving" tree to the food bank during the holiday season. The contribution helps the food bank supply needed goods to help people throughout the winter months.

To raise funds, the Woodbury Lions hold their annual car show in June and "Haunted" Hay rides during October. This past year the club had a "Super Bowl" raffle to raise funds to sponsor a Fidelco dog. This, the club hopes, will be an annual event.

## History of District 23-B Projects

American School for the Deaf

In 1973 District Governor Milan Knight, appointed a committee to determine the possible involvement of the District in Hearing Conservation. The District Governors following continued the association with the American School for the Deaf. This includes a project to bring the computers and other equipment used at the American School for the Deaf up to date and available for use by the hearing impaired to aid in their education. Since that time the District has supported the school by making further contributions.

Tree Planting at the University of Connecticut

During his term as District Governor, PID Otto Strobino instituted a project at the University of Connecticut in Storrs involving the planting of trees on campus. This was in response to the Lions Clubs International President that year seeking environmental projects around the world.

Originally a "forest" of trees was planted, and since that time a tree has been planted each year in honor of the then International President.

*To plant a seed*
  *To grow and mature*
    *To give fruit and die,*
*This is the essence of Life.*
*To give birth to a child*
  *To grow and flourish*
    *To make a life and die,*
*This is the essence of Life.*
*Death comes to all living things yet*
  *There will always be Life*
*The warmth of the sun – the nourishment of water*
  *– the hand of God will make it so,*
*This is the essence of Life.*
    *Otto P. Strobino*

Fidelco Guide Dog Foundation

Lions in District 23-B have always supported Fidelco. During the early 80's, CLERF awarded Fidelco a start up grant, and for several years, starting with PID Scott Storms, the current District Governor was invited to sit on the Fidelco board.

When Keith Wuerthner was District Governor during the 1991-1992 Lions year, the first of several vans was purchased for Fidelco by the Lions of District 23-B. While Fidelco is not solely a District 23-B project, the District and many individual clubs make annual contributions to the organization.

The Berlin Blues Festival

The origin of the Berlin Lions Blues Festival started with a dream of a young boy. His dream was to someday find a playground where children with and without disabilities could meet and safely play together.

Proceeds from the first Berlin Blues Festival held in 2001 were donated to a community wide fund raising project. The New Britain Lions Club also contributed to the Berlin Lions project, and these funds along with funding from LCIF allowed the dream of a child to come true. When sufficient funds were raised, the construction of a "Boundless Playground" a playground for children of all abilities became a reality.

Responding to an urgent call for help, the Berlin Lions used the Berlin Blues Festival as a means of raising necessary funds for the Connecticut Lions Low Vision Center. The Berlin Lions invited other Lions Clubs from District 23-B to assist as well. Lions from Berlin along with Lions from throughout Northern Connecticut contributed over $100,000 during a three-year period (2002-2004)

Nine months of planning are involved in the preparation for this one-day event. The Berlin Blues Festival has become one of the "Premium" New England Blues Festivals. The committee has invested countless hours selecting, contacting and negotiating with local and international performers. Other committee members actively solicit corporate sponsorship, coordinate food activities, coordinate traffic flow with the Berlin Police Department, prepare parking areas, and meticulously groom the Berlin Fair grounds.

A car show was added in 2002. This venue has grown in popularity with the assistance of the newly formed Hartford County Motorcycle Lions Club.

BESB and CRIS Radio

Through the years, the Lions of District 23-B have made significant contributions to two organizations physically located in the District but also supported by Lions Clubs from throughout Connecticut.

The Board of Education and Services for the Blind and CRIS Radio are both of great importance to the sight impaired population of Connecticut, and the Lions of this District appreciate the significant contributions of both organizations.

## Chapter 5 - History of the Lionism in District 23-C

## History of the Bolton Lions Club

In the "Spirit of '76" the Bolton Lions Club was organized on April 6, 1976.

The Bolton Lions have had a history of giving both to local as well as international charities. A significant local project is the Bolton Lions Elmer Wilson Memorial Scholarship named for Past President Elmer Wilson and the Scott Minicucci Memorial Scholarship in memory of Lion Dave Minicucci's son. Over the past nine years, $14,400 was granted to assist 18 local college students.

Additionally the club has purchased an impedance audiometer for the elementary school, and furniture and books for the town library. The cost of eye exams and eye glasses have been met by the town when warranted, American flags were purchased for classrooms, and a fence for the little league ball field was constructed. The club has also provided assistance to families when disaster struck, and provided labor for house repairs for needy families. Funds were also donated to purchase defibrillators for town buildings.

Two significant civic projects deserve special mention, namely the construction of a pavilion in Indian Notch Park and the construction of two "regulation" bocce courts at the Senior Center.

The pavilion project began in early 1978. The architectural plans of Lion Alan Wiedie were followed with the construction under the supervision of the late Lion Ernie Reed, Lion John Schlaefer and Lion Tim Brahaney. Lions Charlie and Dave Minicucci and Lion Jack Whitman installed water pipes, completed electrical work as well as landscaping. On May 31, 1981 there was a dedication ceremony directed by Lion President Loren Otter. The dream became a reality. The Lions emblem on the building brings out the sense of pride in all Bolton Lions.

The members of the Bolton Lions Club have also provided continuous financial support for all major Lions projects.

The most successful fundraisers during the last dozen years have been the club's famous pasta suppers, an annual golf tournament and an annual bass fishing tournament. Others have included raffles, light bulb sales, chicken barbeques, a concession stand at the Hebron

Harvest Fair, dances, a cabaret evening, Las Vegas Nights, antique car shows and the sale of Christmas wreaths.

The Bolton Lions Club honors two of its members: Lion Lawrence Converse III and Lion Loren H. Otter.

Lion Larry served as Charter President from March, 1976 to June 1977   He was influential in the construction of the pavilion in Indian Notch Park, and went on to serve as Zone Chairman, 1982-1983.

Charter member Lion Loren H. Otter was elected Secretary in 1977 and, except for the 1980-1981 year when he served as President, held that office continuously through the 2001-2002 year. Lion Loren has served on the cabinet as Zone Chairman, Region Chairman, Vice District Governor and ultimately as Governor for the 2004-2005 year.

## History of the Bolton Regional Lions Club

The Bolton Regional Lions Club was organized on June 5, 1992. For twelve years prior to that date, this group of community minded citizens was known as the Bolton Lioness Club, and continue to this date as a small but very active organization. Eight of the Bolton Regional Lions were charter members of the original Lioness Club, and each has in excess of 20 years of service. They are proud of the fact that four of their members are Melvin Jones Fellows and one, Yvonne Bass has served the District as a Zone Chairman. Their membership looks forward to Lions conventions and conferences to expand their involvement in inter district and international activities.

Back home, this club has immersed itself into supporting town projects. For example they contributed a microwave for their town's Community building and raised funds for a playscape, which was donated to a town school. Funds were donated to the Enfield Battered Women's Shelter when they had emergent needs, and when local residents lost their homes in a huge fire, the Bolton Regional Lions Club was there helping them meet emergency financial needs. The club also raised a significant amount of money in support of a Bolton scholarship fund, and the Bolton Library "Summer Reading" program.

In Bolton, the local fire department is very important to the well being of the towns people, and this Lions Club proudly contributed to the needs of this organization.

The Blackfoot Lacota Indian Tribe was in need of clothing for winter warmth, and the Bolton Regional Lions once again responded to a community need.

These Lions have been rather innovative in finding ways to raise funds for their many projects. There have been several "Las Vegas Nights" in conjunction with the Bolton Lions. There has also been the annual spring auction, pancake breakfast events, trips on a casino boat, and trips to Radio City, their very exciting 50's dance, a "Tax Relief" dance, a variety show, and the sale of entertainment books. But look further! Look at their service activities:

Glaucoma screenings, collecting hats, gloves and socks for the homeless, contributing goods to the local food shelter, contributing Christmas baskets to the needy, and providing eye glasses for needy local residents.

Their tireless efforts have made the name of "The Bolton Regional Lions Club" a household name in the town of Bolton and beyond.

Perhaps the heart and soul of this club is the sensitivity of its members to respond to a need. Collectively the club members have sent packages, phone cards, and cards of hope and praise to our troops abroad, reaching across the sea to help during a time of need.

## History of the Canterbury Lions Club

The Canterbury Lions Club was organized on June 12, 1972 and has been a household name since its inception. As an integral part of the community, the members are active organizing school dances for the Baldwin Middle School during the school year and conducting children's games at the annual Forth of July celebration.

This club has been instrumental in constructing tennis and basketball courts for the high school over a three-year period. The club constructed a walking track at River Park, resurfaced the parking area and track, and installed a flagpole as a memorial to the club's deceased members.

During December holiday baskets are provided for the needy, and during the year the members serve lunches at the geriatric center.

When needed, eyeglasses are paid for by the club, and when the families cannot afford adequate clothing for their children, the Canterbury Lions are there to assist.

Camperships have been provided for Camp Hemlocks, and when sponsors were needed to organize a Girl Scout and Boy Scout troop, the Canterbury Lions were ready to assist.

A nearby high school was in need of both an audiometer and a Braille typewriter as well as funds to purchase basketball back boards; The library was in need of book shelves and large print books. The Association of Retarded Citizens was in need of a ping-pong table, and the senior citizens van needed new tires. All knew that the Canterbury Lions, part of the greatest service organization in the world, would not let them down.

The list goes on and on. The club raised funds for the construction of a playscape at the Canterbury Elementary School and for the purchase of a resuscitator for the Fire Department and the purchase of lumber so that the Boy Scouts could construct benches at River Park.

Funds are always set aside for Lions projects such as the CLERF, CRIS, LCIF, Fidelco, and Hearing and Speech. The club has participated in the Lions Youth Exchange Program.

To pay for all of these services, the Canterbury Lions hold pancake breakfast events, and sell Christmas wreaths. Flower and food booths are set up at the Hebron and Brooklyn Fairs, and during the year the club sponsors an Easter dance, a musical variety show, sells dinner coupon books, as well as a community calendar. Additionally, funds are raised by participating in antique and arts and crafts shows.

The Canterbury Lions Club is nothing less than a household name within their community.

## History of the Clinton Lions Club

The Clinton Lions Club was organized September 25, 1960, and has served their coastal town with enthusiasm ever since. Their contributions to the community exceed $9,000 per year, and the grateful recipients include the Clinton "Dare Program" of which the Clinton Lions are the primary funding source; The Henry Carter Library's Large print books section, and the Morgan High School annual graduation celebration.

Each year two college bound students receive a $1,000 scholarship, and through the years this has allowed numerous students to meet the high cost of furthering their education.

To raise funds, the Clinton Lions are proud of their annual golf tournament, the fried dough booth at the annual "Blue Fish Festival," and the annual "Eye Fund" appeal.

Annually, the Clinton Lions place luminaries on Main Street during the celebration known as "Christmas in Clinton" and provide hot chocolate and cider to all who brave the weather. The club members also maintain the three gazebos and pavilions in Clinton and recently the members painted the library's conference room.

The Clinton Lions are proud of what their membership has accomplished throughout the decades, and look forward to their continued support of the community they love, as well as the numerous International, District and Multiple District Lions' causes.

## History of the Colchester Lions Club

The Colchester Lions organized in August 1949, is extremely proud of the thousands of dollars of charitable contributions made over the years. This includes academic scholarships, music scholarships for gifted students, eye examinations and glasses, band uniforms for Bacon Academy and Central School, as well as a myriad of youth sports activities. Other recipients include the American Legion, Boy's State, Camp Hemlocks, Camp Rising Sun, Youth Exchange, Christmas Seals, and Large Print Books for the local library. The Colchester Lions have provided gift baskets for the less fortunate, as well as support for the Colchester Historical Society, Campaign Sight First, CRIS Radio, D.A.R.E., CLERF, Hole-in-the-Wall Camp, Lions Low Vision Center, Public Health Nursing, and Quest Skills for Adolescents. In a single year the club raised $20,000 to sponsor a Fidelco Guide Dog.

Service activities provided by this organization include Halloween parties, Banana Split socials and fishing derbies for children, sports nights for coaches and athletes, health fairs, drug free parties and the morning after breakfast for graduating seniors, diabetic screenings, and a youth exchange with Canada.

Their civic activities include developing and maintaining the town skating pond, refurbishing the gazebo on the town green, installation of a commuter bus shelter in conjunction with an Eagle Scout project, installation of a drinking fountain on the Green and placing of benches in the town park. Annually the Lions provide a holiday sign on the green as well as Christmas tree lighting.

All of these projects require many fund raising projects, including Lions Day solicitations, the sale of Lions' mints, pancake breakfast events, raffles, tag sales, concert food sales, carnivals, the Diabetes Shoot Out, food booths, gold tournaments and a horse show.

The Colchester Lions are continually involved in most Lions' activities within Connecticut as well as Internationally. There is usually a sizable delegation to the Mid Winter Conference and State Convention as well as USA/Canada Forums and International Conventions.

Through the diligence of Club Coordinator, Lion Mark Saternis, and his committee, the Colchester Lions became a "Model Club" for Campaign Sight First, one of only 40 such clubs in the United States.

To accomplish this, the club raised over $36,000 in a little over four months, the highest amount of any club in the District.

Members have been honored with numerous Melvin Jones Fellowships and Knights of the Blind. The club is also proud of being the home of three Past District Governors, namely, Lions John W. Damm, Stephen Steg and Eric Jacobson. PDG Eric, among other honors, is the recipient of the International Presidents Leadership Medal, as well as the International Presidents Medal.

## History of the Columbia Lions Club

The Columbia Lions Club, sponsored by both the Willimantic and Lebanon Lions Clubs, was organized May 23, 1955 and received their charter one month later.

Funds are raised by sponsoring a chicken barbecue, a pancake breakfast, the bingo concession at the Hebron Fair, a scholarship fund raffle and an annual mail campaign to support CLERF.

The many community services of the Columbia Lions include providing for eye and audio examinations as well as eyeglasses and hearing aids where the need exists. Camperships to Camp Rising Sun are funded annually and the club sponsors a Boy Scout Troop as well as local teachers in the "Lions Quest" Program.

Throughout the town of Columbia there are signs with the Lions motto, "We Serve."

It all started with the Veterans Memorial and the flagpole with its light to illuminate the Flag of the United States during the darkened hours in front of Yeoman's Hall. Later came the planting of maple trees on both sides of Route 87. In 1988 the Gazebo was purchased by the Columbia Lions, and turned over to the Town in July of that year.

Each year since, the Gazebo has been decorated with glittering lights during the holiday season. At the official lighting ceremony, the Lions jointly sponsor a Carol Sing with a local bank and the town government. Six benches were donated in 1990 and they were located by the Saxton B. Little Free Library, the Gazebo, and along a proposed walkway between the Town Hall and the Gazebo. The Walkway became a reality in the fall of 1993. The Gazebo, benches and walkway are identified as "Presidents Projects." In recent years, the Presidents of the Lions Club have had the honor of identifying a project to be accomplished during their term in office.

Also situated on the Green is the Saxton B. Little Free Library, the sight of another President's project. In need of financial assistance to qualify for a state grant to computerize library records, The Lions contributed $5,000 toward the goal in 1992. This along with a $10,000 state grant, helped to modernize the Library and to improve its services to the community.

The original library, now known as "The Meeting Place" was also the recipient of Lions assistance. As the town's library was painted, some of the interior work was accomplished by members of the Columbia Lions Club. When it was renamed "The Meeting Place" the landscaping was done by the Columbia Lions. Space has been reserved in the "Meeting Place" to house and display Lions Club memorabilia that has been collected over the years. This includes the original charter and a deceased Lions memorial plaque.

The Columbia Lions Club serves as a model for community involvement.

## History of the Coventry Lions Club

The Coventry Lions Club, which was organized on September 30, 1952, takes great pride in having served their community for over half a century. The club built and maintains a band shell at Patriots Park, which is used for activities such as concerts and children's activities, and the club provides funds to help sponsor summer concerts at the park as well. The members built benches, which were installed at several locations in Coventry including the town Senior Center. The club purchased and installed flag poles in front of the town hall to display the state and town flags. Members cleared brush at Camp Creaser and helped with the construction of a pavilion, which is used for picnics and group activities by local citizens.

These Lions made major repairs to the Community House at Patriots Park, which is used by many town organizations for meetings and social functions. The club provides funding for eye exams for needy town residents and conducts glaucoma screenings at the annual town Health Fair held each October.

Members spend numerous hours collecting and cleaning used eyeglasses.

Last year alone over 1500 pairs of glasses were collected, cleaned, and sent to third world countries for distribution.

The club has helped needy families in town with winterization projects such as weather-stripping, glass replacement and insulation. Club members are also involved in a mentoring program at Coventry Grammar School. They support the "Reading Is Fundamental" (RIF) program at the Grammar School and at the G.H. Robertson School by funding the purchase of books for distribution to children. Coventry Lions provide scholarships through "Dollars for Scholars" to deserving students going on to higher education. The club maintains the "Lions Den" area in the children's section of the Booth and Dimock Library and recently funded the purchase of two new computers, a scanner/printer and software used by the children's librarian.

The Salvation Army "bell ringers" raise funds to support needy families. During the most recent holiday season, over 50% of the bell ringers were Lion members.

The Coventry Lions sponsor the town's children's fishing derby in conjunction with the recreation department. They purchase fish to stock the pond at Camp Creaser and provide refreshments and prizes to the participants.

The club's major fundraisers include a pancake breakfast on Memorial Day, the Equinox Golf Tournament in September and an antique doll and toy show in May. The monies raised by these activities go to support numerous Lions activities such as LCIF, FIDELCO, CRIS, CLERF, Diabetes and Camp Rising Sun, among others, as well as community projects.

## History of the Cromwell Lions Club

The Cromwell Lions Club, sponsored by the Berlin Lions, was established on November 13, 1948 with 26 charter members. During their close to 60 years of serving their community, they have developed several types of fundraisers to finance their services for their town and the International community.

From comedy nights to the Riverport Festival, from antique car shows to Spaghetti dinners; from light bulb and broom sales, to candy sales and pancake breakfast events with the Easter Bunny. The members of this club worked, and raised funds for a myriad of services, eye exams and glasses are provided for those in need, as are scholarships for Cromwell students. During the holidays, food baskets are delivered to the least affluent members of their town. The youth of Cromwell are never forgotten as is illustrated by the Lions support of the Girl Scouts, Boy Scouts and the Sea Scouts, and in providing athletic and good citizenship awards to both a male and female student.

People come from miles around to sample the Cromwell Lions French Toast Breakfast events and spaghetti dinners.

The members started and financed a Little League baseball team, constructed dugouts for the team and sponsored midget football. They also provided support to the Boys State program. The Middlesex Hospital was the grateful recipient of an eye treatment room donated by the Cromwell Lions, and to encourage a safe "after the prom" event, these Lions sponsored the "after prom" party for the high school.

As we travel through Cromwell, we are reminded of the Lions work as we gaze at the park benches donated by the club, or the pavilion they built at the Grove picnic area.

Lions charities have not been forgotten. Contributions are regularly made to Fidelco, Camp Rising Sun, CRIS Radio, the Low Vision Center, and CLERF to name a few.

During the Durham Fair, the Cromwell Lions accepted the responsibility for staffing the BESB booth and provided the public with pertinent information concerning that agency.

The Cromwell Lions have honored Wellingon Greaves as Cromwell's only life member, and they are especially proud of favorite son, Fred Curtin, who not only served as District Governor during the 1974-75 Lions year but also served two years as the President of the Connecticut Lions Eye Research Foundation.

## History of the Danielson Lions Club

The Danielson Lions Club was organized in March 1954. This club through the years has purchased eyeglasses for the less fortunate, large print books for the local library, and contributed generously to CLERF.

Donations have been made to charities such as the ambulance corps and the police department, but the club is especially proud of their investment in the community that allowed for the establishment of "Lions Park."

The park was the result of the efforts of Lion Chuck Prest. He was able to persuade the town to transfer title of a section of land located next to his home, which included a pond. The Lions provided equipment and manpower to clean the area and the city agreed to install slides and recreational equipment. The Danielson Lions also established a $25,000 fund and the interest from this fund has been designated for the maintenance of the park.

In the 1980's this club was remembered as the organization that set up a rest stop on Rt.52 during the Labor Day weekend and served their patrons dozens of donuts and gallons of coffee and lemonade.

Fundraisers have included pancake breakfast events, a beer fest, a wrestling match, spaghetti dinners, yard sales, a carnival, food concessions and a spring festival.

The Danielson Lions Club honors H.Wallace Crook who served as President of the club and later District Governor. He passed away in 1984, and in his memory, the Danielson Lions created the H. Wallace

Crook Award, which is annually given to an outstanding citizen of Danielson. His widow Evelyn presents the award each year at a recognition dinner.

More recently, Danielson Lion David St Martin served his club as a 100% President, and served as District Governor during the 1997-98 Lions year.

Lion David was the recipient of an International Certificate of Appreciation as well as the prestigious Leadership medal. At his testimonial, the Danielson Lions honored him with the H.Wallace Crook award for outstanding community service.

Lion David Burgess was also a 100% President and served as District Governor during the 2005-06 Lions year and in the following year, served as Counil Chairman. He has also served as Fidelco chairman, and is the recipient of an International Presidents Certificate of Appreciation.

The Danielson Lions are proud to have served their community for over 50 years.


## History of the Deep River-Chester Lions Club


The Deep River-Chester Lions Club has enjoyed the privilege of serving the towns of Deep River and Chester since September 1,1950. The club members have raised and returned to the communities they serve more than $320,000 over the past 55 years helping the sight impaired and needy residents of their communities. The members have and continues to support beautification projects, eye research, and District, State and International projects as they strive to fulfill our International motto, "We Serve."

This club has supported 100% of the district projects and fundraisers over the years. Those currently being supported include Camp Rising Sun, Hearing and Speech, CRIS Radio, Diabetes, Fidelco, Journey for Sight, and the Low Vision centers. CLERF alone has received $37,280. Also high on the list is the Yale Eye Center Building fund, Yale Macular Degeneration Research, and the UConn Vascular Center. On the International level, the club has continually supported Sight First and LCIF.

The Deep River-Chester Lions built a gazebo along the waterfront, a brick war memorial in Deep River, and helped finance a memorial in Chester, bathhouses at Chester's Cedar Lake, and a press box and concession building at the regional high school.

During the early years, the club sponsored trips for their Jr. Drum Corp and soapbox derbies. More recently the club has been recognized for sponsoring a senior appreciation dinner each year. During this event, as many as 250 seniors have had a night out with a complimentary dinner and entertainment. As part of their ongoing service, the club sponsors eye screenings each year.

Scholarships are provided for local school children and the club has financed the renovation of a baseball field for the Little League team that they sponsor.

Emergency equipment has been purchased for the local fire departments, and significant funding was provided for the purchase of an ambulance.

Eye care is provided for those in need, and food baskets are distributed to the less fortunate each and every Thanksgiving and Christmas.

Two families are adopted each year and provided with gifts for the holidays, and four times a year club members volunteer at the local soup kitchen.

To finance these many projects and activities, the members work together selling Christmas trees, selling flowers for mother's day, and operating a food booth at a local carnival. Additional funds are raised holding tag sales, running a golf outing and soliciting the community by mailing a "sight" letter each year.

This club is the proud home of two Past District Governors, Frank DiStefano and Arthur Davies, and the entire membership is dedicated to continue serving the less fortunate and sight impaired during the years that follow.

## History of the Durham Lions Club

Under the sponsorship of the Portland Lions, the Durham Lions Club was organized in October 1951. During their over 50 year history, the Durham Lions have been involved in numerous fund raisers, the longest running and most profitable being their food booth at the annual Durham Fair.

Other fund raising events include light bulb sales, fruitcake sales, pancake breakfast events, St. Patrick Day dinners and a refreshment stand at the towns Memorial Day parade.

Through the years, the Durham Lions have donated eye-testing equipment to local schools and also met the cost of eye exams and glasses, when local residents could not afford the cost. They have regularly supported the American Red Cross, Boys State, CLERF, LCIF, the Inter Church Holiday Drives, Junior Classical League and numerous other community and sight related organizations. This club has also involved themselves in the Lions Journey for Sight as well as the Peace Poster contest.

Since 1958, this club has annually awarded scholarships to graduating seniors who are residents of Durham. This community service alone accounts for about $4,000 in contributions a year. For several years the Durham and Middlefield Lions Clubs joined forces in providing graduation parties for both eighth graders and high school seniors in the regional school district.

The Durham Lions are proud of one of their longest running service activities, that being the construction and maintenance of a skating rink for the town.

## History of the East Haddam Lions Club

The Haddam Lions are credited with sponsoring the East Haddam Lions Club, organized on February 21, 1955.

The club's civic activities include a backstop, pitching machine, concession stand and lighting at the Legion field. The fire department would not have the tools that they require without the East Haddam Lions. The club purchased a rescue vehicle, the "Jaws of Life" and a thermal imaging camera among other accessories. A bus was donated to provide needed transportation for senior citizens, and when renovations were needed at the local library, the Lions were there with the necessary funds. The East Haddam Lions were instrumental in establishing an eye treatment room at Middlesex hospital as well as a fuel bank for the town. A pavilion was erected at the town beach, and an ambulance service was established for the town.

This club has supported District, State, and International Lions projects. During the Sight First campaign the club pledged $10,000 to this International project to prevent blindness, and $5,000 to CLERF for Macular Degeneration as well as $5,000 to CLERF for the UConn Vascular Center. Camp Rising Sun has benefited greatly from the generosity of this club as well.

In all, the East Haddam Lions Club budgets about $30,000 annually for projects and services. A portion of these funds are distributed for scholarships, Thanksgiving and Christmas food baskets, convalescent home visits, the American Legion, Nutmeg State, Boys and Girls scouting programs, Little League, as well as a myriad of other civic activities.

Fundraising to support these projects include the annual summer auction, Christmas tree sales, a food booth at country fairs, a golf tournament, direct mail solicitation, and the publishing of a local telephone directory.

Through the years, this club has named 28 members as Melvin Jones Fellows and 9 as Knights of the Blind. Lion Ed DesRosiers, a charter member served as Deputy District Governor, and Lion Bill Delehanty as District Governor. Lion John Kromish served the District Cabinet for 20 years, and CLERF in particular for18 years.

Others who served on various cabinets include Ed Barry, Zone Chairman, Fred Gagnon, Youth Exchange and Sight First chairman,

Robert Rhodes, Deputy District Governor, Bill Nelson, Zone Chairman; Jerry Demi, Zone Chairman and Paul Maxwell, District Governor among other positions.

The members of this club attribute their success to leadership, pride in a job well done, and the enthusiastic involvement of the members. They are proud that in the 1981-82 Lions year, the District Governor named their club as the best Lions Club in District 23-C.

## History of the East Haddam Community Lions Club

Although May 29, 1992 is the date that the East Haddam Community Lions Club was officially organized, the history of these dedicated citizens actually began many years before.

It all began on June 29, 1964; the date the East Haddam Lioness Club was formed under the sponsorship of the East Haddam Lions. During the early years the East Haddam Lioness raised funds primarily with bake sales and food booths during local festivities. As the club became more experienced, larger and more ambitious projects became the norm; among them the sales of an entertainment book and notepaper designed by local artists. The major fundraisers were Military Whist and a fashion show.

The Lioness supported many civic projects. They ran a drug awareness program as well as a children's finger print identification program at the elementary school. The club also contributed to families with special needs and supported a holiday food basket program.

When Lions Clubs International invited all Lioness Club members to become Lions, the club voted to form the East Haddam Community Lions Club, and with 36 charter members, a new chapter in this civic organization began.

The first officers were Diane (Pettit) Bielski, President, Jane Maxwell First Vice President, Hazel Shurleff Second Vice President, Angie Borgnine, Third Vice President, Judy Trotochaud Secretary, and Dorothy Davies, Treasurer.

Now as a Lions Club, the East Haddam Community Lions continued their commitment to the community, District, and International projects. Locally the Lions support the town libraries, local schools, youth groups, and annual LEPH screenings. Projects of special note: Meals on Wheels, delivering hot noon meals to the elderly who are home bound. They were instrumental in the formation of a local food bank providing a helping hand to those who experienced temporary or long term financial hardship.

On the District and International level the club supports CLERF, the Low Vision Center of Eastern CT, LCIF and Sight First, just to name a few.

This club has had two of its members serve the District with distinction.

Barbara Davis served as Zone Chairman in 1999-2000, and Diane (Pettit) Bielski served in numerous positions culminating with District Governor 2002-2003 and Council Chairman in 2003-2004. Additionally she chaired the USA-Canada Forum and the Connecticut Lions Mid Winter Conference, and is currently serving as the Second Vice President of the Connecticut Lions Eye Research Foundation.

This inspired group of citizens, first as Lioness and now as Lions has been a credit to their community, to our District and to Lions Clubs International.

## History of the East Hampton Lions Club

The East Hampton Lions Club, sponsored by the Portland Lions Club, was organized March 30, 1957 and have continually served their community since that date.

The club collects eyeglasses, and thousands have been shipped to help those in third world countries. Lions projects including CLERF, Camp Rising Sun, LCIF, the Low Vision Center, Sight First, Diabetes, and CRIS have received continuous support.

Even with this continuous and faithful support, the club members pay close attention to the needs in their town. Books in Braille have been purchased along with an eye testing device and school supplies. Funds were provided for a computer connection from the local library to the State Libraries for children, and a hiking trail from East Hampton to the Comstock Bridge was developed.

Significant assistance has been given to the food bank and soup kitchen, and eyeglasses have been provided for those in need. The club has supported the Little League, soccer, the Ambulance Association and drug awareness programs. Additionally, benches for the elderly housing complex were provided, and at Christmas time, toys have been purchased for underprivileged children. The club helped provide a float for the "Old Home Day" Parade, and helped the Veterans of Foreign Wars, Police Explorers, the American Legion, as well as a camp trailer for the Boy Scout troop. These Lions not only furnished a room at the library in memory of Lion Burt Bisantz, but also provided funds for food and clothing for families dislocated by fires and for the historical restoration of the "Goff House."

Hands on projects included a gazebo in the center of town, organized and constructed by Lions Joe Becker and Ron Christopher in memory of Lion "Moe" Lanzi. In 2004 Lion Joe Becker designed a picnic pavilion, which the club constructed at Sears Park on Lake Pocotopaug. The building was dedicated just days before Lion Joe passed away.

The club also provides lighting for the local skating pond and has provided lighting and security improvements at the East Hampton Firemen's Association Grounds where the East Hampton Lions held several beer fests.

Members have also constructed wheelchair ramps for the handicapped. The Lions sponsor a golf tournament each year with proceeds used for scholarships. They also participate in the Thanksgiving Day "Lake Jump" for the fight against AIDS.

The members work together cooking for fundraising events such as opening day for fishing at the Salmon River, Old Home Day, the Antique Engine Show, Dirt Bike and Motor Cycle Rally, and the Haddam Neck Fair, as well as the annual Fidelco open house.

## History of the East Hampton Village Lions Club

The East Hampton Village Lions Club was chartered in June 1992. Its membership consists of several original members of the East Hampton Lioness Club, as well as a core of new energetic members, with several husband and wife teams.

Nicknamed "The Village," the club is proud to have contributed to the numerous District and International causes. Whenever possible the Village Lions respond to community needs. For example, due to state cutbacks to senior citizens' transportation, the club began an "Adopt-A-Senior" program. The initiative solicited donations from the community to pay for rides for low-income seniors for visits to doctors, pharmacies, and grocery stores.

The club sponsors a "Citizen of the Year" program to pay tribute to community volunteers. The recipient is honored at the club's annual officer installation dinner. Their name is added to a plaque displayed at the public library.

Another Village Lions civic project includes an essay contest for third graders at the Memorial Elementary School. After reviewing numerous essays, the club presents awards and recognitions at a year-end awards assembly to some 40 students for their success in writing.

The club has conducted many types of fundraisers from cheesecake, light bulbs and mint sales to hosting Military Whist card games. Once known for their "Spring Fling" dances, the club is now known for its annual "Taste of Italy" event. Complete with strolling minstrels, patrons enjoy a spaghetti dinner in an Italian setting. In the fall, the club also provides hot refreshments for the Middletown Regatta crew races.

The club's most notable fundraisers have been their goods and services auctions. They joined forces with two different service organizations to raise tens of thousands of dollars. These funds benefited not only local endeavors but also global programs to eliminate polio and eye related diseases.

The East Hampton Village Lions are proud to honor charter member Mary Krogh who served as District Governor 2003-2004, Lion Sandra Nesci who served as the 1994-1995 Cabinet Secretary-Treasurer, and numerous other cabinet positions, and Lion Gloria

Tourville who was the Districts First Lady during the year husband Robert served as District Governor.

In only a few years the club has grown not only in membership but has gained a solid foundation both in their community and within Lions Clubs International.

Members of the East Hampton Village Lions show up in force at the
2002 Mid Winter Conference. The oriental theme for the conference
was chosen to support the 2002 Lions Clubs International Convention
in Osaka, Japan. ID Sid Scruggs and his wife Judy were our guests
from Vass, North Carolina, who is accompanied by PID Otto
Strobino.

## History of the Essex Lions Club

The Essex Lions Club was organized on August 24, 1950 with 29 charter members, including President Arthur E. Price, Secretary James Bombaci, and Treasurer Carl Sprafke.

Since its beginnings, the club has raised thousands of dollars with fundraisers such as light bulb sales, shrub sales, pancake breakfast events, teddy bear and car shows as well as golf tournaments.

For more than 20 years, the club's largest fundraiser has been an out door festival held during the summer months. The first such event was known as the "Essex Island Festival" held at the Essex Island Marina. With a lively musical background, chicken and beer were served to the waiting audience.

In 1982 the club held a pig roast at the Essex Town Park on Main Street.

The following year the format was changed to a Lobster bake, and the annual event has continued ever since. This year it included a "Thomas the Train" special at the Valley Railroad and was the most successful event to date.

In November the club's "Eye Research Fund" letter was mailed, and the club is optimistic as to the resulting income.

Projects completed by the Essex Lions Club include a handicapped access ramp at the Ivoryton Playhouse and the gazebo in Town Park. Upon purchasing the materials for the Gazebo, the structure was constructed by the Eagle Scouts.

Throughout the year the club has made substantial donations to the Essex Fire Department, the Essex Ambulance Association, Shoreline Soup Kitchen, as well as many other community organizations.

The club sponsors educational programs such as Boys State and Girls State and the D.A.R.E. program. Over the years this club has contributed over $50,000 to CLERF and has regularly supported the Fidelco Guide Dog Foundation. Residents in need can always depend on the Essex Lions for eye exams, eyeglasses and vision related medical treatment.

The local library has been the recipient of Essex Lions generosity with the purchase of large print books, as was a local resident with multiple sclerosis for whom a wheel chair was purchased.

The Essex Lions have provided for annual eye examinations in the schools, glaucoma screenings for town residents, and has participated in a telethon for the Middlesex hospital.

Other civic activities include substantial donations to purchase a Zodiac rescue boat for the fire department, fluoride treatments at the elementary school as well as flood relief.

The Essex Lions Club, for over 50 years has been a household name in Essex Connecticut. The tireless efforts of the membership have resulted in a quality of life that might not have been possible without this organization's presence.

## History of the Franklin Lions Club

The Franklin Lions Club was organized on March 16, 1968. Franklin is a rural town of fewer than 2,000 people. This club has served their community well and has supported both District and International projects.

The club prides itself in not only contributing money but in providing manpower as well for various town projects. To promote town pride, for example, the Franklin Lions Club organized and ran the first and second "Franklin Days." They assisted the town's recreation commission by cutting trees for a new road and parking lot, and helped the school's music program raise $1,000 for the department. Over the years they have participated in the "Diabetes Golf Shoot Out," and raised over $350 to help a young man who was injured in a bicycle accident. Since 1985, the club has held "Community Service" days during which time the elderly and disabled are provided with assistance in performing yard work or in the completion of small projects in their homes. Since 1983 the club has participated in walk-a-thons to raise money for CLERF. Franklin Lions Club members have also provided their labor at the annual Special Olympics swim meets as well as the 1995 International Special Olympics.

For more than 25 years the Franklin Lions Club has sponsored a Senior Citizens Holiday party, which includes a meal cooked by members as well as entertainment. For the 8th grade children, the club provides the annual "Sportsmanship" award.

During their rich history, the club has hosted banquets for the members of the Senior League baseball team along with their families.

During the 80's, the club accepted the challenge of assisting a young paraplegic and his family. At that time the members provided manpower and funds to re-roof his home, paint his house, install new gutters, build ramps and a porch, and repair his specially equipped van.

A special needs child in town needed a computer, printer and software, and the Franklin Lions responded. In 1995 the members helped a vision impaired young woman to acquire a seeing eye dog and are proud of the fact that their help resulted in her being able to attend the college of her choice.

The club continues to improve the town recreation field including the horse ring area. They also constructed a basketball court as well as horseshoe pits..

The major fundraiser for the Franklin Lions Club has been the annual horse show. Other fundraisers have been walk-a-thons, tag sales, raffles, dances, dinners and breakfast events.

Although increasing the number of members has been an ongoing challenge, club members have attended Mid Winter Conferences and have involved their community by sending young people to Canada as part of Lions "Youth Exchange."

The Franklin Lions have had a positive impact on their community through years of dedicated service to the people of a small rural town.

## History of the Griswold Regional Lions Club

The Griswold Regional Lions Club, sponsored by the Plainfield Lions, was chartered on March 30, 1988. Since that time they have had a profound effect on the communities they serve.

Services provided by the Griswold Lions include eyeglass collection, donation of computers to disabled individuals, Christmas parties for the homeless and giving support to both soup kitchens and the homeless shelters.

The DARE program in area schools is totally supported by the Griswold Regional Lions, who also provide scholarships for graduating students in their community. Every December, the club hosts "Jail Your Boss" with all proceeds used to furnish winter clothing to needy children in the Jewett

City area. This Lions Club also has a "Blind Outreach" program and members volunteer their time for Special Olympics, CRIS Radio, and the Lions Low Vision Center.

The Griswold Lions hosted the first and second "Lions Journey for Sight" in District 23-C in 1993 and 1994. The first year of the walk-a-thon, five clubs participated and raised $3,000 for the Low Vision Center. The second year nine clubs participated, and raised $6,000 for Campaign Sightfirst. Today the walk-a-thon is one of the most popular and successful district projects raising several times the amounts raised during the initial years.

In March 1992, the club formed and sponsored "The Eastern Connecticut" Leo Club. The Leos have assisted the Lions in their fund raising, and have projects and fundraisers of their own. Several members act as Leo Club advisors and support the Leos in their undertakings.

Financial support for the club's projects and charities comes from fund raising such as pancake breakfast events, spaghetti suppers, and comedy and crafts shows. For the younger set, the club has held dances at the Middle School and sponsored fishing derbies. The Griswold Regional Lions also provide food at local events, and holds two auctions each year.

A club as active as the Griswold Regional Lions has many outstanding members. The club over the years has honored many as "Lion of the Year." They are Lions Betsy Arpin, Lawrence Mclean,

William Graham, Cathy Cedarette, Marie Salpietro, Clair Maynard, and Phyllis Brown.

Many of the club's members have served on the District Cabinet in various positions including Lions George Salpietro, Phyllis Brown, Lawrence McLean, Joel Zuckerbraun, Bill Graham and Marie Salpietro. International Presidents Certificates of Appreciation have been awarded to both Lions George and Marie Salpietro.

## History of the Groton Lions Club

Lionism and all it stands for came into being in Groton on October 10, 1929. The Groton Lions Clubs' first fundraiser was a minstrel show which netted the club $62.98. The Depression era caused a drop in membership, yet the remaining members never lost sight of their desire to better serve the community and promote Lionism.

The Groton Lions have been involved in numerous fundraising activities. During the early years, they were involved with collecting clothing and tin cans. More recently they have held a myriad of events including pancake breakfast events, golf tournaments, Christmas tree sales, chowder sales at Mystic Seaport, fried dough sales, mystery dinners, and calendar sales. The club has also raised funds during "Sight Saver" days and the annual "Journey for Sight."

Because of their many lucrative fundraising events, the Groton Lions have been able to generously fund Christmas and Thanksgiving baskets, support Hospice of Southeastern Connecticut and provide eye examinations and glasses as well as surgical procedures for those in need.

The club annually funds Scholarships for students of the local high school as well as the alcohol free graduation parties.

At the District and International levels, contributions are made to Hearing and Speech, CLERF, Camp Rising Sun, Diabetes, CRIS and Fidelco.

Members of the Groton Lions Club stand behind their 2004 contribution to the town's Lawrence & Memorial Hosptial. The $8,000 check represents a part of their $40,000 commitement needed to help with the cost of equipment needed at their Pequot Medical Center. This check was presented to William T. Christopher, the Hosptial's President (shown third from the left in the front row) and CEO at the annual recpetion for the club members and L & M administration. Past President Ken Smith is shown at William Christopher's left.

Throughout its seventy-four year history, club membership has grown and community activities have been continuous and innovative. The club members have been involved in the "Adopt a Highway" program, the creation of comfort stations, the development of Washington Park, the collection of used eyeglasses and community eye screenings.

There is great fellowship at club meetings and numerous social events that include family members. The club honors those members who have given of themselves for the betterment of the community. Many Groton Lions have been named as Melvin Jones Fellows, Knights of the Blind, as well as Ambassadors of Sight.

The Groton Lions Club has a grand mixture of strong energetic youth and wise and prudent elders. The club celebrated its 75th anniversary, during which time the members looked forward to creating an even greater legacy of Lionism within their community.

## History of the Haddam Lions Club

Under the sponsorship of the Deep River/Chester Lions, the Haddam Lions Club was organized on September 12th 1951 and received its charter on November 27,1951. The presentation was made by PDG.'s Al Urbinati, and T. Joseph Puza and Lion Michael Monte. Lion Emerson Carpenter served as the club's first President.

Visitors to the Higganum Green are immediately made aware of the presence of the Haddam Lions in this community. In 1998 the members of this organization donated a gazebo to the town of Haddam and erected it on the Green to be used for community activities and events.

The presence of the Haddam Lions is evident with their involvement in the Haddam Lions Eye Drive, "Rollin on the River" car show, and concerts on the Green. Other fundraisers include their annual Christmas tree sales and semi annual pancake breakfast events.

The Haddam Lions have consistently supported Lions related charities including CLERF, Fidelco, The Lions Low Vision Center, CRIS Radio, and Camp Rising Sun.

Support is also given to community projects including the Haddam Meadows Skating pond, Haddam Volunteer Fire Department, Haddam Ambulance, Haddam Public Health Annual Health Fair,

Middlesex Hospital Cornerstone project, High School achievement awards, Project Graduation, Haddam Little League, and the Youth and Family Services "Pumpkin Run."

This organization celebrated its 50th anniversary in 2001 and continues to live up to the Lions motto, "We Serve."

## History of the Hebron Lions Club

There are but a few service organizations in existence that have donated in excess of $1,000,000 to charitable causes. The Hebron Lions Club, organized December 3, 1969, is one such organization. They have been most generous with their funds, but have also donated their labor and equipment where needed.

The clubs largest fundraising activity is the "Hebron Harvest Fair." Members are quite busy during other times of the year selling Christmas trees as well as operating a flea market, and running a pancake breakfast.

There are currently 30 Melvin Jones Fellow in the Hebron Lions Club as well as 28 Knights of the Blind.

The first priority of the Hebron Lions Club has always been the local organizations that offer support and assistance to the community. Some of these include Youth Services, the Douglas Library, Hebron Interfaith Human Services, Hebron Fire Department and Senior Center.

Through the years the club has provided eye exams and glasses for those in need. Eye and Ear testing equipment has been donated to both schools and health organizations. Scholarships are awarded each year to promising high school graduates.

Lion's charities include CLERF, LCIF, Fidelco, and Camp Rising Sun.

The club's hands on services have included installation of a soccer field and track at RHAM High School, the installation of a handicap ramp at the Douglas Library, serving food at Camp Rising Sun, and volunteering at the annual Connecticut Special Olympics.

The Hebron Lions are most proud of their members, both past and present. Wilbur Dennis, who passed away, served as District Governor. Everett Clark served five terms as Secretary-Treasurer and served as District Governor. The Hebron Lions bestowed Life

Membership on him in 1992. Among numerous awards, he was the recipient of the prestigious International Presidents medal.

Robert Dixon Jr. served the District as Zone Chairman as well as Secretary Treasurer and held several management positions at the Hebron Harvest Fair. He also was awarded life membership.

Charles Barrasso, known as an outstanding District Tail Twister, served his club and District and served as Superintendent and Fairgrounds electrician for the Harvest Fair.

Phillip Bradley served both his club and the District including Zone Chairman and Lions Tale editor, and served the Harvest Fair as An arts and crafts Superintendent and treasurer.

If we were to enter the Hebron Lions Den, located on the fairgrounds in Hebron, we would find the following plaques, certificates, awards, and letters of thanks or special recognitions hanging on the walls including State of Connecticut Governor William O'Neill, Governor Roland, CT General Assembly, LCIF, American Diabetes Association, Town of Hebron, Boy Scouts of America, American Legion, Hebron Youth Baseball. RHAM High School. The list goes on and on.

These are but a sampling of the lives touched by the members of the Hebron Lions Club. There are so many more, and dozens of members who have made their mark in Lionism and the community.

The Hebron Lions are shown on their float
in the Annual Memorial Day Parade.

## History of the Hebron Harvest Fair

The Hebron Harvest Fair, now known as The Big "H", began as a small "district" fair in 1971, sponsored by the newly formed Hebron Lions Club. It was held on Wall St. in Hebron on property owned by a Lion. The public response that year was most gratifying, so much so that the Hebron Lions committed themselves to a 10 year bank loan for the purpose of buying 84 acres of land on Rte 85. This proved to be the beginning of an almost legendary growth that has become the 3rd largest agricultural fair in the State of Connecticut.

Two years before the first loan was re-paid, 16 additional acres of land were purchased. This additional land allowed room for the expansion of the parking area as well as a second entrance to the fair grounds from Rte 85.

In its third year, the fair qualified as a "major" fair, meaning a required number of animals were exhibited and premiums paid for all competitions which met or exceeded "major fair" minimums.

The Fair steadily grew, and each year additional area was cleared and buildings added including permanent booths to replace canvas covered frames. A stage was built and bathroom facilities were constructed. This was followed by an electrical building and a large open sided building, which was closed in with canvas siding. At a later date this building was enclosed with permanent siding, and became the Antique Farm & Home Equipment Building, with the "Lions Den" at one end.

In 1983 the attendance had increased from less than 5,000 in 1971 to an estimated 130,000 individuals. The thousands of hours donated by Lions coupled with an extraordinary public response has resulted in the addition of many more buildings. The purchase of tractors, mowers, backhoes trucks and other necessary machinery made it necessary to build a large maintenance building to house and service the equipment.

On January 5, 2005, vandals committed major crimes on the fairgrounds. Arson resulted in destroying the largest building on the grounds with all its valuable contents including vintage cars, boats, a forklift, golf carts, picnic tables and other Lions property. Major property damage caused by driving a large dump truck into almost every building resulted in over $600,000 damage.

The Lions faced a huge challenge, clearing away and rebuilding and replacing damaged buildings. With massive assistance from community and Lion volunteers and donors of materials, labor and money, the fair was rebuilt on time, and bigger and better than ever!!

The Hebron Lions have always attempted to deliver more for the price of admission. This was the first agricultural fair to have farm tractor pulls (the President of The Ct. Farm Tractors Pulling Assoc. was a Hebron Lion.) It was also the first fair to have a "Fair Princess," the first fairgrounds to have a State of Connecticut building, and the first fair to have a multi-band radio communication center.

The 2007 Hebron Harvest Fair will have all concessions using coupons instead of cash, and booths will be selling coupons for all sales on the grounds.

From a small district fair that ran for three days in 1971 on a lot on Wall Street in Hebron and drew a few thousand people, a giant has grown.

The Hebron Lions Club is extremely proud of one of the greatest accomplishments in Connecticut Lions history. As a result, numerous community and Lions charities are recipients of funds to serve the residents of their community and communities throughout the world.


## History of the Killingly Quiet Corner Regional Lions Club

The Killingly Quiet Corner Regional Lions Club, sponsored by the Griswold Regional Lions Club, was chartered on February 28, 2004 with 34 members. Their Guiding Lion, Region Chairman Armand LaFleur has been an invaluable asset to this new organization, which, during their first year participated in the Journey for Sight Walk-a-thon, and the multi-club Flea Market as fundraisers, and purchased a food trailer for future events.

During their first year they also very ambitiously prepared for and held a live goods and services auction. The members, some of whom are transfers from other Lions Clubs, work well together, and it is evident that this organization will have a bright future.

## History of the Killingworth Lions Club

The Killingworth Lions Club was organized November 18, 1970, and its members have demonstrated a love for community since that date. This is an organization dedicated to helping others in the community as well as improving the quality of life of their residents, and a desire to see their community grow and prosper.

To attend one of their meetings is to witness camaraderie like few others. The members have a love and respect for each other that is quite remarkable and certainly a delight to witness They work hard and play hard, and one gets the feeling that each would be lost without the commonality they share, being members of the greatest service organization in the world.

The smiling faces of the Killingworth Lions team can be found at the Durham Fair as they perform their duties in their food trailer and at other times as they sell raffle tickets, run a turkey shoot, operate the annual jazz festival and manage their car shows, air shows and the St. Patrick's day dance.

Funds raised have been applied to scholarships, eyeglasses for those in need, youth baseball, the town library and the Society for the Prevention of Blindness.

Contributions have been given to the town welfare fund and to the Killingly Ambulance Association. The club has also contributed towards the cost of the annual Christmas tree lighting, and performed work on the town's recreation fields.

To view the Killingworth Lions is to witness the joy of serving ones community.

## History of the Lebanon Lions Club

The Lebanon Lions Club was sponsored by the Colchester Lions, and was organized on January 31, 1952 with 32 charter members.

This club is best known for its annual Lebanon Country Fair, which comes to life every summer. The club has operated the Fair since 1959, and through the years it has remained their major fund-raiser.

In 1955 the club purchased 38 acres of wooded land for $2,000. Members cleared about eight acres, built a three-acre pond, and opened a recreation area for the town's use.

The club needed substantial revenues to carry out their work. Because Lebanon was basically a farming community of about 4700 people, it did not have a strong base to support charitable activities. The club needed outside revenues, and this led to the decision to start a fair.

The first Lebanon Country Fair was held in 1959 on the Lebanon Town Green. Attendance was approximately 2,500. It was a success and has continued to be a success ever since now attracting in excess of 30,000 people each summer.

After ten years on the Green, the Fair was moved to its permanent home on land previously purchased.

Other fundraisers during the years include horse shows, auctions, food booths, raffles, Christmas tree and light bulb sales, a road race, and country breakfast events.

The Lebanon Lions Club has contributed towards scholarships, Boy Scouts, Girl Scouts, elementary and high school band awards, the Windham Community Hospital, and purchased large print books for the library. Additionally it continues to meet the cost of eye examinations and glasses for those in need, District and International charities include CLERF, LCIF, Campaign Sight First, Diabetes, Hearing and Speech, Camp Rising Sun, Low Vision Center, CRIS Radio, and Fidelco.

Many Lebanon Lions have served with distinction. Charter member Lion Edward O. Clark was a past President, and, served on the District Cabinet for 12 years. Three of those years he served as Deputy District Governor. Lion Ed was the prime mover in starting the Lebanon Fair and served as its superintendent for 37 years.

Lion Kenneth Craig served as District Governor in 1992-93, and during his term, he was instrumental in the creation of the Districts' Lions Low Vision Center.

Francis Adamcewicz served as District Governor during the Lion's year 1998-99 and Lion Marjorie Adamcewicz served as Cabinet Secretary-Treasurer during the 1995-96 Lions year.

Each Memorial Day, the Lebanon Lions proudly march in the town's Memorial Day Parade, and as they pass in review, there is a resounding applause from by standers in appreciation of what this organization has meant to the residents of this small rural town in Connecticut.

19919819881988198198819881988

1988198819881988

## History of the Ledyard Lions Club

The Ledyard Lions Club, sponsored by the Mystic Lions, was chartered on October 17, 1960 with 24 members. Charles J. Cavanaugh served as the club's first president.

Since their inception, they have waged a continuous battle against diabetes and other causes of blindness, and have strived to serve those in their community who are in need.

The Ledyard Lions Club is fortunate that one of its founding members continues to be active. Lion Howard Kaminske has epitomized the motto "We Serve." He has been involved in numerous club activities from parades, auctions, Christmas shopping, as well as serving hamburgers and hot dogs from the kitchen or food trailer. He served on the inaugural "Block Party" committee, which began raising funds for a Fidelco guide dog. The Ledyard Lions have since raised and donated funds for two guide dogs, both of which have been donated.

Each Memorial Day, the Ledyard Lions pay tribute to departed service men and women, and organize the annual Memorial Day Parade. The club has received recognition for this in the Lions International magazine.

The Ledyard Lions have continually supported their community with college scholarships totaling over $12,000. Each year the Ledyard Lions accompany children and parents during a Christmas shopping spree. At that time school age children in need, purchase clothing of their choosing which is paid for by the club. In excess of $9,000 is spent each year.

Additionally the club has met the cost of eye exams and glasses. In addition thousands of used eyeglasses are collected and shipped to developing countries each year.

Support is given community charities. To name just a few, contributions are made to Ledyard Parks and Recreation, Girl Scouts, The Senior Citizens Luncheon, Clara Barton Camp for girls with juvenile diabetes, Ledyard libraries, and the Ledyard Senior Center.

Lions charities include LCIF, CLERF, CRIS, and the Fidelco Guide Dog Foundation to name a few.

The District is thankful to the Ledyard Lions Club, which, under the direction of Past President Leonard Matzdorf, inaugurated the annual statewide Melvin Jones Dinner in 1993.

The Ledyard Lions are proud of the now deceased Morris M. Smith who served as District Governor during the 1985-86 Lions year.

Recently, the Ledyard Lions Club celebrated their 45th anniversary, and can look back on an extremely proud past. The men and women who make up this great organization have given their all through the years from country auctions, to book and record sales and giant tag sales to pancake breakfast events and a weekly bingo. They work because of their love for community and an opportunity to help their fellow citizens.

## History of the Lyme Old Lyme Lions Club

The Lyme-Old Lyme Lions Club, sponsored by the East Haddam Lions Club, was organized on April 11, 1972 with 31 charter members. The clubs Charter President was Peter G. Chapman.

Early fundraisers included sponsoring an antique show for eight years as well as a Las Vegas Night for several additional years.

Many years ago the club purchased a used pop up camper, which they converted, to a mobile unit for the preparation of food. This innovation has served the club continuously as a fundraiser preparing hot dogs, hamburgers and beverages. It has been utilized at fairs, model airplane competitions, antique shows, model train shows, and various other community activities.

More recently the club has sponsored the annual Super Bowl Sunday Pancake Breakfast and other events raising funds for their scholarship fund.

In 2005 they held their first annual Antique Car Show fundraiser, which coincides with the Town of Old Lyme's annual Memorial Day parade.

One of the club's proudest accomplishments is having been the driving force behind the formation of the Southeastern Connecticut Low Vision Center for District 23-C. The center officially opened in 1993.

The Lyme Old Lyme Lions Club worked hand in hand with the Town of Old Lyme on the Special Olympics of 1995 and hosted the Olympians from the country of Guyana.

As a direct result of the Special Olympics, the club refurbished ten wheelchairs donated by the Chelsea Foundation of Niantic. These chairs were then shipped to the handicapped of Guyana.

This club has provided scholarships to graduating seniors of the Lyme - Old Lyme High School for over 20 years. More recently their scholarship program has provided two $1,000 scholarships each year.

Annual donations are made to LCIF, Sight First, CLERF, Fidelco, Camp Rising Sun, and the Low Vision Center to name a few. The club's main focus continues to be the support of their local community. A few such projects include holiday food baskets, sight and hearing testing, as well as glasses and hearing aids for those in need.

Locally support is also provided for the Little League, "Bikes for Kids," The Council of Churches fuel Fund, and the Lyme Old Lyme Public Libraries.

Currently the club is performing a public service by maintaining a three mile stretch of roadway in the shoreline area, by becoming members of the adopt a highway program of the State of Connecticut.

This is a club that works so very well together. Walking into a room where the Lyme Old Lyme Lions are meeting, there is feeling of warmth as they extend their hands in worldwide friendship. They are, in the truest sense, "Lions of the World."


## History of the Mansfield Lions Club

There was excitement in the spring of 1952 in anticipation of Charter Night for the state's 100th Lions Club - The Storrs Lions Club at the University of Connecticut on May 10th, 1952. Honored participants included Senator William Benton, Congressman Horace Seeley-Brown, University President Albert Jorgensen, International Director Curtis Lovell, and District Governor T.Joseph Puza. The Charter President was Delmas Cookson.

The club name was changed to the Mansfield Lions Club in February 1959 to better define the area being served.

In 1989 Past President Ward Cornell was killed in a helicopter crash while on active duty with the National Guard. Memorial gifts totaling thousands of dollars were received by the club and used for additional soccer fields and to provide water and electricity for a recreation facility. Other special support projects included a grant of $9,000 to Windham Community Hospital to purchase electrically operated beds. Grants were also made to the senior center for landscaping and the installation of a handicapped entrance door.

The Mansfield Lions have supported Lions projects including CLERF, Diabetes, Lions Low Vision Center, Camp Rising Sun, Youth Exchange, and LCIF.

Additionally community support has been provided to "Lions Park" Camp Hemlocks, Boy and Girl Scout camperships, baseball teams in the town's recreation program, the local soup kitchen, an interfaith social service program, and recreation programs for senior citizens including an annual theatre party at the UConn Summer Theatre with Lions serving as escorts.

Funds for financial support come from a short list of fund raising projects. The Fall Festival including an auction, tag sale, refreshment stand, harvest products stand, and chicken BBQ, held on the grounds of a recreation facility donated by Lions Lloyd Duff and Dudley Hamlin, sale of Vermont cheddar cheese, the "Eye Fund" appeal, roast beef dinner, and the walkathon.

In addition to naming Melvin Jones Fellows and Knights of the Blind, the club has given special recognition to Charter Treasurer, Hartley Fitts with a Life Membership. Lion Gordon Allan has been honored with an International President's Certificate of Appreciation primarily for his outstanding work as the Cabinet Chairman of Camp Rising Sun. The most outstanding Lion Plaque was awarded to Lions Gordon Allan, Philip Knowlton, Lloyd Duff, Paul Kozelka, Dignor Piner, Warren Sargent, Donald Nolan, George Norman, Thomas Sheehan, James Stallard and Edward Casoni.

The Mansfield Lions are best identified in town by the observations of Mayor Audrey Barberet delivered at the 25th Anniversary celebration in 1977: "No organization in town has more fun doing more good for more people than the Mansfield Lions Club."

Past President Dick Burnham presents the Outstanding Lion plaque to Mansfield Lion James Stallard for a decade of distinguished service, including two terms as President, fundraising chairman, program chairman, treasurer and auctioneer.

Middlefield Lions Club runs their food booth fundraiser.

# History of the Middlefield Lions Club

The Middlefield Lions Club was chartered in January 1957, but the charter members simply couldn't wait for the formality, and completed their first community project four months before the official date.

Since that date the club has become an intricate part of their community and lend their support where needed. Over the years contributions have been made to the Mystic Community Center, the Levi E. Coe Library, the Senior Center, the volunteer fire Department and the Community Service Council to fund food baskets for the needy. Other community organizations benefiting from the clubs generosity are the Middlefield Garden Club, the Old Home Days committee, the Coginchaug High School Scholarship Fund and "Project Graduation." This club also provides support to the Special Olympics as well as projects helping handicapped groups.

On the District and International level, the Middlefield Lions support the Low Vision Center of Eastern CT, Camp Rising Sun, Fidelco, LCIF, and CLERF.

The Middlefield Lions have raised their funds through a variety of events including light bulb sales, carnivals on the Green, Sight Drive campaigns, chicken barbecues, a fishing derby and the highly successful food booths at the Durham Fair.

The members of this club proudly tell all that Middlefield is "A better place to live" because of the clubs many community projects, such as the Dom Ferretti Pavilion, the Little League field house, bleachers, and backstops, and a covered bridge constructed for safe access over the brook to Peckham field. Other projects have included repairing the public address system for the Park and Recreation Department, preparing the skating pond for winter, helping the Easter Seals Telethon as well as the Easter egg hunt and Halloween party for the community's young people.

The Middlefield Lions strive to serve their community and the citizens of Middlefield appreciate their presence.

## History of the Middletown Lions Club

The Middletown Lions Club, organized in May 1929, is the second oldest chartered club in the State of Connecticut, and have, since that date, continuously carried on their proud tradition of supporting Lions projects, as well as local humanitarian causes.

In the 1950s, in cooperation with representatives from the Middletown school system, Lions Sebastian Mazzotta and Thomas Moore began the first community project for graduating seniors called "After The Ball." Lions, their spouses, and school personnel provided a safe environment for seniors to eat, dance and socialize through the night. This has since grown into a community-supported event.

In 1961 a $500 donation established the first Big Brothers/Big Sisters organization in the State of Connecticut. Today the Nutmeg Big Brothers/Big Sisters, as it is now called, is the 10th largest Big Brothers/Big Sisters agency in the United States, serving approximately 60% of the State of Connecticut. Middletown Lions continue to support this organization with generous annual donations.

The Middletown Lions have always emphasized helping youths in their area, as a way of encouraging healthy development. Some of these projects include efforts in the schools supporting the Quest Program with funds from a spring pancake breakfast. They also support the Y. M. C. A. program for troubled youth, and the 4-H Pork Pals among others

Lions Park, which was established when Lions Stephen Kayser and Thomas Wilcox chaired an effort in 1963 to create a park and picnic area, is still enjoyed by many visitors each year.

Lions Joe Milardo and Audrey Scotti have accepted responsibility for the management of vendor services for the annual Regatta. In addition, in 2002, the Middletown Lions assumed the lead roll in managing the Columbus weekend event, which is the largest one-day crew race in the world and attracts participants from around the globe.

The Middletown Lions Club supports an annual medical screening for seniors, and helps to inform visually impaired individuals as to what devices are available for them. Eyeglasses and hearing aids are provided for those in need as well.

Through the efforts of this Lions Club, eyeglasses are collected and sent to third world countries or reground and refitted through the eyeglass grinding and fitting program at Middlesex Community College.

According to the Middletown Lions, "Lions Serve" is their motto, and their tireless efforts are celebrated with camaraderie beyond comparison.

## History of the Middlesex Community Lions Club

The program reads, "Thank you for participating in the Middlesex Community Lions Second Annual Concert on the Green." The narrative goes on to explain that the proceeds of this fund raising event will be used to provide services to the residents of Middletown.

The motto of Lions International is "WE SERVE," and the Middlesex Community Lions Club is dedicated to fulfilling that motto with hands-on projects and services. In the past year we have provided eye screenings, cooked and served holiday meals to homeless, provided eyeglasses, hearing aids, prescriptions and transportation to medical appointments for people in emergent need. We have funded teens who wanted to participate in the "Safe Sitters" certificate program. We're proud of our accomplishments as a 'young' club and look forward to even greater service to Middletown"

The club was a mere two years old when that was written, and had already accomplished so much. We salute this Lions Club, which was sponsored by the East Haddam Lions Club, and chartered in September 2002 with 22 members. Shortly afterbeing chartered, the club sponsored a children's Christmas party at the youth center on December 21, 2002. Early in the following year they sponsored a vision screening, and shortly there after a health fair in May 2003. Less than a year after being chartered, the Middlesex Community Lions Club held its first concert on the Green. And in the following year presented an original one man hit show, "Antipasto!" a Sicilian Celebration, as a club fund raiser.

## History of the Montville Lions Club

Under the sponsorship of the Norwich Lions, the Montville Lions Club was organized on June 11, 1958. With a total of 24 charter members, William Kirby served as the club's first president.

In 1976 they sponsored the Montville Lioness Club and in 1996 they also sponsored a Leo Club for the town's youth.

Since its inception, this club has been involved with numerous fund raisers such as Christmas tree sales, Thames River Raft Race, Montville Fair, pancake breakfast events, Montville Harvest Festival, corned beef dinners, the annual Valentine's Day dance comedy nights, herb sales, pasta dinners, military whist, and an entertainment book. The largest sum ever raised by one event was the $9,000 realized at the 1980 Montville Harvest Festival.

As a result of these fundraisers the Montville Lions Club has been able to make contributions in excess of $110,000. Funds have been used to purchase eye glasses for the less fortunate, sponsor a Little League team, sponsor an individual for Girls State, purchase eye testing equipment for local schools, sponsor a youth exchange with Canada, and award three $1,000 grants to high school seniors. This club has also been an annual contributor to CLERF and LCIF.

Service activities include helping to move three elderly couples into elderly housing, donating and installing an air conditioner in the housing recreation room, donating and installing air conditioners in the Montville Senior Center, sponsoring a Christmas party for 150 disabled individuals, assisted the local chapter of the Center for the Blind during their monthly dinners, and providing food for Thanksgiving and Christmas baskets.

Civic activities include installing lights at the Montville High School football field, constructing stage and dressing rooms at the Camp Oakdale pavilion, and creating a new Community Center. This project alone required $8,000 of the funds raised by the Montville Lions Club.

For the Montville seniors, the members remodeled the Senior Citizens hall and also donated tables and chairs. At the request of the Montville Historical Society, this club along with others helped moved an historical structure to a new location

The Montville Lions are proud to have provided several district chairmen for the Cabinet as well as four Zone Chairmen, Two Deputy District Governors, Two District Governors and a Multiple District 23 Council Chairman. The Montville Lions Club is also proud to have named nine individuals as Knights of the Blind, ten as Melvin Jones Fellows, and two as District Ambassadors of Sight.

## History of the Montville Mohegan Pequot Lions Club

The Montville Mohegan Pequot Lions Club was chartered in 1992. The organization however had its beginnings several years prior to that date.

In 1976 the Montville Lioness Club was created, and had the distinction of being only the third Lioness Club in the world.

This club has been best known for their famous brunches. Lions come from far and wide just to sample the many delicacies created by the members.

Those who attend the Montville Fair each year are also able to sample the best-baked potatoes this side of the Thames, and partake in one of their great breakfast spectaculars as well.

Perhaps of greater importance are the outstanding deeds performed by the club's members. As a Lioness Club, and subsequently a Lions Club scholarships were awarded to students attending both Montville and St. Bernard's High School. Funds were donated to the Raymond Hill Library for the purchase of large print books, and the club purchased an EKG device for the seniors of their town.

The members participated in a health fair, sponsored dinners at the Community Center at Camp Oakdale and the Center for the Blind, and sponsored several bloodmobiles as well.

To raise funds for these events, the members held Valentine and St. Patrick's day dinner dances, compiled and sold their own Lion's cook books, and held benefit bingos at Foxwood's bingo hall.

Upon being chartered as a Lions Club, their fundraising activities continued, as did their contributions to most Lions charities. The clubs very popular fashion show was famous for its very distinguished models such as their Zone chairman, Region Chairman,

District Governor, and of course their number one Guiding Lion, PCC Frank Mauro.

The club has initiated a project to raise $20,000 for a Fidelco guide dog. Their project was called "Raising Friends for Life" and sucessfully completed it.

The Montville Mohegan Pequot Lions Club and their predecessor the Montville Lioness Club have continually responded to both District and International charities. The District chairs are invited to their club in May of each year where checks are presented, as each chairperson describes their program.

With all of their activities, the club members faithfully attend many of our Mid Winter Conferences and State as well as International conventions. They are very proud of their charter member, Charles Spicer who was named as a Melvin Jones Fellow in 1996. Regrettably, Charles passed away in 2003. In lieu of flowers, donations were requested for their "Raising Friends for Life" program, and Lions and friends from throughout the area responded generously.

## History of the Mystic Lions Club

On September 14, 1949, the Mystic Lions Club was officially chartered with 20 members. Merle Bradley, a Mystic businessman organized the club, was the first President, and later served as District Governor. He was also one of the organizers of the Connecticut Lions Eye Research Foundation. This club is pleased to have named 10 individuals as Melvin Jones Fellows and 12 as Knights of the Blind.

To the members of the Mystic Lions Club, the motto "We Serve" has meant vigorous participation in their community. For 55 years the Mystic Lions Club has raised hundreds of thousands of dollars and made their community a better place to live. They have held Beer Festivals and Pancake Breakfasts; they have sold light bulbs and brooms; held Monte Carlo Nights, Bloody Mary Brunches, and Hot Air Balloon Festivals. Currently the club holds an annual Golf Tournament, a "Swing Dance" and silent auction. They hold Steak Nights, and sell hot dogs at various events. Wine Tasting Events are held periodically along with tag Sales, and raffles. Proudly the club returns all profits to the community.

The Mystic Lions Club has participated in many community improvement projects throughout their area. They have strongly supported the development of the Mystic River Park, a community funded venture to enhance family life.. They helped develop and construct playground equipment, donated a Lion-shaped children's drinking fountain, and donated and setup park benches dedicated to past members.

The club members painted day care centers and various community buildings. They repaired downtown flower boxes, donated to the Groton Food Locker and held various joint club events with Lions Clubs in their area of the State. They have also supported local families by providing for their eye care needs, as well as contributing food baskets and Christmas toys and trees.

Recently, the club held its first joint Free Public Health Fair along with the Groton and North Stonington Lions, providing vital tests, as well as information on subjects such as Lyme Disease.

Over the years the Mystic Lions Club has donated to help those less fortunate locally as well as to state, national, and international projects.. It has been one of the largest contributors to the Connecticut Lions Eye Research Foundation (CLERF), and has contributed generously to other charities including: Camp Rising Sun, CRIS Radio, Diabetes, Hearing and Speech, Easter Seals Camp Hemlock, FIDELCO, LCIF, the Joslin Diabetes Center, Lawrence & Memorial Hearing Bank, the Lions Eye Health Program, Lions Low Vision Center, the Macular Degeneration Fund, as well as numerous community charities.

The Mystic Lions Club has been a vital force in their community for over half a century. They have the spirit of community, which today is stronger than ever.

## History of the New London Lions Club

The New London Lions Club was organized August 5, 1922. During the past 85 years, this, the oldest club in District 23-C, has been serving the New London community and communities throughout the world. These Lions have collected thousands of pairs of eye glasses and raised hundreds of thousands of dollars which has enabled them to support worthy causes such as the Connecticut Lions Eye Research Foundation as well as the blind in their community.

For many years the New London Lions Clubs' primary fundraiser was the New London Annual Flower Show. Today they participate in the Home Show at Connecticut College and annually hold a wine tasting and silent auction at Ocean Beach Park. Funds are also raised by sponsoring pancake breakfast events as well as tag sales.

Each year the New London Lions award three scholarships to graduating New London High School students.

This club has sponsored numerous other Lions Clubs. During the years 1929 and 1930, the club sponsored clubs in East Lyme, Groton, Niantic, Old Lyme, Old Saybrook and Newport, RI. The Norwich club was sponsored in 1939 and the New London Ocean City Lions Club was sponsored in 1992.

During the club's 50th year, the New London Lions were proud to have one of their members serve as District Governor. Although this club had provided many Deputy District Governors, Zone Chairmen, and other cabinet members, Joseph L. Raub was their first District Governor. This individual went on to serve as an International Director. At a later date, New London Lion member, Ernest Kopec also served as District Governor.

When attending a meeting of the New London Lions Club, it becomes quite apparent that there is great camaraderie among the membership, and this explains why they have enthusiastically participated in all programs and projects decade after decade.

## History of the Niantic Lions Club

On September 27, 1949 the Niantic Lions Club was officially chartered with an initial membership of over 50 members. This club is well known for their annual "Lobsterfest" which originated in 1978. In 1989 the Niantic Lions describe the adding of barbecued chicken to their menu as a major event as it was prepared by master chef Lion Gerry Burkhardt using a well-guarded secret recipe for the special marinade. Because of Lion Burkhardt's secret recipe, each year people come from miles around just to enjoy this special treat.

Through the years those who have benefited from the Niantic Lions fundraising are too numerous to list. Let it be said, however that all of Lions District and International charities have benefited greatly through these many year, as have numerous charities within East Lyme which are much better off today, because there has been an organization called the "Niantic Lions Club."

The Niantic Lions Club is honored to have had several members active in the District 23-C Lions Cabinet as well as in the Multiple District. Lion William Allen served as District Governor in 1983-84 and went on to serve two years as President of the Connecticut Lions Eye Research Foundation. He is also a Past President of the Lions Low Vision Center of Eastern Connecticut.

Lion James Harris has served as a Zone Chairman as well as a Leo Advisor; Ernest Hopkins served as District Governor 1954-55; Howard Parkhurst is a Past Council Secretary Treasurer, and also served as President of the Lions Low Vision Center; Lion Edward Tanguay has served as a Zone Chairman as well as Information Technology Chairman. Lion Tanguay is also a past President of the Connecticut Lions Pin Trader's Club which was founded and chartered in 2003.

The Niantic Lions have not only contributed thousands of dollars to their community, but provided their time and talent as well. These Lions worked together building the George Seabeck Pavilion on the town picnic ground, they constructed showers and baths at the "Hole in the Wall" Beach Park; rebuilt bleachers for the East Lyme High School athletic field; built picnic benches for the town pavilion; installed a gazebo on the East Lyme Town green, and built a storage shed near the pavilion on the Town picnic grounds. They built park

3

benches for the East Lyme Senior Center, and the East Lyme town hall, and built a storage shed for the Senior Center.

The Niantic Lions have left their mark in so many ways and are proud of their outstanding history.


## History of the North Stonington Lions Club

In March 1967 Lion President John Vogt signed the charter to affirm the founding of the North Stonington Lions Club in the presence of the 35 charter members.

One of the club's first acts was to serve as co-sponsor of the Memorial Day parade that year. That undertaking evolved very quickly into a Lions Club annual event. It has been the tradition of this club not only to feature a grand marshal leading the line of march, but to invite both the District Governor and the Vice District Governor and other guests to ride in the parade and to have honor seating at the post parade ceremony.

Initial fund raising began with a program of vaudeville, presented by a small group of very talented members. It was greatly appreciated by all who attended.

As obligations to the community grew, the club broadened its fund raising program. Thus began their relationship with an equine association to sponsor horse shows beginning in the seventies and lasting through the nineties. Over this three-decade period, the club also sponsored beer fests, and breakfast and dinner events whenever additional funds were needed. During this period as well, the club funded numerous annual events including Senior Citizens Dinners, Flu Clinics, D.A.R.E, YMCA leadership program, public school improvements, youth outreach, as well as Christmas toy and ornament contributions.

Ongoing programs that commenced in the early decades are numerous, such as the college scholarship award for a graduating senior, eyeglass collection and shipment to the Lions recycling program, diabetes screening, White Cane Day, Peace Poster contest, and the Grange Annual Agricultural Fair Parking Project. They added "Meals on Wheels" and an annual Christmas package that would provide either a fully decorated tree with presents for a family in need, or paid-up credit cards to be distributed by the Senior Citizens Center to low income seniors. Also continuing from the earliest decades, the club provides contributions to the Diabetes Foundation, LCIF, Fidelco, the Little League, Cub Scouts, Town Recreation Committee, Town Volunteer Fire Department, Town Volunteer Ambulance Association., Low Vision Center, Town Historical Society, Wheeler Library, High School "Alcohol Free" Dance, and the Senior Center.

Recently the club added CRIS Radio, Habitat for Humanity and the Hearing Aid collection and distribution program. A new feature has produced interest within the membership and the public alike. A self guided farm tour program illustrating the changing pattern of the local farm community.

This club is dedicated to the true meaning of the words, "We Serve."

## History of the Norwich Lions Club

The Norwich Lions Club was chartered on April 11, 1939.

A unique project started during the 1950's was called the "Lighthouse for the Blind." Every other week club members traveled throughout their city picking up blind men and women including patients residing at Norwich Hospital. Each individual was treated to a good home cooked meal that was prepared and served at Norwich's Mohegan Park. For recreation there was always bingo and entertainment provided by Josie Urbinati, the wife of PDG Alfio Urbinati. Norwich Lions also performed errands for the blind and accompanied many to the voting booth as well. The "Lighthouse" continued for many years with great success.

Other sight projects included purchasing equipment and providing financial assistance for the Backus Hospital totaling over $60,000.

The club purchased Braille typewriters for the visually impaired, and provided scholarships for both the Norwich Free Academy and Norwich Technical School students. They provided for the construction of bleachers for the soccer and little league fields, and purchased rescue boats for the Norwich Fire Department.

Each year members deliver holiday food baskets to the blind and elderly in Norwich, and throughout the year purchase eyeglasses for both visually impaired children and adults.

The Norwich Lions supported the annual "Rose Arts Festival" with hands on as well as financial assistance. Three members of the club, PDG William F. O'Neil jr., and Lions Ruby Bokoff and Nozzi DiBattista also served as President of the festival. Other members spent hours creating floats for the annual "Rose Arts Parade."

In 1963 a devastating flood wrecked havoc throughout the heart of Norwich due to the collapse of Spaulding Dam. Most merchants did not have insurance to cover flood damage and were devastated when their businesses were virtually destroyed. The Norwich Lions enlisted the aid of the then famous John Cameron Swayze who taped an appeal, which aired on radio stations throughout New England. As a result, the club raised thousands of dollars for the affected merchants.

The Norwich Lions have donated over 10,000 pairs of used eyeglasses to assist those in third world nations.

In 1994 the club agreed to establish, manage and coordinate the operation of the Norwich Satellite Studio of the Connecticut Radio Information System. For the next six years PDG Joel Ragovin managed the radio station and trained all volunteer readers who broadcasted daily to the blind and print handicapped.

Seven Norwich Lions, Al Abraham, T. Joseph Puza, Alfio Urbinbati, William F' O'Neil Jr., Mario Gualtieri, Joel Ragovin and John J. Connor have served with distinction as District Governors. Lions O'Neil, Gualtieri and Connor went on to serve as Council Chairmen. Both William F. O'Neil Jr. and Mario Gualtieri also served two-year terms as President of the Connecticut Lions Eye Research Foundation.

These individuals are representative of the dedication of all Norwich Lions throughout the years.

The Norwich Lions Club presents a flag and poll to the Norwich Senior Center/ Raising the flag for the first time is PDG John Connor, PDG Joel Ragovin, PDG Mario Gualtieri and Nullario D. Battastra.

## History of the Old Saybrook Lions Club

Sponsored by the Niantic Lions Club, the Old Saybrook Lions Club was organized on June 27, 1950.

Membership currently consists of about thirty active members who have enthusiastically organized activities such as big band concerts (Stan Kenton, Guy Lombardo, etc.) road races, food booths, candy sales, overnight river races, a motorcycle raffle, and annual fund raising mailings. During this past year alone, the organization raised upwards of $12,000.

Funds raised are used for scholarships for promising high school students, Easter egg hunts for the town's children, a local soup kitchen, the famous annual Memorial Day Parade, as well as eye exams and glasses for the less fortunate.

Each year the club is quite generous with their support for Camp Rising Sun, Fidelco, Diabetes, Hearing and Speech, CLERF, LCIF and other Lions charities.

During the early 90's, the Old Saybrook Lioness Club's members were combined with the Old Saybrook Lions Club. Each group had their individual strengths, but together they became an even greater vital force serving their community and Lions Clubs International.

The goal of this Lions Club is to improve the quality of life in Old Saybrook and the neighboring communities by participating in activities involving fundraising and charitable distribution. Such activities include two eye screenings a year, one during the winter months and another during the spring.

This club is proud of their roll in the community with the hope that their efforts will help ease some of life's burdens for their neighbors.

Enthusiastically the members embrace the Lions International motto, "We Serve," as their own.

## History of the Pawcatuck Lions Club

The Pawcatuck Lions Club, sponsored by the Norwich Lions Club, was organized on October 25, 1950.

Each year the club donates a Christmas tree to the town and serves its youth with programs at the Pawcatuck Middle School, including "Lions Quest." The members annually take a group of students to the Veterans Hospital in West Haven and pay for e transportation and lunch for the students and chaperones. The club has participated in the District 23-C Peace Poster Contest, in cooperation with the teachers and students at the Pawcatuck Middle School.

The Pawcatuck Lions have sponsored a Little League baseball team each year since 1953, have donated funds to the Boy Scouts, Girl Scouts and Brownies and has hosted Christmas parties at the Mystic Oral School.

The annual "Blind Drive" was established with the slogan, "Be Thankful You Can See." Money raised is used for the purchase of eyeglasses and hearing aids, as well as medical examinations.

The club has also donated funds to the Town of Stonington, to upgrade the electrical service at the Pawcatuck River Park, which serves as the staging area for the club's annual road race.

Scholarships are awarded annually and the club hosts a breakfast for graduating high school students.

In 1999 under the leadership of President David Capizzano, a service project with the Westerly Lions Club helped the Boy Scouts rebuild their kitchen, which was lost in a fire at their Camp Kitchetau location. A pasta dinner raised and estimated $2,000.

The Pawcatuck Lions played a major roll in the creation of the Pawcatuck Neighborhood Center which opened in 1975, Not only is this a human services center for the town, it is also used periodically for senior luncheons and dinners.

In 1999, the club agreed to renovate the former Pawcatuck Italian American Club. The renovations were completed in February 2001. The hall now serves as a central meeting location for the Pawcatuck Lions as well as the location for LEHP screenings.

As a result of donations to the Connecticut Lions Eye Research Foundation, the club has honored seven members as Knights of the

Blind. Donations to LCIF allowed the club to honors six members as Melvin Jones Fellows.

Angelo Miceli was the recipient of a special Presidential Leadership Award authorized by President George W. Bush. The award was presented at the District Governor's Award Banquet of 2004.

Four members of this club have served as District Governor, namely Lions Thomas Shackley, George MacKnight, Joseph Pescatello, and Angelo Miceli. Angelo Miceli also served as Council Chairman of Multiple District 23 and as President of the New England Council. During his year as Governor, and in cooperation with the American Cancer Society, Lion Angelo adopted Camp Rising Sun as his project.

The 2006 four women presidents from the Pawcatuck, Groton, North Stonington and Mystic Lions Clubs. Shown from left to right are Bella Miceli, Stacy Haines, Lee Paradis and Susan Jensen.

## History of the Plainfield Lions Club

This club was originally chartered as the Moosup Lions Club on December 13, 1951, but in 1978 became the Plainfield Lions Club. The membership felt that this more accurately reflected the area as well as the people represented and served.

Through the decades that followed, these Lions worked hard and played hard. They enjoyed socializing at formal dances and dinners, Mardi Gras celebrations, barn dances, clambakes, bazaars and fairs.

As fundraisers they sold light bulbs and Christmas trees, and operated their food trailer at events such as the Brooklyn and Hebron Fairs. The baked potato booth at the Hebron Fair continues to this day.

More recently the club has sponsored comedy nights, and pancake breakfast events. The food trailer is used at various events such as the multi club flea market, Journey for Sight, and golf tournaments.

In the late 50's, a sizable contribution was awarded to the community volunteer ambulance group, which enabled them to purchase a new ambulance. In 1983, $41,000 was raised by the Plainfield Lions to construct an addition to the local medical center.

In support of children's activities, the Plainfield Lions donated a building at the Moosup Little League field in 1958, and in 1973 provided a bus for the recreation department. A playscape and gazebo were placed in a field next to Town Hall and this area is now known as "Lion Park."

In 1999 the Plainfield Lions sponsored the Plainfield Leo Club, which has been active since its inception. Annually, the Plainfield Lions Club participates in the "Lions Peace Poster" contest.

The club has through the years supported Lions projects. Contributions have been made to the Low Vision Center, Fidelco, CLERF, Diabetes, Camp Rising Sun, CRIS Radio, and LCIF.

In the community individuals with hardships have received help from a crisis fund, and food baskets are distributed during the holidays. Used eye glasses have been collected and are currently being sent to a project in Haiti.

Last year $10,000 was contributed for the repair and reopening of the indoor swimming pool at the town hall, benefiting all age groups.

Over the years life memberships have been bestowed on two Lions, Irving R. Barber Sr. and Harry Bigonesse.

The Plainfield Lions are proud that two of their members have served as District Governors, namely Theodore Coolidge and Robert Erickson. Eight of their members have been named as Melvin Jones Fellows and four as "Knights of the Blind."

Arthur L. Nadeau was designated as an Ambassador of Sight as well as a Knight of the Blind and a Melvin Jones Fellow. He was known as Plainfield's "Mr. Lion." and his untimely death in January 2003 left a void, which will not soon be filled. Lion Arthur played a significant roll in his club and the District.

In 2003, the Plainfield Lions Club, Lion Mike Finnemore presented a check for $10,000 to Plainfield First Selectman Kevin Cunningham in support of the town's Pool Restoration Fund.

The Plainfield Lions Club held an Eye Screening as a part of the Lions Eye Health Program (LEHP), which is performed in the community to help stop preventable blindness. Shown is the district's FDT field of vision testing equipment. This is a helpful diagnostic tool to discover the onset of glaucoma and other eye related problems.

## History of the Pomfret Lions Club

The Pomfret Lions Club was organized in September 1954, and has had a history of supporting Lion's causes including LCIF, CLERF, The Lions Low Vision Center, Camp Rising Sun, and Fidelco. They have been most sensitive to the needs of the people in their town and their need for eye care. The members acknowledge the citizens and businesses of their town that support local eye care through donations to the club.

Other contributions are used for Lion's scholarships. The Pomfret Lions have supported many of the community's youth activities such as the "Frog Rock" basketball league, the Pomfret Little League, and the Girl Scouts and Boy Scouts.

The Pomfret Community School was also a major recipient of the Pomfret Lions generosity. Additionally cheer leading equipment was donated to the Pomfret School, and rocking chairs were purchased for the birthing room at Day Kimball Hospital.

The Pomfret Lions have also supported Opera New England, the Community Kitchens of Northeastern, CT, 4-H camperships and community concerts.

Service activities included the annual Pomfret "Man of the Year" award, and the donation of a plaque dedicated to veterans of the Vietnam and Korean wars. During the holiday season, the Pomfret Lions were responsible for "Santa" house calls with toys and gifts for those being visited.

Some of the major fund raisers have been the spring and fall golf tournaments, chicken barbecues, pancake breakfast events, the community birthday calendar, "Positively Pomfret" Day, the chili booth at the Woodstock Fair, and the Town of Pomfret quilt sales project.

The Pomfret Lions honor their first President, Thomas Hanley, who was born in Pomfret in 1902, and died in 1976.

The devotion of the Pomfret Lions exemplifies their Spirit of community.

## History of the Portland Lions Club

The Portland Lions Club was sponsored by the Cromwell Lions and chartered July 25, 1950. From the beginning this club has been involved with community and civic activities. They have raised funds as well as club awareness through fundraisers. The most notable was the Portland Fair, which started as a Grange project in the 1920's and became the Portland Fair in 1981 under the direction of the Portland Lions Club.

During their first year the fair had about 30 concession stands, and a paid attendance of 9,000. By 1983 the number of concession stands exceeded 75 and attendance was well over 21,000.

Today the club raises funds by selling Christmas trees, Halloween candy, light bulbs, and brooms. They prepare and sell donuts at the Hebron Fair, have spaghetti dinners and pancake breakfast events, and annually raise funds for eye research through mail solicitations.

Money raised by the Portland Lions is used to support scholarships, eye exams and glasses, holiday food baskets, the Little League and the Cub Scouts.

The Portland Lions constructed a field house at the local athletic field, and contributions have been made to the Portland Fire Department, the Portland Food Bank, the Portland DARE and a lifeline for seniors.

This club contributes to CLERF, Lions Low Vision, Drug Awareness, Diabetes, Campaign Sight First, Hearing and Speech, and Camp Rising Sun. The Lions in this club are proud that two of their members served as District Governor, namely, James J. Amato (1972-73) and Frank DeStefano (1980-81)

## History of the Putnam Lions Club

The Putnam Lions Club was organized on September 29, 1949. Lion George Shaw, one of 25 charter members, served as the club's first President.

This club has had a most positive impact on their community. In 1954, the members recognized an urgent need, and raised $10,000 to purchase the town's first ambulance. In the 60's they raised $10,000 to outfit a room at Day Kimball Hospital. An additional donation of $2500 was made to the hospital's diabetes department in memory of Past President Joseph Gadbois.

Their community work has continued through the years. The club has sponsored a Boy Scout Troop and trips to Fenway Park for the schools patrol boys and girls, as well as a little league and a soccer team.

Each year the Putnam Lions spearhead a LEPH screening. They also help celebrate the high school's "Project Graduation" by serving breakfast to the Putnam High School seniors and also award three $1,000 scholarships.

The Putnam Lions replaced the sound system at high school's gym and contributed to a fund to improve a local athletic field.

The local food bank receives the club's financial support, and additionally the club sponsors the collection of non-perishable food for the organization.

A rather unique project involved acquiring an old car with the help of Lion Greg King, owner of an automobile dealership. The car was painted with Lion's colors, and at various times was parked in the Wal-Mart shopping center as well as the K-Mart parking lot and was utilized in the collection of used eyeglasses.

Each year the Putnam Lion's Golf Tournament is a significant source of revenue for the club and fun for the community. The Power boat race is sponsored each year by the club as is the Charity Volley ball Tournament at the Pomfret School Racquet Club.

The Lions colors are spectacular as their float is seen rolling through the streets of Putnam during the Memorial Day and Christmas light parade.

The smell of gourmet onion rings fills the air each year at the Woodstock Fair, and during other festivities as well.

The Putnam Lions are proud to have sponsored two Past District Governors, namely Lions Francis Gregoire and Ronald Hemingway. It is also noted that several members of the club have been honored as Melvin Jones Fellows.

Not only has this club been an avid supporter of the community, they have also supported District, Multiple District, and International projects including LCIF, CLERF, CRIS, Lions Quest, Hearing and Speech, and the Lions Low Vision Center of Eastern Connecticut. In all contributions total over $20,000 annually.

## History of the Salem Lions Club

The Salem Lions Club has fostered and maintained a focus of community service since its charter in June 1973. This is most certainly a unique club as a high percentage of the services that they offer to the community are "hands on." Service projects supporting town agencies and elderly and handicapped residents have included remodeling the Center School and Historical Society kitchens; the erection of a fence between the parking lot and the new recreation field; small remodeling and repair jobs; small construction; painting and yard work; providing transportation and maintaining a wood bank.

A call from an elderly woman on a cold day has brought the Salem Lions to action, immediately responding to the need, doing what was necessary to provide wood to get her through a cold spell. To the Salem Lions this is all in a days work.

Their civic activities have included painting the Salem school and the Easter Seal Rehabilitation center in Uncasville, assisting the building of dugouts at the baseball field, installing storage shelves in the Salem Historical Society vault, installing benches at the base ball field, planting trees at the Salem Green Cemetery, and maintaining a skating pond at the recreation field.

In addition to supporting all Lions sponsored programs, Salem Lions support includes scholarship to graduating Salem students, civic awards to 6th and 7th grade students; A Grange award to an eighth grade student, Salem Easter egg hunt; Salem Secret Santa; Salem Memorial Day parade, Youth baseball team sponsorship, Salem Food Bank, and the Salem community calendar.

Fundraising to support their programs has varied over the years from St. Patrick's Day dances, wood raffles, pancake breakfast events, community calendars with the sale of advertisements, hay rides, annual tag sales and the Journey for Sight.

The "Salem Lions Club" is a household name in the town of Salem, and its value to the residents of this town is nothing less than "Priceless."


## History of the Somers Lions Club

Upon being sponsored by the Stafford Lions Club, the Somers Lions Club was organized on January 30, 1953.

This club has served their community for over 50 years. Among their more notable projects is the sponsorship of a local Boy Scout troop and annually awarding scholarships to two high school seniors.

During the holiday season, the Somers Lions are responsible for the annual tree lighting on the Green, and provide holiday baskets for needy families.

In addition to funding several projects, the Somers Lions provide hands on assistance, such as building dugouts for the Little League baseball program. They also sponsor several town sports programs including the youth basketball program.

The senior citizens are also a focus of their services as each year the Somers Lions  sponsor a holiday party for seniors from throughout the town., and the club is responsible for the  "Citizen of the Year" program.

To support all of these projects, as well as the many District, State and International programs, the Somers Lions host an annual golf tournament, and throughout the year hold various other fundraisers.

The Somers Lions are a spirited group of community minded individuals who enjoy the camaraderie of working together as a group, and serving the town that they love.

## History of the Stafford Lions Club

The Stafford Lions Club was organized in July 1951. Although they began serving their community immediately, it was during the latter part of he 1950's that the club was recognized for a humanitarian act. It was at that time that the Stafford Lions donated a large amount of money to a family whose small daughter fell off the back of a truck, and was severely and permanently injured.

Through the years this club has purchased equipment for testing the eyes of children in the Stafford School system. Whenever the equipment became obsolete, they voted to replace it.

Interestingly, the Stafford Lions became involved in the Miss Connecticut contest. In 1969 the club sponsored Carol Norval as their candidate for "Miss Stafford." Not only was she selected as Miss Stafford, she went on to become Miss Connecticut and this indeed made the members proud.

Each year, the Stafford Lions Club provides a $500 scholarship for a deserving Stafford High School graduate, and this has helped many to continue their education.

Beginning in the 1980's the Stafford Lions initiated a program for delivering food baskets to needy families in Stafford and Willington at Thanksgiving and Christmas. In addition toys and clothing are provided for several children during this holiday season.

This club also provides a great service to the residents of Stafford. Every two years about 5,000 large print telephone directories are printed.

The members of the club go door-to-door delivering the books and mail others to those living in the rural areas. They also leave copies of the directory at several locations in their town for those who may have been missed in the initial distribution. Not only is this a great service, but also in addition, the club realizes several thousands of dollars from advertisers.

"The Spirit of Stafford" is the annual 5K and 10K road race held on the fourth of July and is sponsored each year by the Stafford Lions.

A seven by eight foot community bulletin board erected at the center of Stafford, is the clubs latest project. All local organizations now have the opportunity to post information concerning upcoming events.

Girls of elementary school age have the Stafford Lions to thank as each year they sponsor the Father/Daughter Valentines dance.

Many of the projects initiated by the Stafford Lions are unique to this club. Stafford is a small community, and their concentration is less global in nature, but designed for the needs of this small rural community in Connecticut. They have made their mark and continue to meet the sometimes-unique needs of the community they call home.

## History of the Taftville Lions Club

The Taftville Lions Club was organized on June 30, 1998 after being created in "two hours of door to door interviews by PCC Angelo Miceli and PDG Frank DiStefano" Their work resulted in 38 men and women becoming part of the greatest service organization in the world. This club has continued to grow since its inception.

The members enjoy referring to their village as "The Center of the Universe" and each month the members join forces for what has become a very lucrative fund raising event. Their mainstay is the monthly pasta supper, but in addition they also offer a mothers day brunch, and a fall harvest brunch which collectively have provided the bulk of the $40,000 in revenues needed to support both Lion's charities and local needs.

Each December the townspeople gather at what was a neglected grotto next to a Little League field. A Christmas tree is erected by the Lions and decorated by the children of the town who join others for the carol sing. All of this occurs during the annual Christmas party. During national holidays, the Taftville Lions join together in a flag project during which time American flags are placed at each intersection of the town. In addition the members created two signs for the town; the first one welcoming all to Taftville and the second asking for the support of their local Boy Scout "Eagle Scout" project rejuvenating a neglected city owned lot into a park. This club also supports the local school PTO's, Fire Department and individual special needs by dedicating proceeds of various pasta suppers to specific causes.

The Taftville Lions have a spirit of community unmatched by many of our other clubs. Their energy is contagious and their future is bright.

## History of the Thompson Lions Club

It was on April 29, 1953 that Lions International Special Representative Alfio Urbinati organized the Thompson Lions Club with the Putnam Lions Club serving as the sponsor. Adrian Valade served as the club's first President with Marcel Beauregard serving as club secretary.

The Thompson Lions have contributed countless dollars and hours to a variety of causes and charities over its more than 50 year history. Contributions have gone towards eye examinations and eyeglasses, Boys and Girls Scouts, Boys and Girls State, Little League, 4H Camp, Hole in the Wall Camp, diabetes research, Lions Quest, Special Olympics and scholarships. The club has fully supported Lions causes including LCIF, CLERF, and Camp Rising Sun.

These Lions are especially sensitive to the needs of their community including the Day Kimball Hospital, the Thompson Youth Center, and projects such as Thanksgiving and Christmas food baskets.

In 1994 the Thompson Lions, spearheaded by Lion Skip Faucher, celebrated their 40th anniversary by raising over $23,000 to build a Gazebo (Bandstand), which was donated to the Town of Thompson and dedicated to the fond memory of deceased members. For their 50th anniversary, the club built a storm shelter on the "Mill Pond."

Fundraisers included the annual Golf Tournament, chicken barbeque, roast beef supper, raffles, as well as working with their food trailer at three major fall events, and dinner and entertainment events.

The Thompson Lions are proud to have named five of their members as Melvin Jones Fellows. One member, Lion Don Antonson has not only served his club with distinction, but has also served the District. Lion Don has been Youth Exchange Chairman for over 15 years and club Treasurer for over 30 years. Lion Rene Morin served as Campaign Sight First Co-Chair and Lion Paul Hoenig as Zone Chairman.

All work and no play simply does not describe the Thompson Lions Club. Fun events have included trips to Block Island, Boston Harbor, Newport, R.I. and Stockbridge, MA. The club also sponsors fall and spring extravaganzas which are always sold out.

The Thompson Lions Club with their many projects has become part of the landscape of this rural town near the border of Massachusetts. They are proud of their past, and in this, their 52$^{nd}$ year, the current King Lion, Kevin Valade carries on a tradition. It was his grandfather who served as the club's first president, and his father as well was a long time member of the Thompson Lions Club.


## History of the Tolland Lions Club

The Tolland Lions Club was sponsored by the Stafford Lions and organized on November 10, 1969.

In the town of Tolland, there is a Little League field that bears the name of "Lions." One of the Tolland Lions Club's projects is to maintain, and when necessary, upgrade the field so that it is always ready for use, and can deservingly bear the name "Lions."

The Tolland Lions have provided annual support for the High School Scholarship program, Tolland's "Project Graduation," and the youth soccer, baseball and basketball programs.

Annual support is given to those who participate in Boy's State and Girl's State as well as the Boy Scout Eagle projects.

The Tolland Lions have faithfully supported Lions projects including the Low Vision Center, CLERF, CRIS, Fidelco and Camp Rising Sun.

When requests are received for food and clothing, or for vision screening and eyeglasses for those in need, the Tolland Lions respond on an as needed basis.

The club has accepted responsibility for the annual Tolland "Citizen of the Year" banquet as well as the prestigious award granted to the finalist.

Funds are raised for these projects by holding a pancake breakfast, pumpkin and corn stalk sales as well as the annual "Spirit of Spring" road race; however, their biggest ongoing fundraiser is renting and erecting tents.

The Tolland Lions are proud to have honored their charter President Lion Dave Serluco with a Lions Life Membership, as well as charter member Lion George Tornatore who since the club's inception has had perfect attendance.

The Thomson Lions Club built a gazebo on the Thomson town green in fond memory of their deceased members.

Vernon Lions are shown at work, repairing scoreboards at the Rockville High School.

## History of the Vernon Lions Club

The Vernon Lions Club was chartered on April 27, 1987 and has served the towns of Vernon and Ellington since that date.

Perhaps the Vernon Lions are best know for their annual Goods and Services auction which has become their mainstay for income. With over 100 attendees, and 250+ items and wonderful support from friends and the community, they are currently raising over $7,000 a year. In addition, they co-sponsor an annual bowling tournament with the Manchester Lions Club which directly benefits Fidelco.

The club's fundraising efforts evolved over the years from humble beginnings of operating a hot dog cart at every event that would allow them to participate, selling mints, light bulbs, and eventually moving into a food trailer and serving the worlds best hot dogs and kielbasa. Unfortunately, the food trailer met an untimely death a few years ago, and has not been replaced.

This club has the distinction of having one of the most unusual members in Lions history. In 1990, the club sponsored the first of two great fundraisers. After receiving "official" approval, the club inducted "Hugo" a massive gray elephant as a member. Hugo helped the club with a multiple Lions Club tug of war against Lion members from neighboring towns. While he is no longer a member, the club remembers him fondly, even though he was never "officially" counted as a member when reporting to LCI.

Through the years, the Vernon Lions have named four individuals as Melvin Jones Fellows, and the members of this club have always been visible in their community.

The Vernon Lions Club is composed of active fun loving Lions that live the "We Serve" motto each and every day.

## History of the Waterford Lions Club

The Waterford Lions Club had its beginnings in 1952. On June 11th of that year the club was organized upon being sponsored by the Niantic Lions Club.

This civic-minded group of men and women provides eyeglasses and examinations to residents who cannot meet this need themselves. In April of each year the Waterford Lions can be found at the Crystal Mall taking donations for the "Hospice Tree of Life." During the summer, the members hold a picnic for the visually impaired at Camp Harkness, and they have been doing this for the past 35 years.

For the past 26 years during "Waterford Week" the club has sponsored the "Lions 5K Road Race."

Each year the Waterford Nurses Association sponsor "Health Day " exams, and the Waterford Lions can be seen assisting with the examinations, truly a public service.

At years end the Waterford Lions gather together at Town Hall, decorating the tree they purchased. They preside over the lighting of the tree, and take responsibility for Santa Clause who distributes candy to the children in attendance. In the weeks just prior to this event, the Waterford Lions are busy distributing Thanksgiving turkeys to the town interfaith food locker and the Salvation Army.

This club has averaged over $9,000 per year in donations to Lions programs and community projects and organizations. This has been made possible by various fundraisers including the annual craft show that has just celebrated its twentieth year.

The Waterford Lions are proud that of all the clubs participating in the annual "Journey for Sight" walk-a-thon, they have, for three consecutive years raised the highest amount in District 23-C. Quite an accomplishment.

Finally, in addition to the annual "Be Thankful You Can See" seal drive, the Waterford Lions can be found operating a concession stand during the Waterford Soccer tournament, and preparing pancakes at their annual breakfast in April.

Since 1990, the club has named eight individuals as Melvin Jones Fellows, two as Loyal Shepherd Fellows, and one "Knight of the Blind."

## History of the Waterford Regional Lions Club

The members of the Waterford Regional Lioness Club voted in 1992 to leave the Lioness organization and become a Lions Club.

Under the sponsorship of the Waterford Lions, the club was organized on June 30, 1992. President of the newly formed club was Sheri Ann Grills, Christine Campbell, 1st V.P., Judi Dousis, 2nd V.P., June Mostowy, 3rd V.P., Mary Ann Peter, Secretary, Derri Proctor, Tail Twister, and Jeanette Martin, Lion Tamer.

Service activities have included Christmas Caroling at local nursing homes, assisting Waterford Nurses with their "Health Day," participating in the "Niantic Light" Parade, volunteering at the SNET Golf Tournament as well as the Low Vision Center donut booth at the Hebron Fair. An ongoing service activity has been the collection of eyeglasses.

Contributions have been made to the Waterford Ambulance Service, Hospice of Southeastern CT, scholarships at Waterford and East Lyme High Schools, Southeastern Connecticut Center for the Blind, and the Waterford Historical Society.

These Lions have given their support to District, State, and International Lions causes. Contributions have been made to Camp Rising Sun, CRIS Radio, FIDELCO, CLERF, Diabetes, LCIF, Hearing and Speech, Lions Low Vision Center, Lions Journey for Sight annual walk-a-thon, and the Macular Degeneration Research Center at Yale.

The club has named three individuals as Melvin Jones Fellows and one as a "Knight of the Blind."

To support their many services to the community, the members are involved in several fund raisers including bake sales, Christmas wrap sales, The Crystal Mall Hometown Fair, pancake breakfast events co-sponsored by the Waterford Lions Club, an annual fundraising letter, Bingo Nights at the Casinos, car washes, 50/50 raffles and the annual Holiday Crafts Show.

Although the Waterford Regional Lions Club has only been in existence since 1992, most of the members have served both as Lioness and Lions for many additional years. During the Lions year 2004-2005, they celebrated their 25th year of serving their community and communities throughout the world. They plan to commemorate their 25th year of service with their first "Friendship" banner.

The Waterford Regional Lions are a unique group. Although the number of members in this club has remained low but constant, this is perhaps the most "united" club in the District. The percentage of members attending conferences and conventions has been significantly higher than most other clubs. The members have continually participated in all Zone, Region, District, and State functions. They simple love working and playing together, and most of all, their love of Lionism is most impressive.

## History of the Westbrook Lions Club

The Westbrook Lions Club, one of our newest clubs, was sponsored by the Essex Lions and organized on February 13, 2004. Their first endeavor at raising funds was what they termed as the "First Annual Potato Fest" and the club realized a hefty profit.

The Westbrook Lions has continually grown since its inception, and during a recent "Invitation Drive" they added several new members to an already thriving organization.

The leadership of this club is willing to accept nothing less than excellence, as they serve their community and the communities of the world, and we can all expect greatness from this group of civic minded individuals who are proud to call themselves "Lions."

Members of the Westbrook Lions Club
are shown at their Potato Fest food booth.

Willimantic Lions Club President Shirley Mauro presented a Life
Membership to Lion Fred LeBeau.    Looking on is PCC Diane (Pettit)
Bielski and PCC Frank Mauro.

## History of the Willimantic Lions Club

In 1941, the Willimantic Lions Club was organized under the sponsorship of the Norwich Lions with Raymond Coutu serving as charter president.

During the early years, the club was involved in activities aimed at helping the war effort. Books and puzzles were collected and sent to boot camps across the country. Funds were also raised to aid the blind and visually impaired in their community.

Every spring, for over 40 years, the club held a dinner honoring local athletes.

During the 50's, the members held their first Christmas party for the blind at Mansfield Training School and also purchased an ambulance for the community at a cost of $10,000.

Willimantic Lion PDG Richard Case, was instrumental in the establishment of the Connecticut Lions Eye Research Foundation, served a term as President, and was the first person to be honored as a "Knight of the Blind."

The club established an outreach program to assist blind residents. Rides to medical appointments were provided and the club hosted two evening socials each year. To this day the club continues to provide eye exams and glasses for residents in need.

Currently the club holds three pancake breakfasts events each year, and donuts are sold at the Hebron Lions Fair.

In 1996 the Willimantic Lions formed a twinning relationship with the Senkadagala Lions Club of Sri Lanka. The club's members arranged for the shipment of surgical instruments, and their twin club was able to establish a cataract surgical center, still in operation today.

The club also sponsored a Leo club in 1996.

The Willimantic Lions continue to support local charities, assisting the Salvation Army each Christmas and providing funding for community organizations. Each year the club also hosts the Windham Special Olympics Swim Meet.

These Lions support all District, State and International projects. They have participated in Campaign Sight First, Campaign Sight First II, completed a 5-year commitment for the CLERF Macular Degeneration Project and contributed to the Vascular Eye Research Center at UCONN.

Locally the club adopts a family every Christmas, providing gifts for the entire family, a tree, lights, and ornaments.

Five Willimantic Lions have served as District Governor, namely Richard Case, Charles Hitchcock, James Mackey, Frank Mauro, and Edwin Fisher. One member, Frank Mauro, also served as Council Chairman.

Lions International has recognized the service of several club members; PCC Frank Mauro has received the International President's Medal, International Presidents Leadership Medal, four International Presidents Certificates of Appreciation, the Governors 100% Award and the Governors Excellence Award. PDG Edwin Fisher was awarded two International Presidents Certificates of Appreciation and an International Presidents Leadership Medal. Lions Gunnel Stenberg and Shirley Mauro are both recipients of International Presidents Certificates of Appreciation. Dr. Keith Lemire received two and Wilfrid Lebeau and Sue Fisher each received three International Presidents Certificates of Appreciation.

Several members of this club have been honored as Melvin Jones Fellows, Knights of the Blind, FIDELCO Loyal Shepherds, and Ambassadors of Sight.

## History of the Woodstock Lions Club

The Putnam Lions were pleased to sponsor the Woodstock Lions Club, which was organized on January 16, 1956. As this club approaches its 50th year of service to the local and worldwide community, their focus continues to be on projects which will enrich the lives of both the youth and adult population in Woodstock.

The Woodstock Lions each year award scholarships to two seniors planning to enroll in a college or university, but unlike other clubs, the Woodstock Lions Club also provides scholarships for those who require attendance at the Child Care Center. In addition each year a candidate is sponsored for "Boys State."

When the club was approached to assist with the "Walk for Life" cancer program, the Woodstock Lions rented and installed a tent for the occasion.

The E.M.T.'s as well as the fire department needed jump suits, and the Woodstock Lions did not hesitate to purchase them. And let us not forget the Woodstock Lions each year provide both food and toys at Christmas time to the less fortunate in their community.

Each year the Woodstock Lions look forward to the "Woodstock" Fair, where for the past 40 years, their greatest fundraiser has been their ice cream booth. Additional funds are derived from their annual pancake breakfast.

## History of District 23-C Projects

The Lions of District 23-C are not only active in various projects in their communities but also participate and support the activities endorsed by District 23-C. The following describes some of these activities:

Journey for Sight Walkathon

Journey for Sight was originally endorsed by Lions Clubs International and was started as a club and zone project by then Griswold Lion Marie Salpietro. In 1994 it became a District 23-C project under then District Governor Eric Jacobson. Lions Clubs' members get pledges for various amounts, walk the route established in various locations in Eastern Connecticut, and give half the money raised to several district projects and the other half to projects in the Lions Clubs' communities.

### LEHP and Health Screenings

Clubs throughout the district run Lions Eye Health Program Screenings as a service to the people in their communities. In addition to checking eyes, tests for hearing, blood pressure, diabetes and other health related issues are performed based on the availability of health care professionals. Most, if not all, of these tests are performed free of charge. Serious health or vision problems discovered at these screenings are referred to professional healthcare providers for further evaluation and/or treatment. Brochures on eye diseases, the symptoms of and treatment for diabetes and hearing problems are distributed at these screening as well as at club meetings by the district chair people responsible for these duties.

### Miscellaneous

In addition to the projects listed above, the Lions of District 23-C contribute their time, talents and money to Youth Exchange and Youth Projects, Sight Saver Day (to raise funds for the CT Lions Eye Research Foundation), Low Vision, CRIS, Camp Rising Sun and the Fidelco Guide Dog Foundation. Many of the Clubs participate in the International Peace Poster Contest. For the efforts of these outstanding club officers and special Lions, the District Governor holds an annual awards night to thank them for all the hard work that they and their club members do and for their dedication to helping those in need in their communities, their district and their state.

# Chapter 6 - History of Lioness and Leo Clubs in Connecticut

## The History of the Leo Club Program

The objective of the Leo Club program is to provide the youth of the world with an opportunity for development and contribution as responsible members of the community.

It all began in 1957 when the first Leo club was formed by two Lions, namely Jim Graver and William Ernst of the Glenside, PA Lions Club. The club was made up of 26 students from the Abington High School, where the school colors were maroon and gold. And thus from that day forward, the Leo colors would forever be maroon and gold.

Ten years later in October 1967, the Leo Club program became an official program of Lions Clubs International.

Leo clubs are classified as either "Alpha" (club members between 12 and the legal age of majority in their country) or "Omega," (Members between the legal age of majority in their country and age 28.) Each Leo club operates under the sponsorship of a Lions Club.

Leo members most often stand out from other members of their peer group as they develop skills as organizers and motivators. Leos learn the importance of cooperation through the performance of community service. It is evident that membership in a Leo club provides young people with a chance to excel, to develop character traits and receive recognition for their contributions to the community.

Currently Leo clubs can be found in 134 countries, where there are over 5500 Leo clubs with over 137,000 members. Within our Multiple District there are 12 clubs in District "A", 18 in District "B" and 7 in District "C."

The involvement of Leo members in Multiple District activities is best illustrated by this letter from a member of the Shoreline Leo club addressed to Zone Chairman Jim Harris of the Niantic Lions Club:

*Hello Mr. Harris,*

*I just got back from the Leo Convention and Training Conference. I had such a great time! I really enjoyed speaking with the other Leos from across Connecticut.*

*The day started out with a 16 year-old named Matt speaking about bullying. He said some very powerful things about his own experiences as a disabled person, which made me feel very lucky to have such an open-minded and understanding community in East Lyme and Salem. All were assigned to random lunch groups and mine consisted of 2 seniors from Montville (who were looking for Jeff!), 2 members of the Foundation Leo Club, one 7th grade Windsor Locks Leo, and a junior from Woodbury. We had a great time getting to know each other and talking about our own Leo Clubs. Megan, President of the Montville Leos, shared her idea to recruit new members. She suggested that each senior recruit a person to replace their spot. I thought this was a good idea to prevent the loss of Leos. We all agreed that we would enjoy more joint events with towns and cities all over Connecticut.*

*After lunch, we listened to a seminar about leadership in conflict situations. Mr. Mauro lead us through a list of guidelines for dealing with confrontation and conflict and explained that all leaders (he described the Aggressive, Democratic, and Permissive types) will be faced with conflict. I find these guidelines helpful, as being mature about confrontation is a characteristic of a good leader.*

*By the end of the day, I felt as if I had really enjoyed myself and feel I can use the advise from the speakers in my own life. The conference was well organized and I am looking forward to attending the Connecticut State Leo Convention and Training Workshop next year.*

*Thank you for letting me know about the convention!*


*Alexandra*

In 2005-2006, Connecticut was recognized for being among the top 10 in the world with the greatest net gain in new clubs, and as a result, Council Leo Chairperson Lion Blanche Sewell received a "Top Ten" Leo club service pin from Lions Clubs International.

## History of Leo Clubs in District 23-B

It was not until June 30, 1993 that the first Leo Club in District 23-B, the Bloomfield Leo Club, was chartered under the sponsorship of the Bloomfield Lions Club. Although the club was very successful in many of it's endeavors, beginning in the year 2000 the club's membership started to diminish, and the club became inactive. The sponsoring club through its Leo advisor, Lion Beverly Grever-Clements is attempting to reactivate the group.

The East Hartford Leo Club was chartered on March 7, 1995 with the East Hartford Lions serving as their sponsor. On October 2nd of that year the Windsor Locks Middle School Leo Club was chartered. This club, sponsored by the Windsor Locks Lions Club, has been extraordinarily active serving the needy in their community, and this was the subject of an article in *The Lion Magazine*.

The Windsor Locks High School Leo Club was also chartered on October 2, 1995 with the Windsor Locks Lions Club as their sponsors. This Leo club works along side their sponsors helping to keep their town clean. The club has also been involved in many other service projects as well as fundraising activities.

The Watertown Swift Jr. High School Leo Club was chartered on March 22, 1996 upon being sponsored by the Watertown Lions Club. The club is proud that each and every year, the members faithfully attend the Connecticut Lions Mid Winter Conference.

The Woodbury Middle School Leo Club was chartered on February 17, 1997 and this was followed on March 11, 1997 when the East Windsor Jr. High Leo Club received its charter.

On May 2, 1997, under the sponsorship of the South Windsor Lions Club, the South Windsor Leo Club was chartered. This was followed on June 20, 2000 when under the sponsorship of the Winsted Lions Club, the Gilbert School Leo Club received its charter. This club is known for the work that they have done for cancer patients and the elderly. If you can remember your own senior prom some time in years past, this Leo club decided to sponsor a "Senior" prom for, who else but "seniors" at the local senior center. Needless to say, the club whose liaison is Lion Blanche Sewell, has been very active in the community.

The Nonnewaug High School Leo Club was chartered on January 25, 2001 with the Woodbury Lions serving as their sponsor.

The Fermi High School Leo Club was chartered on April 2, 2003 with the Enfield Lions Club as their sponsor. The members have created a special program for children that are in the school's special education program, and this has been done under the direction of educator, Ms Cokkinias, an advisor, and Lion Trish Holmes, the Enfield Lions Club liaison.

The Granby Lions sponsored the Granby Memorial High School Leo Club, which was chartered on December 9, 2003. The Terryville Lions Club sponsored the Terryville High School Leo Club and this organization was chartered on October 25, 2004.

The East Hartford Lions sponsored the Two Rivers Magnet Middle School Leo Club, which was chartered on January 26, 2005. Shortly there after on February 14, 2005 the Griswold Middle School Leo Club received its charter from sponsor, the Rocky Hill Lions Club.

## History of the Colchester Leo Club

Created in the spring of 1998, The Colchester Leo Club was born under the guidance of Leo advisors Charlene Picard, Rita Anastasio, Julie Shilosky, and Steve and Mary Gillis. They were officially chartered in November 1998 with 12 members under the leadership of club President Jayme LaGrega.

As their first fundraiser, the club held a tag and bake sale, and donated the $500 raised to the Colchester DARE program.

Two years later the club shrank to only four members, and this prompted the remaining Leos to develop a new and unique way to both serve their community and raise funds. Lion Chuck Taylor and the advisors attended "Clown College" and passed on the art of clowning to the Leos. This revived the club, and with 15 Leos strong, they took their show on the road , performed, and raised funds. This was the first Leo Club to perform in this manner, and in the spring of 2004, the members attended clown school to hone their skills.

Fundraising activities included face painting and applying tattoos at the Colchester Lions carnival. They also held a bake sale at a Colchester Lions pancake breakfast, and collected pennies that were ultimately donated to the local food bank.

Service projects include Thanksgiving and Holiday food baskets for the residents of Dublin and Ponemah Village, and participating in the Memorial Day parade. The club is also know for their "Haunted Hay ride" event during Halloween and for their support of the DARE Program, The Senior Center, and "Project Oceanography."

The Colchester Leo Club have paved the road to the future and those who will follow. They are, without exception a credit to their community.

## History of the E.O. Smith Leo Club

In 2006, Kousanee Chheda was a Peace Poster contest winner. As a result, both she, her mother Nayna, and her sister Sumaali became interested in the Lions organization. They spoke to members of the Mansfield Lions Club who not only explained what it meant to be a Lion but also reported how Leo Clubs around the world interact with their communities.

Thus the seed was planted for the formation of a new Leo Club. Kousanee, Sumaali and their mother Nayna were the force behind the creation of this club. In fact Nayna herself was invited to become a member of the Mansfield Lions Club and accepted the invitation.

Three individuals volunteered to serve as advisors, namely Linda Lombard, a teacher at the E.O. Smith High School, Lion Doryann Plante, and the newest member of the Mansfield Lions Club, Lion Nayna Chheda. Also instrumental in the formation of this club was Mansfield Lion Joyce Passmore.

Officers elected were President Kousanee Chheda; Vice Presidents Janice Tate and Sumaali Chheda; Secretary Aileen Yang; Treasurers Ariana Levin and Mariam Mian; Tail Twister Madhushree Gnanasambandan; Membership Chair Victoria Chen and board member Cristobel Ortega. During the months of September through December, 2006, the members assisted at the Lions Fair, the town Halloween party, the UNICEF penny drive, the Mansfield Lions pancake breakfast, the Lions bell ringing for the Salvation Army, the Senior Center's Bazzar, and the Senior Center's gift wrapping project.

They collected food for the Covenant Soup Kitchen, and warm coats for the Windham Area Interfaith Ministry. Additionally, these Leos also collected eyeglasses for third world countries in all Mansfield Public Schools as well as the town hall and the children's piano teacher's home.

The members participated in the "Adopt-A-Family" program by collecting gifts from local businesses and individuals. In the planning stage at the date of this writing was an E.O. Smith movie night, ice skating fundraiser, a talent show and a pasta dinner ... and to think, all of this over the course of less than four months. Certainly nothing less than remarkable.

These Leo members are tremendously enthusiastic, and a tribute to the Lion name.

## History of the Eastern Connecticut Leo Club

Since the club's certification on March 26, 1992, it has had an ever-increasing influence on the sector of the community it serves. The club has grown not only in members, but also in its knowledge of Lionism and the meaning of serving their community. These young individuals from area schools have learned from their sponsoring club, the Griswold Regional Lions and the club's advisors what the Lions motto, "We Serve" truly means.

In the early years, their first fundraiser, a walk-a-thon to benefit a local youth, raised a total of $3,600, a truly great beginning. Since that first fundraiser, the club has had the opportunity to be involved in other benefit walk-a-thons as well as another successful fundraiser, which involved a dance for students in grades 5 and 6.

With monies raised from their various activities, the Leos have contributed to International and District projects, including CLERF, Fidelco, LCIF and a donation to the Lions Low Vision Center of Eastern Connecticut, which itself was in the very generous amount of $1,000, truly a tribute to the young members of a young organization.

The Eastern Connecticut Leo Club's main thrust is service. The members have established an ongoing clothing and canned food drive for area shelters. Additionally, they have assisted senior citizens with household chores and assisted in yard work for those unable to perform these tasks themselves.

The Leo President at the time of certification was Leo William Graham followed by Leos Kristy Requin, Stacy Graham, John Cadarette, Beth McLean, and Ben McLean, Jennifer Mitchell, Nicole Lamarre, and Rachael King.

Those who have been honored as "Leo of the Year" include Leos John Cadarette, Stacy Graham, Kristy Reguin, Jacob Switzer, Tara Mitchell, Jennifer Mitchell, Nicole Lamarre, and Robert Maynard.

As we view the work of the Eastern Connecticut Leos, we are viewing the future of America, and the future of these soon to be adults who have rapidly learned the meaning of serving mankind.

## History of the Foundation High School Leo Club

The Foundation High School Leo Club was chartered in 1999. The Milford and Orange Lions Clubs of District 23-A, together served as the club's sponsors and representatives of both attend meetings along with school advisors. This is the first Leo club organized for students with special needs.

Leo members who wish to seek an office are nominated, and conduct a campaign, which includes delivering numerous speeches. Following an election the new officers are installed each fall at the beginning of the school year. Meetings follow an agenda set by the officers and include the Lions four point opening (pledge of allegiance, verse of America, invocation and Leos toast). General meetings are held twice a month and officers meet weekly.

One of the members of the Foundation High School Leo Club received the honor of "Leo of the Year" in 2004, one of only eleven in the entire world. The members of this club attend the Connecticut Lions Mid Winter Conference each and every year where they have a chance to meet, socialize and attend workshops with Leo members from throughout Connecticut.

Some of the charitable undertakings of this Club include a beach cleanup in the spring, collecting eyeglasses in conjunction with Lens Crafters, collecting soda can tabs for Ronald McDonald House, a food drive, and filling baskets for needy families at Thanksgiving. The members conduct a pet food drive for the Milford Animal Shelter and they also sponsor a family through "Operation Hope" for the holidays.

These Leo members have helped the Orange Lions Club serve dinners to seniors at Thanksgiving and serve food at their "Taste of Amity" fundraiser in May. The members have taken part in the "Walk for Diabetes" at Lighthouse Park for the past eight years, have adopted several acres of rain forest and, this year, and adopted a whale. The Leo members collected teddy bears for the children in Russia and raised and donated $1,000 for both the victims of the tsunami and Hurricane Katrina. This in itself is a magnificent achievement.

Guest speakers are invited to attend many of the club's meetings. Examples of those invited to speak include representatives from the State Police and the Milford Canine Units, The Fidelco Guide

Dog Foundation, Canine Companions, the Milford Library, the Animal Shelter, as well as Lions from both the Milford and Orange Lions Club. The Club hosts an end-of-the-year luncheon to conclude the year's efforts and activities.

The Foundation High School Leo Club has not only performed with excellence, but serves as an example of how best to serve the community, and at the same time prepare these young adults for the years that follow.

## History of the Killingly Area Leo Club

The Killingly Area Leo Club, with an average membership of twelve, raises an average of $1,000 a year, but more importantly contributes over 1,000 hours of community service.

Each year the club adopts a family and provides not just basic necessities, but gifts as well.

The club members work with the American Cancer Society raising funds, and assisting that organization with the local "Relay for Life" event at the Woodstock Fairgrounds. The funds raised are donated directly to the American Cancer Society.

Members of this Leo club also assist at any and all Lion's events, and it is said that they "are the backbone of food events" by being part of the wait staff, busboys, dishwashers, and servers.

Funds have been raised for Lion's charities including CRIS, Fidelco, Diabetes, Hearing and Speech, and the Lions Low Vision Centers.

The club members each year perform a service project such as working at the food bank, or park clean up. During the past year the members assembled tote bags for children entering Foster care to assist with a sometimes-difficult transition. Items include toiletries as well as clothing.

With only a fraction of the potential number of members, this Leo Club has accomplished a great deal in a short period of time. Their potential is almost limitless, and the future for this club appears to be extremely bright.

## History of the Montville Leo Club

Sponsored by the Montville Lions Club, the Montville Leo Club was chartered in June 1996. The organization started with twenty charter members, and today consists of students from both the middle school and the high school. Three members of the Montville Lions Club serve as Leo advisors.

Annually the Montville Leos sponsor Halloween Parties for area children, volunteer at Montville's Youth Day, participate in "Journey for Sight" as well as the "Relay for Life." Collecting eyeglasses is an ongoing activity for this club. The members also assist with dinners at the Center for the Blind, and sponsor dances held at the Montville Middle School. Funds are raised by sponsoring car washes, bowling for pledges, and conducting yard and bake sales. The club has been innovative in establishing "Leo Landscaping," a small "business" that accepts donations from the community by raking leaves, shoveling snow and performing various odd jobs. They have sponsored hay rides and pictures with Santa, and have participated in the Montville Fair, as well as assisting the Montville Recreation Department with Easter festivities.

Families are adopted for the holidays and cards are created and then delivered to nursing home patients. The Leos also assist the Montville Lions Club with dinners, pancake breakfasts and Christmas tree sales. The club has adopted a road in Montville and quite frequently you can see these Leo members removing litter from the side of the road.

When a local family lost their home due to a fire, the Leo members stepped in to assist the family.

The Montville Leos have reach out to other Leo Clubs in the area and enjoyed joint meetings with both the Willihelm Leo Club and the Shoreline Leo Club. Those who attend a Lions Midwinter conference will always find members of this Leo Club taking an active part. Two members of the club also participated in the Youth Exchange with Canada.

Funds raised are donated to organizations such as Camp Rising Sun, Lions Low Vision Center, Fidelco, CRIS Radio, Montville Youth Services, DARE, Literacy Volunteers, the Raymond Hill Library, Connecticut Humane Society, Hospice, American Cancer Society, Southeastern Connecticut Center of the Blind, Connecticut Lions Eye

Research Foundation, Lions Club International Foundation, Hearing & Speech, Diabetes, and the Big Brother/Big Sister organization.

During their short history, five Montville Leos have gone on to become members of the Montville Lions Club.

## History of the RHAM Leo Club

The Hebron Leo Club was incorporated in 1996 with Lion Steve Beauchene serving as club advisor. Among the charter members, Scott Griffin served as President. Other officers included Secretary, Lindsey Cavanaugh, Treasurer, Brigitte Gynther, and Membership Chairman, Jeff D'Atri.

The first six years were quite successful with a membership average of about 25 members. In the seventh year, club membership started to dwindle very rapidly and with a large group of graduating seniors the club became inactive.

Lion Richard Griswold, a retired public school teacher of 35 years, expressed interest in reactiving the club during the 2005 Lions year. Plans were made to recruit a co-advisor from the RHAM High School staff and faculty. A member of the RHAM Guidance department, Jeannie Kmetz, volunteered to serve in this role. With the permission of the RHAM administration, a membership drive began in October of 2005.

The Hebron Leo Club was re-named the "RHAM Leo Club" and re-incorporated in January of 2006 with 13 charter members. Since that date they have recruited 7 additional members. The current officers are: President, Hillary Federico, Vice-President, Alex Moore, Secretary, Kaylee Tomaso, Treasurer, Dan Nissley, Leo Tamer, Courtney Federico, and Tail Twister Rebecca Stuart.

The RHAM Leo Club continues to conduct fundraising activities to help build its financial base. The service projects committee has been actively researching projects and activities for their club to sponsor. Currently the club is committed to assisting the Eastern Region Special Olympics games in May 2006.

It would appear that this club is well on its way to becoming a vital force within the community.

## History of the Shoreline Leo Club

The Shoreline Leo Club was born on April 19, 1993 under the sponsorship of the Niantic Lions Club. Robert Senkow as President of the Niantic Lions Club was the driving force, which helped create the organization. Students from East Lyme, Salem and Waterford joined together as the first members of the club with their goal of working with students and others who needed the hand and heart of a Leo.

Leo Presidents Caryn Levy (2001-2003) and Erica Mahon (2003-2004) served with excellence resulting in increased membership as well as services to the community. Leo President Erica Mahon celebrated the Leo Club's 10-year anniversary with an active membership drive that raised membership above 60 members. Leo President Tess Kohanski (2004-2005) continued with the goal to increased membership with active recruitment of new Leos from both the East Lyme Middle School and High School. The Shoreline Leo Club has become the largest Leo Club in Lions District 23-C with 77 active members as of November 2004.

The Shoreline Leos have been generous with their support of the District's charities as well as community causes. The club has held numerous face-painting fundraisers, and also raised funds through sale of potholders. The members have participated in charity walkathons, and supported car wash fundraisers.

There was a needy family in town, and the members worked together contributing gifts for the adults and toys for the children. Food baskets as well were delivered to needy families Shoreline Leo members manned water stops for numerous town road races, sponsored Middle School dances, held holiday music programs for local senior citizens, and provided ongoing community service support for several local community groups such as the Children's Museum, and the Smith Harris Historical House.

In 2002, the Shoreline Leos instituted an annual Holiday new toy drive for needy kids, and an ongoing program for recycling used eyeglasses collected in local schools. Additionally this club established an ongoing community services awards program honoring East Lyme Middle School students for outstanding volunteerism. The program was expanded in 2004 to honor Middle School student service contributions within the towns of Salem and East Lyme. In 2004, the club established a Shoreline Leo Club $500 scholarship with the East Lyme High School Scholarship Association.

The Shoreline Leos have been recognized for their community service contributions and continues to live up to the motto "We Serve."

## History of the Connecticut Lioness Clubs

From the beginning, women have been active in Lionism. The Lions magazine of March 1920 reported the establishment of a "wives" club, The Lioness Club of Quincy, Illinois. The group was organized for the purpose of helping the Lions of Quincy.

There were hundreds of such auxiliary women's groups around the world before the middle of the century.

In 1974 the International Board of Directors sent a questionnaire to these groups seeking information about their interest in becoming official members of the International organization. The benefits were that they would receive the general support of Lions Clubs International in organizing and recruiting members. They could make use of International awards to members and would have the benefits of the public image associated with Lions.

The response to the questionnaire was overwhelmingly positive, and on October 15, 1975 the first Lioness Club was organized in Pawcatuck, Connecticut. However the first Lioness charter was issued to the Mt. Pleasant (North Carolina) Lioness Club on December 24, 1975.

In 1983 Connecticut had a total of 18 Lioness Clubs, four in District 23-A, five in District 23-B and nine in District 23-C

In 1987 an amendment to the associations constitution allowed women to join Lions Clubs. By October 1991, there were more than 40,000 female Lions worldwide, many of whom were once members of a Lioness Club. At its October 1991, meeting therefore, the board concluded that all Lioness Clubs should be invited to make known their willingness to become members of an existing Lions Club or to take steps to form a new Lions Club.

The board felt that since women could now be members, Lions Clubs International could become even greater if both men and women united under a single banner of Lions Clubs International.

In July 1992, the International Association discontinued the administrative services it had provided to Lioness clubs, Districts and Multiple Districts. It is quite evident that women have had a most positive impact on the International association, and will continue to do so in the years to follow.

## History of the Beacon Falls Lioness Club

Under the sponsorship of the Beacon Falls Lions Club, the Beacon Falls Lioness Club received its charter on April 29, 2000. Susan Mis served as the club's first President. The organization began with 12 members and has continually grown. As of this writing, the Beacon Falls Lioness Club had a total of 36 members.

Since it's inception, the club has contributed almost $30,000 to various charities and individuals. Recipients include the Lions Low Vision Centers (with four Ambassador of Sight Awards), The Woodland Regional High School Concession Stand, a scholarship for a graduate of Woodland Regional High School, the Fidelco Guide Dog Foundation, and the town's youth sports programs.

Other beneficiaries of the club's altruism include the Boy Scouts, the local Junior Women's organization, Friends of the Library, local churches, the Woodland Regional High School Library, the Fine Arts Booster Club, the Connecticut Lions Eye Research Foundation, the American Diabetes Association, and Alzheimer's research.

The Beacon Falls Lioness club has contributed to many non-traditional charities such as the Valley Breast Cancer Woman's Initiative, the Laurel Ledge Elementary School playground, Student Ambassadors, St. Jude, "Wind Over Wings," a holiday assistance program, and the Leukemia Society, among others.

For a number of years they also ran their own thrift store, "Fibber McGee's Closet," located on South Main Street in Beacon Falls. They not only sold clothes and household items at this store, but were also called upon by their police department to help with emergency clothing needs for victims of house fires.

To raise funds, the club has held road rallies, Halloween dances, breakfast events, fashion shows, beer tastings, and holiday shopping sprees. They have also sold baked goods, run raffles for quilts and crocheted tablecloths, and created and sold a cookbook. When not occupied with their own events, the club also quite frequently assists the Beacon Falls Lions Clubs during their fundraisers.

This young club is constantly searching for new ways to serve their community, and has proven time and time again to be masterfully innovative.

## Chapter 7 – Lions Communication


## History of the Connecticut Lions on the Internet

The Multiple District "Promote Connecticut" committee met in 1997 and discussed the need to develop a Lions information system on the Internet. This would consist of a website as well as e-mail services to promote the Connecticut Lions Eye Research Foundation and other projects that are supported by the Lions of Connecticut. PCC Frank Mauro served as chairman of the committee and PDG Dan Uitti volunteered to investigate the costs of establishing the site. It was discovered that these services could be available at minimal cost or perhaps even donated by Connecticut local Internet Service Providers.

For the purpose of maintaining a nonprofit status for potential donors, the committee recommended that the Connecticut Lions Eye Research Foundation be the owner and recipient of these donated services.

The first web pages for the Connecticut Lions appeared in the spring of 1997, using the domain name ctlions.org, which was understood to represent the non-profit status. Shortly thereafter, Lions throughout the world became aware of the existence of the Connecticut Lions website.

These Lions had already formed an information group, called "LionNet International." Lion Noelle Newerth of Maine made contact with the Connecticut Lions concerning participation in this group. Lion Illka Siissalo of Finland also contacted the Connecticut Lions regarding the sharing of information with Lions around the world in the hope of eventually collaborating with others concerning ideas and services.

In April 1998, PDG Dan Uitti, representing Connecticut, joined with Lions from throughout the world to assist in this effort.

In 1998, the Hartford Courant launched its "CTNOW" on-line. When this was first developed, free web pages were provided to community groups. PDG Uitti among others worked with the promoters and assisted dozens of Lions Clubs in the creation of the free websites. Unfortunately, in late 2001, CTNOW ended the project due to a lack of participation.

In early 2000, Lion Dr. Enzar Tore from Turkey began to develop free Internet services for the use of Lions Clubs. This effort encouraged Lions from throughout the world to join a "Lions Club only" service, which was free of sponsor advertising. Many Clubs in Connecticut joined the effort to make and maintain a free website for their clubs, as their participation in CTNOW came to an end.

Further efforts to encourage the Lions of the world to participate on-line, were made when PDG Uitti directed an effort with LionNet International to provide multiple languages at their website during the later part of 2000. Shortly thereafter, French, Spanish, Portuguese, Turkish, German, Finnish and Italian appeared at the LionNet International website.

Lions, who were active on the Internet from throughout the world, first met at the Lions International Convention in Philadelphia in 1997. In 1998, these same Lions met with the goal of providing Internet training at the International Convention of 1998 in Birmingham, England. At this gathering, Connecticut Lions were recognized as the leaders in this area. From that time forward, Internet services were provided at International Conventions as a free service to all Lions. At the International Convention held in Boston in 2006, this service grew to include 30 computers, dozens of volunteers, and worldwide free telephone services through the high-speed connections on the convention floor. From this venue, Lions could send e-mails, make telephone calls, transfer and send digital photos, book and print return flight boarding passes and learn more about the many internet based services that support the Lions effort.

In 2004, a Lions Club Secretary could utilize the service to file District Club Activities Reports. By this time, Lions Clubs International had completed the development of the club's membership report and record system on-line. It was only natural that clubs could use the system to communicate their activities to District Officers and other leaders. PCC Robert Rendenz, was instrumental in designing the system, working side by side with PDG Dan Uitti who possessed the technical expertise.

## History of the Communication Within the Lions Organization

Communication is essential in any society. It is the method used to let others know your strengths and your limitations; your needs and your frustrations.

Within the organizational structure of Lions Clubs International we have lines of communications both to inform the members and to keep the International organization abreast as to what is transpiring within each individual club.

It is essential for today's Presidents and Secretaries to have the ability to access monthly membership reports electronically and to send District Monthly Activities Reports via the Internet. Not only does this expedite the process, it also allows immediate access to club information held by the International Organization.

Although Lions Clubs International has its own very comprehensive and informative web site, it is evident that not all Lions will take the time to examine it thoroughly. Therefore we need to rely on communications within each individual club as well as within the District and Multiple District. It is essential that each club publish newsletters on a regular basis with an attractive format. This will not only serve as a reminder to the membership of the date and place of the next meting, but will also allow the members to review the agenda and if warranted add new items for discussion.

The District has the responsibility of periodically informing the membership as to what is transpiring within the Regions and the Zones, with detailed accounts of outstanding club endeavors.

The fastest and least expensive method of transmitting club news to the membership is the use of e-mail. Almost all members today have access to a computer, and for the few who have not yet entered the electronic age, the bulletin may be mailed.

Communication with both active and inactive members is essential. Those who are not informed and cannot attend meetings regularly will soon loose interest in the organization and ultimately resign.

Although newsletters are an essential element in the communications chain, the human voice is perhaps the most powerful instrument available.

The phone tree should be utilized on a regular basis both to confirm attendance and to relay urgent news as many only read their e-mail three or four times a week.

We also need to communicate to the public who we are and what we have accomplished. A club web site can be established, but the club brochure is most essential to inform prospective members as well as the general public, and can be distributed to the public at every opportunity.

A good communications plan is essential to the success of all Lions Clubs. It has often been said that "Lionism is the best kept secret in the world." Through good communications let us together inform the world as to who we are and the miracles we perform. Lionism is the greatest service organization in the world.

## Chapter 8 – Multiple District Activities

## History of the Peace Poster Contest

Each year since 1989, more than three million children between the ages of 11 and 13, share their visions of peace through the Lions International Peace Poster Contest.

Entries are judged on three main criteria; originality, artistic merit, and expression of the year's theme. After being chosen on the club, district and multiple district levels, the winning posters are judged on the international level. The grand prizewinner, along with family members and the sponsoring Lions Club International President, are presented at Lions Day with the United Nations.

There are also 23 merit award winners. Most winners have included young artist from Guadeloupe, Hong Kong, Indonesia, Italy, Japan, Lebanon, Martinique, Peru, Philippines, Republic of South Africa, Turkey, and the United States. All 24 posters are exhibited at the Lions International Convention and other venues around the country.

## History of the Lions Pin Traders Club of CT (P.T.C.CT)

PDG Curt Fitch had been involved in pin trading for several years and was a member of the Lions International Trading Pin Club as well as several state pin clubs. After conferring with several Connecticut Lions he felt that there was sufficient interest in Connecticut to start a club.

Lion Curt was not certain how to proceed, and therefore contacted Past Council Chairman, Bill Smith, a Virginia Lion who is widely known as the "God Father" of Pin Trading. He willingly guided Curt through the process, and assisted him in creating the constitution and by laws.

At the State Convention of 2001, approval for the Connecticut Pin Club was granted by the State Council, and the first official meeting of the club was held at the Ct Lions State Lions Convention of May 2002.

Officers elected, included President PDG Curt Fitch, Vice President Lion Chris Porter, Secretary Lion Ralph Dolan, Treasurer Lion Blanche Sewell, Two year Directors PDG Dan Uitti, Lion Rose Marie Spatafore, and Lion Trish Holmes. One year Directors, Lion Joe Porier, PDG Sid Schulman, and Lion Len Johnson.

The Mission of the Pin Trading Club is to promote the trading of Lions Club pins with other Lions throughout the world. Among the club's goals is the need to design a pin based on the theme of the forthcoming Lions Club's International Convention. The club also designs and trades their pin trader pins, and subsequently sells the newly created pins to all who desire them.

The newly created club designed their Charter pin, an outline of the state divided into the three Districts A-B-C in the colors red white and blue. A charter pin was given to each charter member. Starting in 1959 the Lions of Connecticut have issued a State pin each and every year.

In August 2004 the P.T.C.CT hosted the Northeast Pin Swap, in Stamford.

The event was a huge success attracting Lions from throughout the United States, and our Connecticut Pin Trading Club now has full national recognition.


## History of Lions Conventions

The Lions of Connecticut have taken an active part in local and International Lions Conventions since July 7, 1922. Very early local conventions were held in various New England States and included Lions from throughout New England. As Multiple District 23 formed and became an entity unto itself, local conventions included only Lions from Connecticut and Rhode Island. With the creation of District 42, Rhode Island in 1949, Multiple District 23 became a single-state district and all MD 23 conventions from that time were attended exclusively by the Lions of Connecticut.

By the close of 2006, the Lions of Connecticut will have taken part in at least 80 International Conventions, been major participants in

85 State Conventions, and will have hosted 55 Mid-Winter Conferences.

Our Association began holding annual conventions in October 1917. With the creation of the first Lions Club outside the United States (Windsor, Canada -1920) the annual convention became an international gathering.

The Lions of Connecticut have not only been represented at all of these conventions since the 1920's, but at times, in very significant numbers relative to the rather small size of our district. In 1972, more than 100 Connecticut Lions traveled to Mexico City to attend the International Convention held there. In 1977 over 120 attended the Convention in New Orleans, and in 1998 over 60 Connecticut Lions traveled to Birmingham, England to take part in that convention. Significant numbers of Connecticut Lions have attended conventions in such sites as Brisbane, Australia, Taiwan, Hong Kong and Japan. When the Convention did come closer to home, as it did in 2006 in Boston, more than 230 Connecticut Lions seized the opportunity to be part of this international event.

The commitment the Lions of Connecticut have shown to the International Convention became most evident in 1954 when they offered as their gift to the Convention, sponsorship of the Connecticut Lions Teenage Dance. They have continued to host this dance for 52 consecutive years and will continue to do so into the foreseeable future.

With the formation of Multiple District 23 in 1922, the Lions of Connecticut began the tradition of participation in their annual State Convention. Generally held in late May or early June, this convention has at times, seen attendance of well over 600 Lions. It provides an opportunity to elect new District and Multiple District officers, to hear of the accomplishments of outgoing officers, to pay homage to Lions who have passed on during the year, to gain knowledge of events, programs and happenings in the world of Lionism through seminars and exhibits, to conduct the official business of the multiple district, to host and be addressed by an International officer, and generally to share camaraderie with other Lions from throughout the State.

While all of the MD 23 State Conventions held prior to 1952 were held in either Connecticut or Watch Hill, Rhode Island, the majority of these conventions over the past 50 years have been held at resort hotels in New York, New Jersey or Pennsylvania. Between 1965 and 1971 State Conventions were held at Banner Lodge in Moodus,

Connecticut, but with the closing of that facility, the convention venue again moved out of State and with very few exceptions, continues to be held outside of Connecticut. Regardless of location, the Multiple District 23 State Convention has continued to be the highlight and culmination of each Lion year in Connecticut.

In 1951 the Leadership of MD 23 decided that a mid-winter gathering of Lions from throughout Connecticut would be beneficial. Thus the MD 23 Mid-Winter Conference was born. This conference provides the attendees the opportunity to hear mid term reports from the Governors, to attend classes and seminars on subjects both Lionistic and non-Lionistic, and to host a second International guest. It is also an opportunity for good fellowship and for the candidates for District office who will stand for election at the next State Convention, to present themselves to the members of their respective districts.

Over the past 55 years the Annual Mid-Winter Conference has gained in popularity and in the past 10 years has regularly been attended by 500 to 600 Connecticut Lions.

Year after year, the Lions of this state have continued to demonstrate their desire to come together with their fellow Lions to share the ideals, accomplishments and camaraderie of Lionism whether it be halfway around the world, three states away, or in the next town. Convention attendance by Connecticut Lions continues to be an indication of their dedication to the cause we serve.

## History of the Connecticut Lions Teenage Dance

The Connecticut Lions Teenage Dance, sponsored by the Lions of Multiple District 23, Connecticut has been held at every International Convention since 1954.

The dance has been held in such far-away places as Osaka, Japan, Brisbane, Australia, and Birmingham, England. Attendance at all Teenage Dances is dependent largely upon the number of high school and All-State marching bands that come to the International Conventions for the purpose of marching in the International Parade. It has proven to be the rule that attendance by these bands at conventions held within the United States is much higher than at overseas conventions. Teenage marching bands are not nearly as common outside the United States and this has always been reflected in the attendance numbers seen at the Connecticut Lions Teenage Dances.

In recent years, one of the largest attendances was at the 1986 International Convention in New Orleans, LA, where almost 3,000 teens gathered for the dance. The Honolulu, Hawaii Teen Dance saw over 1,000 attendees. The Indianapolis, Indiana dance hosted 1100 in 2001 and the Denver, Colorado dance saw an attendance of more than 1200 teens. By far the smallest Teen Dance took place in Osaka, Japan where only 150 teens attended. This was unique because for the first time, the dance was held in a private nightclub and was attended almost entirely by the children of Lions conventioneers.

Generally, the venues for the Teenage Dances have been hotel ballrooms or major public spaces such as municipal convention or civic centers. For the most part, these venues are assigned to the Lions of Connecticut by LCI at no cost to Connecticut. One exception to that rule occurred most recently in Boston, Massachusetts at the 2006 International Convention.

This Convention had to be relocated from New Orleans because of the Hurricane Katrina disaster of 2005 and LCI was unable to provide a venue for the dance. The Lions of Connecticut, with help from Lions in Massachusetts, were able to secure the Reggie Lewis Center on the campus of Northeastern University for this event.

Music for most of the dances through the early 1990's was provided exclusively by live bands, but with rising costs, it has become necessary to use disk jockeys in lieu of live music at many of the more recent dances. This does not seem to diminish the enjoyment of the attendees at all.

In 2003, PDG Francis Gregoire and PCC Alan Daninhirsch collaborated on and published a policy manual for the Connecticut Lions Teenage Dance.

This manual was adopted by the MD 23 Council and made a part of the Multiple-District Policy and Protocol Manual.

The Lions of Connecticut plan to continue to host the Connecticut Lions Teenage Dance at Lions International Conventions for the foreseeable future, wherever the conventions are held. Attendees from Connecticut have always looked forward to their chaperone duties with great pleasure as an opportunity to see teenagers at their best. It has always been and will continue to be a most exciting project of Connecticut Lionism.

# Chapter 9 – Leadership Development

## President/Secretary/Treasurer/Membership District 23-A

Training those selected as the key officers of a Lions Club is of the greatest importance. These are the individuals elected to lead their clubs, be responsible for keeping a record of club business, managing the finances of the organization, and implementing a viable membership plan. Even those officers that have held the office in the past need to subject themselves to the training each year to be knowledgeable concerning any and all changes.

Often training is available for other key positions such as "Tail Twister." New projects such as Campaign Sight First ll often use this arena to explain the program as well as relate how the club's leadership can respond to questions from the membership.

In District 23-A the Leadership Development chairperson consults with the District Governor about the training that they feel is necessary. In an effort to implement the plan, the members of the "MERL" team are asked to participate.

The Presenters are experienced individuals most of whom have received training through the Multiple District's "Train the Trainer" Program. Due to the geographic layout of the District, it is occasionally necessary to present the training in two locations to allow for greater participation.

Training is often held at different times of the year so that those who might not have been available during the first offering could now take advantage of the training.

Clubs throughout the District are encouraged to participate in the program each and every year, as they strive for excellence in leadership.

## History of the Train the Trainer

During the mid 1980's, Lions Clubs International initiated a new leadership training curriculum called "Train the Trainer." The goal of the seminar was to invite future leaders for an intensive session on leadership and presentation skills that would benefit Lions from throughout the world. The first Lion from Connecticut to travel to Oak Brook, Illinois to be trained was PCC Clifford Randall, a member of the Windsor Locks Lions Club.

In 1987, the first Connecticut Lions training session was conducted in Meriden, CT with Lions from throughout the Multiple District invited to attend. They were given instruction in the various techniques necessary for the presentation of seminars to Lions in the Multiple District.

In 1988, the second "Train the Trainer" session was held in Windsor Locks with a new group of leaders chosen by their District Governors to attend the one-day seminar. Topics such as "Basic Strategies for Organizing and Promoting a Workshop," "Satisfactory and Successful Learning Experiences" and "Designing a Training Program" were discussed at great length. At the end of the training each of the groups was asked to present a training exercise before their peers to show what they had learned.

In 1992, the next group of future leaders was invited to Cromwell, CT to be taught by PDG's Angelo Miceli and Frank DeStefano and Lion Frank Mauro. Although this event was also one day in duration, it soon became apparent that future sessions should be expanded to include Friday evening, all day Saturday, as well as Sunday morning, in an effort to allow enough time to train the students adequately.

Therefore the next two sessions in 1994 and 1996 were held in Cromwell with the students remaining overnight Friday and Saturday, returning to their Districts early Sunday afternoon.

In 1998 and 2000 classes were taught by PDG's Eric Jacobson, Michael Del Re and Richard Foote. The 1998 session was taught in Cromwell and the 2000 session was held in Plainville. The 2002 session was taught by PDG's Jacobson and Foote with a new instructor, PDG William Phillips of the Orange Lions Club.

In 2004, as the time approached for the next class of students, it became apparent to the presenters and the leadership of the Multiple District that the material was quite dated and much work would be required to update the presentation. It was decided to revise the material during the next twelve months, updating the flip charts and converting the overheads to PowerPoint slides. As a result, the class of 2005 was the first to received instruction using the new tools and techniques devised by their instructors, PDG's Jacobson, Foote, and Daninhirsch and Lion Kevin Hadlock.

Lions Clubs International was quite interested in the efforts of the Connecticut team, and therefore the instructors produced an additional instructor and student manual and a disk of all the updated material, and presented it to LCI in August 1995.

The project has been well received by all the Lions who were fortunate to have been chosen by the leaders of their District to participate. The skills they learned have come back ten fold allowing our Lions to be well informed.

## History of the New England Council

The New England Council had its beginnings on January 19, 1949 at the Narragansett Hotel in Providence, R.I. The meeting was called to order by District Governor John Booth of District 42, Rhode Island, Chairman pro-tem, with members from all New England states except Vermont. Chairman Booth explained that all District Governors and Immediate Past District Governors were invited.

It was determined that the name of the organization would be the "New England Lions Council of District Governors." The object of the council was to assist in formulating policies to promote Lionism in New England.

The first President voted into office was District Governor John M. Booth and the first Secretary was Past District Governor Sherwood Cronk from District 33Y, East Longmeadow, MA.

It was also voted to have the New England Council hold a "New England" breakfast at the International Convention that was to be held in New York City, and each District would help pay for the expenses.

The first By-laws were formulated March 4, 1951 to officially change the name to "The New England Council of Lions District Governors" It was determined that active members of the Council would be the present as well as the immediate past Governors of New England. All "other" Past District Governors would be "Associate" members. Only active members would have the right to vote.

For administrative and operative expenses, the Council would request $25 from each District.

The officers were a President and Secretary-Treasurer. The President was to be elected by the active members of the council and that individual should be an immediate Past District Governor on a rotation basis. The Secretary would be elected in the same manner.

In 1971 the name of the Council was changed to the "Northeast Council of Past District Governors." The membership was changed to include Present and Past District Governors but there was no change in the voting as stated in the 1971 By-laws.

In 1972, it was determined that each member would donate $1.00 to help defray expenses. Some committees were placed in the by-laws including the Rindge Memorial Service committee, Constitution and By-laws committee, and the Lions Gallery for the Sightless committee.

In 1975 the name was changed to the "The New England Lions Council, Present and Past District Governors." The "Donation" was raised from $1.00 to $2.00 per member and the election of the President and Secretary Treasurer was to be by all members present at the meeting.

In 1977, the By-Laws were change to add a Vice President to be elected along with the other officers.

In 1980, the "donation" from each member was raised from $2.00 to $5.00.

In 1984 the By-laws read that all members of the Council in good standing, present at the meeting shall have the power to vote. Also, a new committee, The New England Lions Breakfast at the International Convention, was added.

In 1992, the Lions Gallery for the Sightless committee was dropped along with the New England Breakfast Committee. Two new committees were added, namely the New England Lions International Convention Committee and the Nominating Committee.

During the 1995-96 Lions year, the Council voted to increase the dues from $5.00 to $10.00.

In 2003 the name of the organization was changed to the "New England Lions Council." It was at that time that all Lions in good standing became eligible to join the organization and were eligible to vote. Only a Past District Governor however would be eligible for appointment to the executive council, which consists of the President, Vice President, Secretary Treasurer, and Immediate Past President, as well as a representative from the remaining states.

Officers are appointed in rotation by state. As of this writing, there were 179 active members in the organization. The President was PDG Don Correia from the State of Massachusetts, the Vice President, PDG Ed Farrington was from New Hampshire, and the CST, PDG Mary Krogh was from the State of Connecticut.

The New England Council as an organization has brought together Lion members from the New England states for the purpose of promoting Lionism and the exchange ideas.

## The Lions Family

Further Observations of a Connecticut Lion
By PDG Dick Foote

Back in '93 during my term as District Governor, my Cabinet Secretary/Treasurer Dave Barbieri and I were returning from the Enfield area, and stopped in at the McDonald's in Southwick, Massachusetts. We were both wearing the cabinet uniform; Navy Blue blazer, blue shirt, and oxford tie.

As we entered the restaurant, a young man sitting with several mends, spotted us and got up from his table. "I want to thank you," he said. I asked him what he meant; stating that we were from Connecticut, and probably hadn't done anything for him. He said that that was OK with him, but he wanted to thank us anyway. It seems that he had been given a week at music camp, sponsored by his local Lions Club, and just wanted to thank the Lions Club generally for their efforts on his behalf.

Dave and I both left Southwick with the feeling of satisfaction that comes from being a member of the Lions family.

## Appendix A—Annual International Conventions

| No. | Year | Location | Date |
|-----|------|----------|------|
| 1 | 1917 | Dallas, Texas | October 8-10 |
| 2 | 1918 | St. Louis, Missouri | August 19-21 |
| 3 | 1919 | Chicago, Illinois | July 9-11 |
| 4 | 1920 | Denver, Colorado | July 13-16 |
| 5 | 1921 | Oakland, California | July 19-22 |
| 6 | 1922 | Hot Springs, Arkansas | June 19-24 |
| 7 | 1923 | Atlantic City, New Jersey | June 26-29 |
| 8 | 1924 | Omaha, Nebraska | June 23-26 |
| 9 | 1925 | Cedar Point, Ohio | June 29-July 2 |
| 10 | 1926 | San Francisco, California | July 21-24 |
| 11 | 1927 | Miami, Florida | June 15-18 |
| 12 | 1928 | Des Moines, Iowa | July 10-13 |
| 13 | 1929 | Louisville, Kentucky | June 18-21 |
| 14 | 1930 | Denver, Colorado | July 15-18 |
| 15 | 1931 | Toronto, Canada | July 14-17 |
| 16 | 1932 | Los Angeles, California | July 19-22 |
| 17 | 1933 | St. Louis, Missouri | July 11-14 |
| 18 | 1934 | Grand Rapids, Michigan | July 17-20 |
| 19 | 1935 | Mexico City, Mexico | July 23-25 |
| 20 | 1936 | Providence, Rhode Island | July 21-24 |
| 21 | 1937 | Chicago, Illinois | July 20-23 |
| 22 | 1938 | Oakland, California | July 19-22 |
| 23 | 1939 | Pittsburgh, Pennsylvania | July 18-21 |
| 24 | 1940 | Havana, Cuba | July 23-25 |
| 25 | 1941 | New Orleans, Louisiana | July 22-25 |
| 26 | 1942 | Toronto, Canada | July 21-24 |
| 27 | 1943 | Cleveland, Ohio | July 20-22 |
| 28 | 1944 | Chicago, Illinois | August 1-3 |
|  | 1945 | NONE HELD |  |
| 29 | 1946 | Philadelphia, Pennsylvania | July 16-19 |
| 30 | 1947 | San Francisco, California | July 28-31 |
| 31 | 1948 | New York, New York | July 26-29 |
| 32 | 1949 | New York, New York | July 18-21 |

| 33 | 1950 | Chicago, Illinois | July 16-20 |
|----|------|-------------------|------------|
| 34 | 1951 | Atlantic City, New Jersey | June 24-28 |
| 35 | 1952 | Mexico City, Mexico | June 25-28 |
| 36 | 1953 | Chicago, Illinois | July 8-11 |
| 37 | 1954 | New York, New York | July 7-10 |
| 38 | 1955 | Atlantic City, New Jersey | June 22-25 |
| 39 | 1956 | Miami, Florida | June 27-30 |
| 40 | 1957 | San Francisco, California | June 26-29 |
| 41 | 1958 | Chicago, Illinois | July 9-12 |
| 42 | 1959 | New York, New York | June 30-July 3 |
| 43 | 1960 | Chicago, Illinois | July 6-9 |
| 44 | 1961 | Atlantic City, New Jersey | June 21-24 |
| 45 | 1962 | Nice, France | June 20-23 |
| 46 | 1963 | Miami, Florida | June 19-22 |
| 47 | 1964 | Toronto, Canada | July 8-11 |
| 48 | 1965 | Los Angeles, California | July 7-10 |
| 49 | 1966 | New York, New York | July 6-9 |
| 50 | 1967 | Chicago, Illinois | July 5-8 |
| 51 | 1968 | Dallas, Texas | June 26-29 |
| 52 | 1969 | Tokyo, Japan | July 2-5 |
| 53 | 1970 | Atlantic City, New Jersey | July 1-4 |
| 54 | 1971 | Las Vegas, Nevada | June 22-25 |
| 55 | 1972 | Mexico City, Mexico | June 28-July 1 |
| 56 | 1973 | Miami, Florida | June 27-30 |
| 57 | 1974 | San Francisco, California | July 3-6 |
| 58 | 1975 | Dallas, Texas | June 25-28 |
| 59 | 1976 | Honolulu, Hawaii | June 23-26 |
| 60 | 1977 | New Orleans, Louisiana | June 29-July 2 |
| 61 | 1978 | Tokyo, Japan | June 21-24 |
| 62 | 1979 | Montreal, Quebec, Canada | June 20-23 |
| 63 | 1980 | Chicago, Illinois | July 2-5 |
| 64 | 1981 | Phoenix, Arizona | June 17-2065 |
| 65 | 1982 | Atlanta, Georgia | June 30-July 3 |
| 66 | 1983 | Honolulu, Hawaii | June 22-25 |
| 67 | 1984 | San Francisco, California | July 4-7 |
| 68 | 1985 | Dallas, Texas | June 19-22 |
| 69 | 1986 | New Orleans, Louisiana | July 9-12 |
| 70 | 1987 | Taipei, Taiwan, Rep. Of China | July 1-4 |

| 71 | 1988 | Denver, Colorado | June 28-July 2 |
| 72 | 1989 | Miami, Florida | June 20-24 |
| 73 | 1990 | St. Louis, Missouri | July 11-14 |
| 74 | 1991 | Brisbane, Australia | June 19-22 |
| 75 | 1992 | Hong Kong | June 22-26 |
| 76 | 1993 | Minneapolis/<br>St. Paul/Bloomington, Minnesota | July 6-9 |
| 77 | 1994 | Phoenix, Arizona | July 12-15 |
| 78 | 1995 | Seoul, Republic of Korea | July 4-7 |
| 79 | 1996 | Montreal, Quebec, Canada | July 9-12 |
| 80 | 1997 | Philadelphia, Pennsylvania | June 30-July 5 |
| 81 | 1998 | Birmingham, England | June 29-July 3 |
| 82 | 1999 | San Diego, California | June 28-July 2 |
| 83 | 2000 | Honolulu, Hawaii | June 19-23 |
| 84 | 2001 | Indianapolis, Indiana | July 2-6 |
| 85 | 2002 | Osaka, Japan | July 8-12 |
| 86 | 2003 | Denver, Colorado | June 30-July 4 |
| 87 | 2004 | Detroit, Michigan/<br>Windsor, Ontario, Canada | July 5-9 |
| 88 | 2005 | Hong Kong | June 27-July 1 |
| 89 | 2006 | New Orleans, Louisiana | July 3-7 |

(changed due to Hurricane Katrina damage in Sept 2005)

| 89 | 2006 | Boston, Massachusetts | June 30-July 4 |
| 90 | 2007 | Chicago, Illinois | July 2-6 |
| 91 | 2008 | Bangkok, Thailand | June 23-27 |
| 92 | 2009 | Minneapolis, Minnesota | July 6-10 |
| 93 | 2010 | Sydney, Australia | June 28-July 2 |
| 94 | 2011 | Seattle, Washington | July 4 – 8 |
| 95 | 2012 | Busan, Korea | June 22-26 |

# Appendix B—Lions Clubs International Past Presidents

| | | |
|---|---|---|
| 1917 | *Dr. W. P. Woods | Evansville, IN |
| 1918 | *L. H. Lewis | Dallas, TX |
| 1919 | *Jesse Robinson | Oakland, CA |
| 1920 | *Dr. C. C. Reid | Denver, CO |
| 1921 | *Ewen W. Cameron | Minneapolis, MN |
| 1922 | *Ed S. Vaught | Oklahoma City, OK |
| 1923 | *John S. Noel | Grand Rapids , MI |
| 1924 | *Harry A. Newman | Toronto, Ontario, Canada |
| 1925 | *Benjamin F. Jones | Newark, NJ |
| 1926 | *William A. Westfall | Mason City, IO |
| 1927 | *Irving L. Camp | Johnstown, PA |
| 1928 | *Ben A. Ruffin | Richmond, VA |
| 1929 | *Ray L. Riley | San Francisco, CA |
| 1930 | *Earle W. Hodges | New York City, NY |
| 1931 | *Julien C. Hyer | Forth Worth, TX |
| 1932 | *Charles H. Hatton | Wichita, KS |
| 1933 | *Roderick Beddow | Birmingham, AL |
| 1934 | *Vincent C. Hascall | Omaha, NE |
| 1935 | *Richard J. Osenbaugh | Denver, CO |
| 1936 | *Edwin R. Kingsley | Parkersburg, WV |
| 1937 | *Frank V. Birch | Milwaukee, WI |
| 1938 | *Walter F. Dexter | Sacramento, CA |
| 1939 | *Alexander T. Wells | New York City, NY |
| 1940 | *Karl M. Sorrick | Springport, MI |
| 1941 | *George R. Jordan | Dallas, TX |
| 1942 | *Edwin H. Paine | Michigan City, IN |
| 1943 | *Dr. E. G. Gill | Roanoke, VA |
| 1944 | *D. A. Skeen | Salt Lake City, UT |
| 1945 | *Dr. Ramiro Collazo | Marianao, Habana, Cuba |
| 1946 | *Clifford D. Pierce | Memphis, TN |
| 1947 | *Fred W. Smith | Ventura, CA |
| 1948 | *Dr. Eugene S. Briggs | Edmond, OK |
| 1949 | *Walter C. Fisher | St. Catharines, Ontario, Canada |
| 1950 | *Herb C. Petry, Jr. | Carrizo Springs, TX |
| 1951 | *Harold P. Nutter | Oaklyn, NJ |
| 1952 | *Edgar M. Elbert | Roselle, IL |
| 1953 | *S. A. Dodge | Bloomfield Hills, MI |
| 1954 | *Monroe L. Nute | Kennett Square, PA |
| 1955 | *Humberto Valenzuela G. | Santiago. Chile |
| 1956 | *John L. Stickney | Charlotte, NC |
| 1957 | *Edward G. Barry | Little Rock, AR |

| 1958 | *Dudley L. Simms | Charleston, WV |
| 1959 | *Clarence L. Sturm | Manawa, WI |
| 1960 | *Finis E. Davis | Louisville, KY |
| 1961 | *Per Stahl | Eskilstuna, Sweden |
| 1962 | *Curtis D. Lovill | Gardner, MA |
| 1963 | Aubrey D. Green | York, AL |
| 1964 | Claude M. De Vorss | Wichita, KN |
| 1965 | *Dr. Walter H. Campbell | Miami Beach, FL |
| 1966 | Edward M. LIndsey | Lawrenceburg, TN |
| 1967 | *Jorge Bird | Rio Piedras, Puerto Rico |
| 1968 | *David A. Evans | Galveston, TX |
| 1969 | W. R. "Dick" Bryan | Sun City West, AZ |
| 1970 | *Dr. Robert D. McCullough | Tulsa, OK |
| 1971 | *Robert J. Uplinger | Syracuse, NY |
| 1972 | *George Friedrichs | Annecy, France |
| 1973 | Tris Coffin | Rosemere, Quebec, Canada |
| 1974 | *Johnny Balbo | LaGrange, IL |
| 1975 | *Harry J. Aslan | Kingsburg, CA |
| 1976 | Prof. Joano Fernando Sobral | Sao Paulo, SP, Brazil |
| 1977 | *Joseph M. McLoughlin | Stamford, CT |
| 1978 | *Ralph A. Lynam | St. John, MI |
| 1979 | Lloyd Morgan | Tauranga, New Zealand |
| 1980 | William C. Chandler | Montgomery, AL |
| 1981 | *Kaoru "Kay" Murikami | Kyoto, Japan |
| 1982 | Everett J. "Ebb" Grindstaff | Ballinger, TX |
| 1983 | Dr. James M. "Jim" Fowler | Mount Ida, AR |
| 1984 | *Bert Mason | Donaghadee, Northern Ireland |
| 1985 | Joseph L. Wroblewski | Forty Fort, PA |
| 1986 | Sten A. Akestam | Stockholm, Sweden |
| 1987 | Judge Brian Stevenson | Calgary, Alberta, Canada |
| 1988 | Austin P. Jennings | Woodbury, TN |
| 1989 | *William L. Woolard | Charlotte, NC |
| 1990 | William L. "Bill" Biggs | Omaha, NE |
| 1991 | Donald E. Banker | Rolling Hills, CA |
| 1992 | Rohit C. Mehta | Paldi, Ahmedabad, India |
| 1993 | James T. Coffey | Toronto, OH |
| 1994 | Prof. Giuseppe Grimaldi | Enna, Italy |
| 1995 | Dr. William H. Wunder | Wichita, KA |
| 1996 | Augustin Soliva | Sao Jose dos Campos, SP, Brazil |
| 1997 | Judge Howard L. "Pat" Patterson | Hattiesburg, MS |
| 1998 | Kajit "KJ" Habanananda | Bankok, Thailand |
| 1999 | James E. "Jim" Ervin | Albany, GA |

| 2000 | Dr. Jean Behar | Sainte-Adresse, France |
| 2001 | J. Frank Moore, III | Daleville, AL |
| 2002 | Kay K. Fukushima | Sacramento, CA |
| 2003 | Dr. Tae-Sup "TS" Lee | Seoul, Rep. Of Korea |
| 2004 | Dr. Clement F. Kusiak | Linthicum, MD |
| 2005 | Dr. Ashok Mehta | Mumbai, India |
| 2006 | Jimmy M. Ross | Quitaque, TX |
| 2007 | Mahendra Amarasuriya | Colombo, Sri Lanka |
| 2008 | Albert F. Brandel | Melville, NY |

* Deceased

## Appendix C—International Officers From Connecticut

### International President From Connecticut

1977-1978   Joseph M. McLoughlin   Stamford

### International Directors From Connecticut

| | | |
|---|---|---|
| 1925-1928 | *Charles M. Bakewell | New Haven |
| 1930-1933 | *William S. Hewlett | Bridgeport |
| 1934-1935 | *Wilbur J. Dixon | New Canaan |
| 1941-1943 | *Kenneth Taylor | New Milford |
| 1948-1950 | *Harold A. Ashley | Waterbury |
| 1954-1956 | *Charles W. Naylor | New Canaan |
| 1964-1966 | *Joseph W. Ganim | Stratford |
| 1970-1972 | *Joseph M. McLoughlin | Stamford |
| 1980-1982 | *Joseph L. Raub | New London |
| 1990-1992 | *Otto P. Strobino | New Britain |
| 2001-2003 | Scott A. Storms | Windsor Locks |

* Deceased

# Appendix D—Annual Multiple District 23 State Conventions

| No. | Location | Date |
|---|---|---|
| 1 | New Haven, CT | July 7, 1922 |
| 2 | Springfield, MA | May 2, 1923 |
| 3 | Providence, RI | May 7, 1924 |
| 4 | Bridgeport, CT | May 6, 1925 |
| 5 | New London, CT | May 5, 1926 |
| 6 | Newport, RI | June 7-8, 1927 |
| 7 | Hartford, CT | May 24-25, 1928 |
| 8 | New Haven, CT | (no date) 1929 |
| 9 | Newport, RI | (no date) 1930 |
| 10 | Bridgeport, CT | June 9-10, 1931 |
| 11 | Watch Hill, RI | June 28-29, 1932 |
| 12 | Watch Hill, RI | June 28-29, 1933 |
| 13 | Watch Hill, RI | June 27-28, 1934 |
| 14 | Watch Hill, RI | June 26-27, 1935 |
| 15 | Providence, RI | June 20, 1936 |
| 16 | Griswold Hotel, Groton, CT | June 23-24, 1937 |
| 17 | Griswold Hotel, Groton, CT | June 21-22, 1938 |
| 18 | Danbury, CT | June 7, 1939 |
| 19 | New London, CT | June 10-11, 1940 |
| 20 | Norwich, CT | June 7-8, 1941 |
| 21 | Hartford, CT | June 6-7, 1942 |
| 22 | Bridgeport, CT | June 13, 1943 |
| 23 | Hartford, CT | June 10, 1944 |
| 24 | Waterbury, CT | June 16, 1945 |
| 25 | Ocean House, Watch Hill, RI | June 29-30, 1946 |
| 26 | Griswold Hotel, Groton, CT | June 20-21, 1947 |
| 27 | Griswold Hotel, Groton, CT | June 19-20, 1948 |
| 28 | Griswold Hotel, Groton, CT | June 25-26,1949 |
| 29 | Griswold Hotel, Groton, CT | May 25-26. 1950 |
| 30 | Griswold Hotel, Groton, CT | June 2-3, 1951 |
| 31 | Copake Country Club, Craryville, NY | June 6-8, 1952 |
| 32 | Copake Country Club, Craryville, NY | June 5-7, 1953 |
| 33 | Copake Country Club, Craryville, NY | June 3-6, 1954 |

| 34 | Copake Country Club, Craryville, NY | June 2-5, 1955 |
| 35 | Banner Lodge, Moodus, CT | June 7-10, 1956 |
| 36 | Copake Country Club, Craryville, NY | June 6-9, 1957 |
| 37 | Copake Country Club, Craryville, NY | June 5-8, 1958 |
| 38 | Copake Country Club, Craryville, NY | June 4-7, 1959 |
| 39 | No records available | 1960 |
| 40 | Griswold Hotel, Groton, CT | June 1-4, 1961 |
| 41 | Copake Country Club, Craryville, NY | May 30-June 3, 1962 |
| 42 | No records available | 1963 |
| 43 | Copake Country Club, Craryville, NY | June 4-7, 1964 |
| 44 | Banner Lodge, Moodus, CT | June 3-7, 1965 |
| 45 | Banner Lodge, Moodus, CT | June 2-5, 1966 |
| 46 | Banner Lodge, Moodus, CT | June 1-4, 1967 |
| 47 | Banner Lodge, Moodus, CT | June 6-9, 1968 |
| 48 | Banner Lodge, Moodus, CT | June 5-8, 1969 |
| 49 | Banner Lodge, Moodus, CT | June 4-7, 1970 |
| 50 | Banner Lodge, Moodus, CT | June 3-6, 1971 |
| 51 | Grossinger's, Liberty, NY | June 7-10, 1972 |
| 52 | Concord Hotel, Kiamesha Lake, NY | May 31-June 3, 1973 |
| 53 | Concord Hotel, Kiamesha Lake, NY | April 25-28, 1974 |
| 54 | Concord Hotel, Kiamesha Lake, NY | June 26-29, 1975 |
| 55 | Concord Hotel, Kiamesha Lake, NY | June 3-6, 1976 |
| 56 | Concord Hotel, Kiamesha Lake, NY | April 28-May 1, 1977 |
| 57 | Grossinger's, Liberty, NY | May 11-14, 1978 |
| 58 | Playboy Resort, Great Gorge, NJ | May 31-June 3, 1979 |
| 59 | Concord Hotel, Kiamesha Lake, NY | May 1-4, 1980 |
| 60 | Grossinger's, Liberty, NY | May 14-17, 1981 |
| 61 | Grossinger's, Liberty, NY | May 13-16, 1982 |
| 62 | Concord Hotel, Kiamesha Lake, NY | April 28-May 1, 1983 |
| 63 | Mt. Airy Lodge, Poconos, PA | April 27-29, 1984 |
| 64 | Americana Hotel, Great Gorge, NJ | May 10-12, 1985 |
| 65 | The Pines Resort Hotel, South Fallsburg, NY | May 30-June 1, 1986 |
| 66 | The Pines Resort Hotel, South Fallsburg, NY | May 29-31, 1987 |
| 67 | The Pines Resort Hotel, South Fallsburg, NY | May 20-22, 1988 |

| 68 | Kutsher's, Monticello, NY | May 19-21, 1989 |
| 69 | Stamford Marriott, Stamford, CT | May 18-20, 1990 |
| 70 | The Pines Resort Hotel, South Fallsburg, NY | May 31-June 2, 1991 |
| 71 | Sturbridge Hotel, Sturbridge, MA | May 8-10, 1992 |
| 72 | Kutsher's, Monticello, NY | May 20-23, 1993 |
| 73 | The Pines Resort Hotel, South Fallsburg, NY | May 19-22, 1994 |
| 74 | The Pines Resort Hotel, South Fallsburg, NY | May 19-21, 1995 |
| 75 | Villa Roma, Callicoon, NY | May 10-12. 1996 |
| 76 | Villa Roma, Callicoon, NY | May 16-18, 1997 |
| 77 | Hastings Hotel & Conference Center, Hartford, CT | May 1-3, 1998 |
| 78 | Marriott Hotel, Farmington, CT | May 14-15, 1999 |
| 79 | Sturbridge Hotel, Sturbridge, MA | May 5-7, 2000 |
| 80 | Villa Roma, Callicoon, NY | May 18-20, 2001 |
| 81 | Nevele Grande Resort & CC, Ellenville, NY | May 3-5, 2002 |
| 82 | Pocono Manor Inn, Pocono Manor, PA | May 2-4, 2003 |
| 83 | Villa Roma, Callicoon, NY | May 14-16, 2004 |
| 84 | Sturbridge Hotel, Sturbridge, MA | May 20-22, 2005 |
| 85 | Hartford Marriott Downtown, Hartford, CT | May 19-20, 2006 |
| 86 | Cape Codder Resort and Spa, Hyannis, MA | May 18-19, 2007 |

## Appendix E—Past District Governors

### Past District Governors
### District 23 – CT & RI

| | | |
|---|---|---|
| 1922 | *George Hewlett | New Haven |
| 1923 | *James H. Readio | Providence, RI |
| 1924 | *Rev. John Davis | New Britain |
| 1925 | *Judge William W. Bent | Bridgeport |
| 1926 | *J. Nelson Alexander | Providence, RI |
| 1927 | *Phillip A. Jakob | Norwalk |
| 1928 | *William S. Hewlett, PID | Bridgeport |
| 1929 | *G. Irving Burwell | Watertown |
| 1930 | *Lucius A. Whipple | Pawtucket, RI |
| 1931 | *Phillip A. Jakob | Norwalk |

### Multiple District 23 – A & B

| | | |
|---|---|---|
| 1932 | *Wilbur J. Dixon (A) | New Canaan |
| | *Daniel Y. Rose (B) | Providence, RI |
| 1933 | *Wilbur J. Dixon (A) | New Canaan |
| | *Dr. Frank Duffy (B) | West Warwick, RI |
| 1934 | *Joseph C. Bailey (A) | Greenwich |
| | *Robert Johnson (B) | Pawtucket, RI |
| 1935 | *William H. Hoyt (A) | Danbury |
| | *Marcus J. Offers (B) | Woonsocket, RI |
| 1936 | *Kenneth F. Taylor, PID (A) | New Milford |
| | *Leo H. Beaulac (B) | Pawtucket, RI |
| 1937 | *Philip C. Rouleau (A) | Bristol |
| | *Charles D. Carlin (B) | unknown |

* Deceased

## District 23 - CT

| 1938 | *Charles F. Stubbs | Bridgeport |
|------|--------------------|------------|
| 1939 | *Howard F. Saviteer | Meriden |
| 1940 | *W. Carl French | New Britain |
| 1941 | *Charles F. Patterson | Torrington |
| 1942 | *Roy M. Van Fleet | Hartford |
| 1943 | *Col. Lott R. Breen | Bridgeport |
| 1944 | *William F. Curtin | New Britain |
| 1945 | *Harold A. Ashley, PID | Waterbury |
| 1946 | *Merrill G. Scott | Terryville |
| 1947 | *David F. Armstrong | Groton |
| 1948 | *Roy L. Heck | Torrington |
| 1949 | *Charles W. Naylor, PID | New Canaan |

## Past District Governors
## District 23-A

| 1950 | | *Joseph Carlin | Springdale |
|------|---|----------------|------------|
| 1951 | | *J. Sidney Wakeley | Waterbury |
| 1952 | + | *Jerome C. Keech | Southbury |
| 1953 | | *Spencer B. Hirst | Meriden |
| 1954 | | *Albert F. Sprafke | Meriden |
| 1955 | + | *Dominic J. Minicucci | Naugatuck |
| 1956 | | *Walter I. Kenney | New Haven |
| 1957 | | *Stewart E. McKinney | Monroe |
| 1858 | + | *William W. Grosberg | North Haven |
| 1959 | | *Joseph W. Ganim, PID | Bridgeport |
| 1960 | | *Joseph H. Darling, Jr. | Madison |
| 1961 | + | *Joseph M. McLoughlin, PIP | Springdale |
| 1962 | | *Fred E. Cronenwett | Stamford |
| 1963 | | *William R. Buckingham | New Haven |
| 1964 | + | *Leo J. Redgate | Bridgeport |

+ Past Council Chair
* Deceased

| 1965 |   | *Edward J. Papandrea | Meriden |
|------|---|---------------------|---------|
| 1966 |   | *George F. Bonnell | Trumbull |
| 1967 | + | *Frederick H. Parr | Newtown |
| 1968 |   | Theodore Hyatt | New Haven |
| 1969 |   | *Edmund E. Forger | Fairfield |
| 1970 | + | Russell H. Weldon, Jr. | Meriden |
| 1971 |   | *Morton Reisenberg | Cheshire |
| 1972 |   | *Edward Hagerty | Bridgeport |
| 1973 | + | *Theodore Samaris | Meriden |
| 1974 |   | Rocco Cingari | Darien |
| 1975 |   | *William L. Roberts | Meriden |
| 1976 | + | *Robert J. Pilot | New Haven |
| 1977 |   | *Emanuel A. Merullo | Danbury |
| 1978 |   | William J. Carroll | Bridgeport |
| 1979 | + | Michael Granatuk | Waterbury |
| 1980 |   | James Halligan Sr. | Derby-Shelton |
| 1981 |   | *G. Thomas Valerio | Orange |
| 1982 | + | William D. Phillips, Jr. | Meriden |
| 1983 |   | *Theodore Beauregard | Norwalk |
| 1984 |   | *Gene G. Poulos, Sr. | Trumbull |
| 1985 | + | Philip G. Flaker | Bridgeport Host |
| 1986 |   | Walter K. Ahearn | Middlebury |
| 1987 |   | Rene H. Tompkinson | Meriden |
| 1988 | + | *Robert E. Hoxie | Brookfield |
| 1989 |   | *Dr. Chester A. Sobolewski | Trumbull Center |
| 1990 |   | Raymond M. Zaleski | Bridgeport Host |
| 1991 | + | Robert B. Gyle, III | New Fairfield |
| 1992 |   | Peter J. Gostyla | Meriden |
| 1993 |   | William A. Phillips | Orange |
| 1994 | + | Jerry J. Osochowsky | Branford |
| 1995 |   | Alfred P. Hazard | Danbury |
| 1996 |   | *David R. Whitehead | Bridgeport Host |
| 1997 | + | Michael J. Del Re, Jr. | Trumbull |
| 1998 |   | James B. Bennett | New Haven |
| 1999 |   | Raymond A. Shea | Beacon Falls |

+ Past Council Chair
* Deceased

| | | | |
|---|---|---|---|
| 2000 | + | Krishnalal I. Nanavaty | Southbury |
| 2001 | | Donald J. Miloscia | Danbury |
| 2002 | | Marinus J. deJongh | Madison |
| 2003 | + | Robert Redenz | New Fairfield |
| 2004 | | John Gagain | Wolcott |
| 2005 | | William M. Carello | Darien |
| 2006 | + | Joseph Porier | Beacon Falls |
| 2007 | | Rose Marie Spatafore | Seymour |
| 2008 | | Joan C. Bennett, VDG | New Haven |

## Past District Governors
## District 23-B

| | | | |
|---|---|---|---|
| 1950 | + | *Paul L. Moran | New Britain |
| 1951 | | *Merrill G. Louks | Newington |
| 1952 | | *Earle J. Glidden | Unionville |
| 1953 | + | *A. LeRoy Anderson | Bristol |
| 1954 | | *Roy G. Matheson | Rocky Hill |
| 1955 | | *Robert G. Irvin | Plainville |
| 1956 | + | *Thomas J. Leonard | New Britain |
| 1957 | | *Ford G. Crosby | Manchester |
| 1958 | | *Mario Boccalatte | Stamford |
| 1959 | + | Marshall Golden | Newington |
| 1960 | | *Elmer (Bob) Bair | East Hartford |
| 1961 | | *W. F. Matulewicz | Thomaston |
| 1962 | + | *Robert E. Miller | Bloomfield |
| 1963 | | Joseph Cimino | Enfield |
| 1964 | | *Howard V. Wry | New Britain |
| 1965 | + | *George Seely | New Milford |
| 1966 | | *Anthony Caparrelli | Plainville |
| 1967 | | *Nunzio P. Rosso | Berlin |
| 1968 | + | Richard J. O'Leary | Windsor Locks |
| 1969 | | *George W. Staib | West Hartford |
| 1970 | | Robert L. Southworth | New Milford |

+ Past Council Chair
* Deceased

| 1971 | + | Ralph C. Fiore | Enfield |
|---|---|---|---|
| 1972 | | Milan M. Knight | Winsted |
| 1973 | | *William S. Jerin | Southington |
| 1974 | + | *Thomas A. Hubbs | Bloomfield |
| 1975 | | *Herbert A. Leibert | Hartford |
| 1976 | | *Theodore S. Boryczki | Berlin |
| 1977 | + | Otto R. Ruppert | Avon |
| 1978 | | *Angelo J. Salvatore | Windsor |
| 1979 | | *Edward S. Smith | Southington |
| 1980 | + | R. Clifford Randall | Windsor Locks |
| 1981 | | *Otto P. Strobino, PID | New Britain |
| 1982 | | George A. Precourt | East Hartford |
| 1983 | + | *Edward J. Dillon | West Hartford |
| 1984 | | *George A. Lomintzer | East Granby |
| 1985 | | *Ronald E. Jones | Enfield |
| 1986 | + | *Kenneth V. Olson | New Britain Evening |
| 1987 | | Richard C. Stathers | East Windsor |
| 1988 | | George "Curt" Fitch | New Milford |
| 1989 | + | Scott A. Storms, PID | Windsor Locks |
| 1990 | | Daniel A. Uitti | Watertown |
| 1991 | | W. Keith Wuerthner | New Britain |
| 1992 | + | George M. Ondrick | Berlin |
| 1993 | | Richard J. Foote | Terryville |
| 1994 | | Ronald F. Storms | Windsor Locks |
| 1995 | + | *Allan W. Dodge | Watertown |
| 1996 | | Donald E. Griswold | Avon |
| 1997 | | George H. Cooper, Jr. | Plainville |
| 1998 | + | Sydney T. Schulman | Bloomfield |
| 1999 | | Marianne D. Bannan | Simsbury |
| 2000 | | Normand J. Messier | Windsor Locks |
| 2001 | + | Alan I. Daninhirsch | New Britain |
| 2002 | | Marilyn L. Minacci | Canaan NW |
| 2003 | | Ronald H. Wolpoe | CT Singles |
| 2004 | + | Carolyn A. Messier | Windsor Locks |
| 2005 | | Francesco Medina | Hartford Evening |

+ Past Council Chair
* Deceased

| 2006 | Robert Weiss | Berlin |
|------|--------------|--------|
| 2007 | Dr. Stephen Polezonis | New Britain |
| 2008 | Len Johnson, VDG | Terryville |

## Past District Governors
## District 23-C

| 1950 | *William McKenzie | Groton |
|------|-------------------|--------|
| 1951 + | *Rev. T. Joseph Puza | Norwich |
| 1952 | *Richard F. Case | Willimantic |
| 1953 | *Merle K. Bradley | Mystic |
| 1954 + | *Ernest F. Hopkins | Niantic |
| 1955 | *Thomas Shakley | Pawcatuck |
| 1956 | *H. Wallace Crook | Danielson |
| 1957 + | *Charles W. Hitchcock | Willimantic |
| 1958 | *Alexander Abraham | Norwich |
| 1959 | *John W. Damn | Colchester |
| 1960 + | *David F. Darling, Sr. | Middletown |
| 1961 | *George MacKnight | Pawcatuck |
| 1962 | *William F. O'Neil, Jr. | Norwich |
| 1963 + | *William F. Shea | Mystic |
| 1964 | *Harold R. Burke | Mansfield |
| 1965 | Clifford D. Stark | Woodstock |
| 1966 + | *Stephen C. Steg | Colchester |
| 1967 | *Alfio C. Urbinati | Norwich |
| 1968 | *James A. Zeppieri | Groton |
| 1969 + | Dr. Louis DeSantis | Stafford Springs |
| 1970 | *Sebastian DiStefano | Middletown |
| 1971 | *Joseph L. Raub, PID | New London |
| 1972 + | Joseph J. Amato | Portland |
| 1973 | *Angelo Garagliano | Groton |
| 1974 | Fred D. Curtin | Cromwell |
| 1975 + | Theodore C. Coolidge | Plainfield |
| 1976 | William J. Delehanty | East Haddam |
| 1977 | *Wilbur Dennis | Hebron |

+ Past Council Chair
* Deceased

| | | |
|---|---|---|
| 1978 + | Mario Gualtieri | Norwich |
| 1979 | *Ernest Kopec | New London |
| 1980 | *Frank L. DiStefano | Portland |
| 1981 + | *James Mackey | Willimantic |
| 1982 | Joseph A. Pescatello | Pawcatuck |
| 1983 | William K. Allen, II | Niantic |
| 1984 + | Donald L. Fuller | Montville |
| 1985 | *Morris Smith | Ledyard |
| 1986 | Robert B. Tourville | East Hampton |
| 1987 + | Angelo S. Miceli | Pawcatuck |
| 1988 | Everett J. Clark | Hebron |
| 1989 | Robert V. Erickson | Plainfield |
| 1990 + | A. Carleton Eichelberg | Montville |
| 1991 | Arthur J. Davies | Deep River/ Chester |
| 1992 | J. Kenneth Craig | Lebanon |
| 1993 + | Frank P. Mauro | Willimantic |
| 1994 | Eric C. Jacobson | Colchester |
| 1995 | Joel J. Ragovin | Norwich |
| 1996 + | Ronald A. Hemingway | Putnam |
| 1997 | David St. Martin | Danielson |
| 1998 | *Francis Adamcewicz | Lebanon |
| 1999 + | John J. Connor | Norwich |
| 2000 | Francis Gregoire | Putnam |
| 2001 | Edwin C. Fisher | Willimantic |
| 2002 + | Diane (Pettit) Bielski | East Haddam Community |
| 2003 | Mary Krogh | East Hampton Village |
| 2004 | Loren Otter | Bolton |
| 2005 + | David Burgess | Danielson |
| 2006 | Paul Maxwell | East Haddam |
| 2007 | Julianne Shilosky | Colchester |
| 2008 | Armand LaFleur, VDG | Putnam |

+ Past Council Chair
* Deceased

Appendix F—Formation of Connecticut Lions Clubs 1922-2007

| Club | District | Organizer | Sponsor | Organized | Members | President |
|------|----------|-----------|---------|-----------|---------|-----------|
| Avon | 23-B | A. C. Urbinati | West Hartford | 6-18-51 | 27 | Raymond Zacchera |
| Barkhamsted | 23-B | Clarence DenHerder | Winsted | 10-20-66 | 24-6 tr. | Donald Lovley |
| Beacon Falls | 23-A | A. C. Urbinati | Naugatuck | 2-27-53 | 16 | Frank Semplenski |
| Berlin | 23-B | H. T. Miller | New Britain | 10-27-41 | 39 | James Macpherson |
| Bethany | 23-A | A. C. Urbinati | Woodbridge | 3-6-52 | 19 | Frank A. Hoff |
| Bethel | 23-A | Philip Jakob | Danbury | 6-6-28 | 50-3 tr. | Harold B. Senior |
| Bethlehem | 23-B | F. Arute, F. Shepard and W. Ring | Woodbury | 5-30-72 | 29 | Robert Overton |
| Bloomfield | 23-B | H. T. Miller | Hartford | 3-5-42 | 31-1C | Lloyd W. Moulton |
| Bolton | 23-C | Wendell Ring | Hebron | 4-5-76 | 44 | Lawrence Converse III |
| Bolton Regional | 23-C | Francis Gregoire | Bolton | 6-5-92 | | Marilyn Washington |
| Branford | 23-A | A. C. Urbinati | Guilford | 5-22-51 | 28 | Lorin A. Higley |
| Bridgeport (Host) | 23-A | H. McKinnon | None | 2-28-21 | 124 | William H. Hewlett |
| Bridgeport (North Bridgeport) | 23-A | J. Ganim, G. Bonnell & C. DenHerder | Bridgeport | 2-7-66 | 90 | Mario V. Rubano |

| Club | District | Organizer | Sponsor | Organized | Members | President |
|------|----------|-----------|---------|-----------|---------|-----------|
| Bristol | 23-B | T. Graham & Sam Woodrow | New Britain | 3-23-26 | 30 | Dr. W. R. Hanrahan |
| Brookfield | 23-A | W. Sherrer & C. DenHerder | Newtown & New Fairfield | 3-3-66 | 30 | Douglas B. Dewing |
| Burlington | 23-B | C. DenHerder | Unionville | 3-12-68 | 38 | Raymond Cmiel |
| Canaan Northwest | 23-B | | Unionville | 6-12-92 | 29 | Elizabeth Kowalski |
| Canterbury | 23-C | W.Ring, D.Ayrton & T. Collidge | N. Franklin | 6-12-72 | 23-1 tr. | Donald L. Ayrton |
| Canton | 23-B | A. C. Urbinati | Unionville | 11-23-51 | 27 | Robert Ferguson, Jr. |
| Cheshire | 23-A | A. C. Urbinati | Southington | 10-19-49 | 61 | Wentworth T. Carter |
| Clinton | 23-C | A. C. Urbinati | Guilford | 9-26-50 | 26 | Carl Weisse |
| Colchester | 23-C | A. C. Urbinati | Willimantic | 8-2-49 | 41 | John W. Damm |
| Colebrook | 23-B | Milan Knight | Winsted | 6-30-80 | 19-2 tr. | Theodore Vaill Jr. |
| Columbia | 23-C | A. C. Urbinati | Lebanon & Willimantic | 5-23-55 | 19-1 tr. | William S. Burnham |
| Coventry | 23-C | A. C. Urbinati | Storrs | 9-30-52 | 30 | Herbert J. Gable |
| Cromwell | 23-C | D. B. Dewar | Berlin | 10-13-48 | 46 | Robert H. DeHart |
| Danbury | 23-A | | Bridgeport | 9-8-27 | 37 | Edmund B. Watson |
| Danielson | 23-C | A. C. Urbinati | Putnam | 4-1-54 | 21 | Arnold A. Molz |

| Club | District | Organizer | Sponsor | Organized | Members | President |
|------|----------|-----------|---------|-----------|---------|-----------|
| Darien | 23-A | Dugaid Dewar | Stamford | 2-17-49 | 41 | Robert C. Grieb |
| Deep River-Chester | 23-C | A. C. Urbinati | Middletown | 9-1-50 | 26 | Silvio J. Zanni |
| Derby-Shelton | 23-A | A. C. Urbinati | None | 3-30-50 | 25 | David Resnick |
| Devon | 23-A | H. T. Miller | Stratford | 4-30-42 | 15 | Howard K. Taylor |
| Durham | 23-C | A. C. Urbinati | Portland | 10-24-51 | 25 | Ferdinand Arrigoni |
| East Granby | 23-B | A. C. Urbinati | Granby | 4-28-60 | 24-1 tr. | R. L. McGoldrick |
| East Haddam | 23-C | A. C. Urbinati | Haddam | 2-21-55 | 25-1 tr. | Edgar H. Bishop |
| East Haddam Community | 23-C | Francis Gregoire | East Haddam | 5-29-92 | 36 | Diane (Pettit) Bielski |
| East Hampton | 23-C | A. C. Urbinali | Portland | 3-30-57 | 25-2 tr. | G. E. Wheeler |
| East Hampton Village | 23-C | Francis Gregoire | East Hampton | 6-30-92 | | Sandra Nesci |
| East Hartford | 23-B | A. C. Urbinati | Hartford | 1-16-50 | 53 | Leon A. Winslow |
| East Haven | 23-A | | Branford | 9-28-03 | 29 | Elbert M. Burr |
| East Windsor | 23-B | A. C. Urbinati | Enfield | 6-29-53 | 23 | Walter E. Colton |
| Easton | 23-A | C. DenHerder | Trumbull | 4-19-67 | 28-3 tr. | Roben K. Monk |
| Elmwood | 23-B | William S. Jerin | West Hartford | 11-7-80 | 24-1 tr. | Bruce E. Goldberg |
| Enfield | 23-B | H. T. Miller | Hartford | 3-31-42 | 20 | Charles E. Monahan |

| Club | District | Organizer | Sponsor | Organized | Members | President |
|------|----------|-----------|---------|-----------|---------|-----------|
| Essex | 23-C | A. C. Urbinati | None | 8-24-50 | 31 | Arthur E. Price |
| Fairfield | 23-A | Larry Slater | Bridgeport & Stratford | 10-20-36 | 47 | Edward A. Tyler |
| Franklin | 23-C | A. Gorreck & C. DenHerder | Lebanon | 3-18-68 | 25-1 tr. | Vincent Majchier |
| Georgetown | 23-A | A. C. Urbinati | Ridgefield | 2-24-50 | 27 | James B. Sullivan |
| Glastonbury | 23-B | A. C. Urbinati | Newington | 3-27-51 | 26 | Raymond G. School |
| Granby | 23-B | A. C. Urbinati | None | 3-20-53 | 23-1 tr. | William A. Benini |
| Greater Hartford West Indian | 23-B | Elba Schulman & Syd Schulman | Bloomfield | 6-29-01 | | Raymond H. Davis |
| Greenwich | 23-A | H. McKinnon | None | 8-28-23 | 31 | Dr. William A. Hillis |
| Griswold Regional | 23-C | | Plainfield | 3-30-88 | | |
| Groton | 23-C | Gillene Bros. | None | 9-24-29 | 20-1 tr.-1 | Dr. Ed. L. Douglass |
| Guilford | 23-A | A. C. Urbinati | Hamden | 4-26-50 | 28 | Edmund L. Stoddard |
| Haddam | 23-C | A. C. Urbinati | Deep River | 9-12-51 | 25 | Emerson J. Carpenter |
| Hamden | 23-A | A. C. Urbinati | New Haven | 11-17-49 | 58 | Ralph Maisano |
| Hartford (Host) | 23-B | H. McKinnon | None | 5-18-22 | 97 | T. Clay Lindsey |

| Club | District | Organizer | Sponsor | Organized | Members | President |
|---|---|---|---|---|---|---|
| Hartford County Fidelco | 23-B | Eric Jacobson | Windsor Locks | 3-5-03 | 21 | Peter Nowicki |
| Hartford County Motorcycle | 23-B | Glenn Boglisch | Windsor Locks | 6-24-03 | 24 | Karen Gerhauser |
| Hartford (Evening) | 23-B | (Wendell Ring) | Hartford | 5-29-74 | 67 | Jose Flores |
| Hartford Hispanic Seniors | 23-B | Elba Cruz Schulman | Hartford Multinational | 6-23-99 | 28 | Eduardo Rivera |
| Hartford Multi-National | 23-B | Norberto Bello | Hartford Evening | 5-29-91 | | Aurelia Hicks |
| Hartland | 23-B | Milan Knight | Barkhamsted | 6-19-78 | 23 | Walter Swanson |
| Harwinton | 23-B | Elmer J. Blair | Litchfield | 1-30-62 | 26-1 tr. | Hurlburt G. Clark |
| Hebron | 23-C | Bert Johnson | Columbia | 12-3-69 | 26 | Raymond J. Burt |
| Kent | 23-B | William S. Jerin | New Milford | 2-3-78 | 27 | Dolph Trayman |
| Killingly Quiet Corner Regional | 23-C | | Griswold Regional | 11-26-03 | 34 | Thomas Kohl |
| Killingworth | 23-C | Bert Johnson | Middletown | 11-18-70 | 36-2 tr. | John F. Kemper |
| Lebanon | 23-C | A. C. Urbinati | Colchester | 1-31-52 | 31 | Carol Tarcauanu |
| Ledyard | 23-C | A. C. Urbinati | Mystic | 8-11-60 | 20 | Charles J. Cavanaugh |

| Club | District | Organizer | Sponsor | Organized | Members | President |
|---|---|---|---|---|---|---|
| Litchfield | 23-B | A. C. Urbinati | Torrington | 1-30-50 | 45 | A. A. MacDonald |
| Lyme-Old Lyme | 23-C | Chapman & Ring | East Haddam | 4-11-72 | 31 | Peter G. Chapman |
| Madison | 23-A | A. C. Urbinati | Guilford | 2-22-56 | 20-1 tr.-4 reinstated | Thomas Gildea |
| Manchester | 23-B | A. C. Urbinati | West Hartford | 6-28-49 | 50 | Charles Mather |
| Mansfield | 23-C | A. C. Urbinati | Willimantic | 4-7-52 | 32 | Delmas B. Cookson |
| Marlborough | 23-B | A. C. Urbinati | Glastonbury | 10-28-52 | 24-1 tr. | Robert J. Farley |
| Meriden | 23-A | H. McKinnon | None | 11-5-23 | 35 | Dr. H. C. Quinlan |
| Middlebury | 23-A | A. C. Urbinati | Southbury | 2-27-52 | 55 | Howard Watts |
| Middlefield | 23-C | A. C. Urbinati | Durham | 5-11-56 | 29-1 tr. | Frank W. Clark |
| Middletown | 23-C | Gillette Bros. | None | 5-28-29 | 38 | Don Cambria |
| Milford | 23-A | A. C. Urbinati | Devon | 7-24-51 | 42 | William L. Gilbert |
| Monroe | 23-A | A. C. Urbinati | Bridgeport & Trumbull | 3-20-52 | 26 | John J. Ryan |
| Montville | 23-C | A. C. Urbinati | Norwich | 6-11-58 | 19-4 tr.-1 reinstated | William Kirby |
| Montville Mohegan-Pequot | 23-C | Francis Gregoire | Putnam | 6-14-92 | | Patricia Rodriguez |

| Club | District | Organizer | Sponsor | Organized | Members | President |
|---|---|---|---|---|---|---|
| Mystic | 23-C | A. C. Urbinati | Groton | 9-15-49 | 39 | Merle K. Bradley |
| Naugatuck | 23-A | A. C. Urbinati | Derby | 12-12-50 | 16 | Mario Schiaroli |
| New Britain | 23-B | H. McKinnon | None | 7-11-22 | 38 | Harry G. Hancock |
| New Canaan | 23-A | Stamford Lions Club | Stamford | 3-15-29 | 35 | Wilbur J. Dixon |
| New Fairfield | 23-A | A. C. Urbinati | Danbury | 12-21-51 | 32 | Charles B. Carlson |
| New Fairfield/ Candlewood | 23-A | A. C. Urbinati | Yalesville/ Wallingford | 4-11-95 | | Hillery Bassriel |
| New Hartford | 23-B | Ben Johnson | Barkhamsted | 9-17-70 | 24-4F | Harry M. Smith, Jr. |
| New Haven | 23-A | H. McKinnon | None | 2-9-22 | 125 | Louis A. Beecher |
| New London | 23-C | H. McKinnon | None | 8-15-22 | 50 | Francis Allanach |
| Newington | 23-B | H. T. Miller | New Britain | 1-26-42 | 26 | Oran S. Parker |
| New Milford | 23-A | Gillette Bros. | None | 4-18-29 | 23 | Paul Barton |
| Newtown | 23-A | D. B. Dewar | Danbury | 11-30-48 | 32 | George Trull |
| Niantic | 23-C | A. C. Urbinati | New London | 8-23-49 | 54 | Mario Orefice |
| Norfolk | 23-B | A. C. Urbinati | Sharon | 1-30-51 | 25 | J. Owen Byrne |
| North Haven | 23-A | A. C. Urbinati | Branford | 3-28-52 | 24 | Frederick Kamp |
| North Stonington | 23-C | Clarence DenHerder | Mystic | 3-27-67 | 33-2 tr. | Maurice F. Browning |

| Club | District | Organizer | Sponsor | Organized | Members | President |
|------|----------|-----------|---------|-----------|---------|-----------|
| Norwalk | 23-A | D. H. Fogg | Stamford, Springdale, N. Cannan | 7-10-46 | 20 | Robert B. Gillespie |
| Norwich | 23-C | Stubbs, McManus | New London | 4-11-39 | 17 | James A. Calcombe |
| Old Greenwich | 23-A | Gov. Dixon | Greenwich | 5-18-33 | 26 | Neil J. Jensen |
| Old Saybrook | 23-C | A. C. Urbinati | Niantic | 6-27-50 | 29 | Wesley E. Porter |
| Orange | 23-A | A. C. Urbinati | Milford | 4-23-52 | 26 | William A. Knight |
| Oxford | 23-A | A. C. Urbinati | Southbury | 3-15-51 | 19-1 tr. | Fred R. Rice |
| Pawcatuck | 23-C | A. C. Urbinati | Norwich | 10-25-50 | 35 | Peter Mitchell |
| Plainfield | 23-C | A. C. Urbinati | Jewett City | 12-13-51 | 22 | Anthony Collelo |
| Plainville | 23-B | H. T. Miller | New Britain | 5-15-41 | 39 | Henry C. Baum |
| Pomfret | 23-C | A. C. Urbinati | Putnam | 9-9-54 | 19-4 tr. | Frank E. Rowan |
| Prospect | 23-A | | Wolcott | 5-9-00 | | |
| Putnam | 23-C | A. C. Urbinati | Jewett City | 9-29-49 | 25 | George S. Shaw |
| Ridgefield | 23-A | Gillette Bros. | None | 4-19-29 | 36-4 Hon. | Francis Martin |
| Rocky Hill | 23-B | Paul B. Isham | Newington | 2-28-49 | 25 | Alfred Y. Lytle |
| Salem | 23-C | Wendell D. Ring | Niantic | 5-17-73 | 39 | George Gillis |
| Seymour | 23-A | A. C. Urbinati | Oxford | 8-27-52 | 24-1 tr. | Frank J.Casagrande |
| Sharon | 23-B | H. T. Miller | New Milford | 4-30-41 | 31 | Clarence Eggleston |

| Club | District | Organizer | Sponsor | Organized | Members | President |
|------|----------|-----------|---------|-----------|---------|-----------|
| Simsbury | 23-B | Henry Shenning & Howard Wry | Bloomfield & West Hartford | 6-15-65 | 15-5 tr. | Bernard E. Francis |
| Somers | 23-C | A. C. Urbinati | Stafford | 1-30-53 | 22 | Walter C. Bliss, Jr. |
| South Windsor | 23-B | A. C. Urbinati | East Windsor | 6-8-61 | 28 | Frank E. Ahearn |
| Southbury | 23-A | D. B. Dewar | Bethel | 12-7-48 | 37-5 tr. | Howard E. Simons |
| Southington | 23-B | H. T. Miller | Meriden | 2-5-42 | 19 | Milton Chaffee |
| Stafford | 23-C | A. C. Urbinati | Willimantic | 7-30-51 | 21 | Nicholas F. Armentano |
| Stamford | 23-A | Thomas Graham | Greenwich | 10-19-25 | 35 | Edward C. Fisher |
| Stratford | 23-A | Gillette Bros. | None | 11-22-29 | 58 | Frank Mercer |
| Suffield | 23-B | A. C. Urbinati | Granby & Agawam, MA | 4-29-55 | | Charles D. Prunier |
| Taftville | 23-C | Angelo Miceli & Frank DiStefano | Norwich | 6-30-98 | 38 | Ulric (Ric) Tetrault |
| Terryville | 23-B | H. T. Miller | Bristol | 6-27-41 | 20-2Comp | Philip F. Atwood |
| Thompson | 23-C | A. C. Urbinati | Putnam | 4-29-53 | | Joseph A. Valade |
| Tolland | 23-C | DeSantis & Johnson | Stafford | 11-10-69 | 23-4 tr.-1F | Dr. David Serluco |
| Torrington | 23-B | Thomas Graham | None | 11-30-25 | 25 | Dr. Harry Hanchett |
| Trinity College | 23-B | Ron Storms | Simsbury & Windsor Locks | 2-9-00 | | Amy Judy |

| Club | District | Organizer | Sponsor | Organized | Members | President |
|---|---|---|---|---|---|---|
| Trumbull | 23-A | A. C. Urbinati | Fairfield | 11-30-50 | 27 | James J.Carrano |
| Trumbull Center | 23-A | | Bridgeport & Sport Hill | 1-26-86 | 38 | Dr. Chester A. Sobelowski |
| Unionville | 23-B | H. T. Miller | Hartford | 11-29-41 | 17 | James C. Tilley |
| Washington | 23-B | H. T. Miller | New Milford | 5-31-41 | 44-1Comp | Myron S. Couch |
| Waterbury | 23-A | H. McKinnon | None | 10-18-23 | 50 | G. Loring Burwell |
| Waterford | 23-C | A. C. Urbinati | Niantic | 6-11-52 | 29 | Albert Nitsche |
| Waterford Regional | 23-C | Francis Gregoire | Waterford | 6-30-92 | | Sheri Ann Grills |
| Watertown | 23-B | A. C. Urbinati | Waterbury | 10-25-49 | 37 | Anthony Brody |
| West Hartford | 23-B | Paul B. Isham | Newington | 3-26-46 | 54-2 tr. | Wallace G. Hale |
| West Haven | 23-A | A. C. Urbinati | New Haven | 4-25-51 | 33 | John G. Cicala |
| Westbrook | 23-C | | Essex | 2-13-04 | | Michael B. Cushing |
| Western Greenwich | 23-A | | Greenwich | 11-21-96 | | Roy Zold |
| Wethersfield | 23-B | A. C. Urbinati | Newington | 11-29-49 | 67 | John F. Mulvihill |
| Willimantic | 23-C | H. T. Miller | Norwich | 3-31-41 | 13-2 tr. | Ray Couter |
| Windsor | 23-B | A. C. Urbinati | Bloomfield | 12-15-49 | 50 | Oliver T. Mather |

| Club | District | Organizer | Sponsor | Organized | Members | President |
|------|----------|-----------|---------|-----------|---------|-----------|
| Windsor Locks | 23-B | H. T. Miller | Bloomfield | 6-6-42 | 22 | Rev. Charles McNerney |
| Winsted | 23-B | A. C. Urbinati | Torrington | 3-16-60 | 36-1 tr. | James E. Condon |
| Wolcott | 23-A | A. C. Urbinati | Waterbury | 4-23-52 | 29 | Carl G. Mattson |
| Woodbridge | 23-A | A. C. Urbinati | New Haven | 5-24-51 | 26 | William J. Cousins |
| Woodbury | 23-B | Larry Slater | New Milford & Torrington | 4-8-36 | 27 | Earle W. Munson |
| Woodstock | 23-C | A. C. Urbinati | Putnam | 1-16-56 | 19-2 tr. | Melzar A. Woodbury |
| Yalesville-Wallingford | 23-A | Clarence DenHerder | Meriden | 12-18-67 | 41-2 tr. | Frank Vumbaco |

Some of the Defunct Lions Clubs mentioned elsewhere in this book:

Ansonia, Bridgeport Beardsley, Bridgeport East Bridgeport, Canaan, Connecticut Singles, Elmwood, Farmington, Greenwich Western, Goshen, Morris, New Britain Evening, New Haven Elm City Evening, New London Whaling City, Portland, Springdale, Stamford North, Thomaston, Sport Hill, Warren, Waterford Quaker Hill, Westport

## Appendix G—LCI Ambassador of Good Will

| | |
|---|---|
| Harold A. Ashley | Waterbury |
| Charles W. Naylor | New Canaan |
| Joseph W. Ganim | Stratford |
| Joseph M. McLoughlin | Stamford |
| Herbert A. Liebert | Hartford |
| Nunzio Rosso | Berlin |
| Joseph L. Raub | New London |
| Scott A. Storms | Windsor Locks |

## Appendix H—Ambassador of Sight Recipients

### Lions Clubs of District 23-A

**Beacon Falls Lions Club**
Richard Adamaltis
William Mis
Edward P. Slemenski
John King
William Unfricht
Gayle Fredericks
Joseph A Poirier, CC

**Beacon Falls Lioness Club**
Edith Minnick

**Branford Lions Club**
David B. DZiUra
Edward F. Farley
Edwin Laughran

**Bridgeport Host Lions Club**
Theodore H. Bresky
Raymond M. Zaleski, PDG

**Brookfield Lions Club**
George Brown
Mark Lyon
Anthony G. Licursi

**Danbury Lions Club**
John J. Allen
Howard Blainey
Al Cipnani
Mellissa Erdtmann
Thomas R. Nolan
Dottie Wildman

**Greenwich Lions Club**
Frances Blaustein
Women's Club of Greenwich

**Madison Lions Club**
Richard Borner
David Longobucco
R. Russell Martin, M.D.
Louis Desseil
Marinus J deJongh, PDG
Richard E Kennedy

**Meriden Lions Club**
David W. Parke, M.D.
William Phillips, PDG
Peter Gostyla, PDG
David Murdy
Joseph E Crowell
Stephen J Riechards
Richard W Carino
Walter Camp

**Milford Lions Club**
Joseph Elmo
Kathy Patterson
Edward Saxon Weise
Joe Valerio
Roberta Weise
Michael Valerio Jr
Dennis Slavin

**New Fairfield Candlewood
Lions Club**
Robert Gyle, PCC
Martin Steinberg

**New Haven Lions Club**
Walter Anderson
James B. Bennett, PDG
Noel V. Roche
Lawrence J. Sheilds
James E Traester

**Newtown Lions Club**
Stanley Wyslock

**Orange Lions Club**
James Mossey
Marion Nugent
William A. Philips, PDG
Kevin Hadlock
Nicholas Bencivengo

**Oxford Lions Club**
William Valentine

**Prospect Lions Club**
Edward Scarpati

**Ridgefield Lions Club**
Roy Cogswell
Harold Hval
Michael J. Liberta
Ann Slade

**Southbury Lions Club**
Michael E. Kindel
Edward Wilson

**Stamford (North) Lions Club**
Harold Topper

**Trumbull Center Lions Club**
Gene Poulos, PDG

**Waterbury Lions Club**
Michael Granatuk, PDG
William Summa
William L. Tobin

**Wolcott Lions Club**
John Gagain, PDG
Thomas Centinaro
Raymond Mahoney
Harry Najarian
Richard Renkun Sr

**Lions Clubs of District 23-B**

**Avon Lions Club**
Donald Griswold, PDG

**Berlin Lions Club**
George Ondrick, PDG
Joseph Pegolo
Robert Weiss, PDG
Gordon Wicke
Tom Retano
Gerard Bienkowski
Glenn Glatz
Gary Schmidt
David Alkas
Paul Kristopik

**Brisol Lions Club**
Roman Czuhta
Ray Frankowski
Arlene Frankowski
Sydney Shafran
George Rindfleisch
V. Everett Lyons

**Burlington Lions Club**
Pam Weaver

**Canaan Northwest Lions Club**
Patricia Bartlett

**District 23-B**
Jeffery Glatz

**East Granby Lions Club**
Tom Short

**East Hartford Lions Club**
George Precourt, PDG
Gerard Mogielnicki
Steven Crecco

**East Windsor Lions Club**
Richard Stathers, PDG
Margaret Sylvester
Gail Dourossette
Dan Goldan
Stu Woodard
Dr. Collo

**Enfield Lions Club**
Gordon D. Holmes

**Glastonbury Lions Club**
P.K. Das

**Hartland Lions Club**
David Neri
Gary Cicognani
Thomas Mirsky
Walter Bell
Francis Rossbach

**Marlborough Lions Club**
Thomas Couture

**New Britain Lions Club**
Alan Daninhirsch, PDG
Faith Ondrick
Otto Stobino, PID
Dr. Stephen Poezonis
Judy Daninhirsch

**New Milford Lions Club**
Mike Wilcox
Donna Lillis
Curt Fitch, PDG

**Plainville Lions Club**
Craig Banks
Donal F. Dickenson

**Rocky Hill Lions Club**
Eugene Rohr

**Salisbury Lions Club**
Kathy Hawley

**Sharon Lions Club**
Carl Marshall

**Simsbury Lions Club**
Bob Gauthier
Fran Gauthier

**Southington Lions Club**
Ed Sauer

**South Windsor Lions Club**
Terri Cocuzzo

**Terryville Lions Club**
William Allread
Richard Foote, PDG
David Barbieri

**Torrington Lions Club**
William Knight
Blanche Sewell
James Upton

**Unionville Lions Club**
David Merrills
Robert Swaine
Dora Cormack
Joe Grevalsky

**Watertown Lions Club**
O'Neil St. Onge
Bernard C. Beauchamp

**West Hartford Lions Club**
James Schwartzhaupt
Claudio Pane
Gerald Sandler
Joey Belanger

**Windsor Locks Lions Club**
George Cooper, PDG
Scott Storms, PID
Normand Messier PDG
Cindy Cooper
Gail Stegman
Ronald Storms, PDG

**Winsted Lions Club**
Malcolm Sewell

**Woodbury Lions Club**
John Naylor
Kenneth Deschino
Joe Geraci
James Trompter

**Other recipients**
David Bates
Trish Holmes
Catherine Merrills
W. Keith Wuerthner, PDG
David Renouf
Carolyn Messier, PDG

**Lions Clubs of District 23-C**

**Colchester Lions Club**
Peter Lewis
Irene Watson
Robert Michaud
Rita Anastasio
Leo Glemboski
Bob Michaud

**Deep River-Chester Lions Club**
Mark Lowrey

**East Haddam Community Lions Club**
Diane (Pettit) Bielski, PDG
Angeline Borgnine
Theresa Kromish
Gerri Hutra
Marilyn Churchill

**East Hampton Village Lions Club**
Mary Krogh, PDG

**East Hampton Lions Club**
Ralph Nesci
Thomas DiStefano
Robert Tourville, PDG
Joe Walters

**District Flea Market Fundraiser**
Rose Marie Lee
William Graham
Bruce Atwater
Joel Zuckerbraum
Karen Costa

**Griswold Regional Lions Club**
Ken Usted
Mickey Lamarre

**Groton Lions**
Stacy Haines
Perley Kent
Nick Utz
Hugh Casey
Richard Kent
Mark Williams
William Foreman
Jan Miller
Marilyn Searle

**Hebron Lions Club**
Mickey Groshart
Ramon Campbell

**Killingly Quiet Corner Lions
Club**
Herbert Elliot

**Ledyard Lions Club**
James Bowersett
Peter Olsen
Laura Rowe
Agnes Dodge

**Lyme-Old Lyme Lions Club**
Barry Williams

**Middlefield Lions Club**
David Wallach
Robert Cabelus
N. Sumner Lerch-Spencer

**Montville Lions Club**
Nathan Beit
Thomas Carlson
Carleton Eichelberg, PDG

**Mystic Lions Club**
June Valenti
George Finlayson
Nancy MacDonald

**New London Lions Club**
Ernest Torhan

**Niantic Lions Club**
John Sullivan
Ralph Fortuna
Paticia Hanney
Larry Updyke
Craig J. Carucci
Wayne Fraser

**Plainfield Lions Club**
Art Nadeau

**Putnam Lions Club**
Leia Faucher
Greg King
Stuart Neal

**Willimantic Lions Club**
David Bergmann
Shirley Mauro
Keith Lemire

**District 23-C Low Vision
Board**
Steve Martin
Howard Parkhurst, M.D.
Angela Tanguay
Sam Linder

# Appendix I—CLERF Knight of the Blind Recipients

## CLERF Named Knights of the Blind

Donna Del Re
Tom Indoe, President,
  Newman's Own, Inc.
Jack Schlechtweg
Marvin L. Sears, M.D.
M. Bruce Shields, M.D.
Beverly D. Talbot

## Lions Clubs of District 23-A

### Ansonia Lions Club
Peter Aquila
Thomas M. Duffy
Harry Feinberg
Henry J. Gambaccini
Brad Harris
Michael J. Impellitteri, Jr.
Joseph A. LaRocco
Peter Lovermi
Delbert H. Rau

### Beacon Falls Lions Club
William 'Bill' Cable
David Cameron
Edward Chicoski
Dr. Thomas J. DeLuca
Robert Doiron
Kenneth Egan
William Fredericks
Peter V. Galla
William Mis
Donald F. Mitchell

Joseph Poirier, PDG
Raymond Shea, PDG
Thomas Trzaski
Douglas Ventimiglia
James Woodward

### Beacon Falls Leo Club
Larry S. Hutvagner

### Bethany Lions Club
Janet Hescock
Robert Kirsch

### Bethel Lions Club
Tulio Belardinelli
Robert Brunner
Richard D. Clausing
Jan Maria Jagush
Charles A. Steck III

### Branford Lions Club
Amos Barnes
David E. Burke
John Cunningham
John Cushing
Dr. David B. Dziura
Donald C. Erickson
Walter Flesche
Ralph Fuller
Norman C. Lacina
Richard Lacy
Dr. James H. Mendillo
Jerry Osochowsky, PDG
Alex Palluzzi
David A. Reed
John J. Wilkinson

**Bridgeport Beardsley Lions Club**
Richard J. Adzima

**Bridgeport Host Lions Club**
Paul N. D'Elia, Jr.
Philip S. DiLeo
Joseph W. Ganim, PID
Cynthia M. Kovacs
Michael Mayo
John E. McCann
Patrick A. Pallotto
Stephen Pickens
Bert Rinck

**Brookfield Lions Club**
John Anderson
Ernest J. Bendana
Patrick M. Blanchfield
Richard B. Blessey
George Brown, Jr.
Joseph Courtney
Tom Daly
William Davidson
Paul Digrazia, M.D.
Robert Dougherty
Amanda Dube
William J. Font
Christopher P. Goodman
Robert Hoxie, PDG
David Keefe
Francis J. Kerwin, Jr.
James D. Kovacs
Richard LaCava
Anthony G. Licursi
Carolyn Lyon
Mark Lyon
Ronald H. Mattson
Gary Missigman
David J. Moissonnier

Gerald Nindorf
Bob Rossi
John Royce
William G. Side
Alan Smith
Candice Smith
Allan Sniffin
Robert J. Sorisio
Craig Stoeppel
Tom Sullivan
Joseph F. Sweeney
Donald Winkley

**Cheshire Lions Club**
Colette M. Anderson
Carol A. Erasmus
Agnes Strobino

**Danbury Lions Club**
John J. Allen
Nancy M. Beck
Alan G. Brown
Edward G. Butterfield
Frances J. Evans
George E. Good
Morris Gross
Alfred P. Hazard, PDG
Julie Ann Johnson
Nancy Lavers
Boyd O. Losee
Robert Lovell
Louis G. Matthews
Victoria Matthews
Emanuel Merullo, PDG
Harold "Mike" Michael
Frank P. Molinaro
Hubert V. Morgan
John J. Murphy
Thomas Nolan
Kenneth G. Saloom

J. Roger Schmiedel
Kathleen S. Shea
Donald J. Skiba
Martin Steinberg
Helene Thompson
Edward Wicks
Arthur E. Wilson
Dr. Mark Wolmer

**Darien Lions Club**
Thomas Bauder
Herbert Brown
Bruce Buening
John Campbell
William M. Carello, PDG
Rocco S. Cingari, PDG
Stirling Collins
Harold S. Curtis
Peter Daigle
Joseph L. DeRocco
Pete Deutsch
Mark Esposito
Martin J. Flaherty
William A. Frate
Stephen Fritsch
Thomas Gecheran
Irving Geddes
Ken W. Gifford
Linda Hagerman
Robert Locke
Kenneth L. Lord
Robert Martin
Michael J. Murray, DDS
Robert Musitano
Lawrence Pakkala
Joel Rappaport
Peter Rogers
Joseph Santelle
Eric Scott

Scott C. Scribner
Frank Sherwood
Paul C. Smith
Thomas Sniffen
Mark Thorne
Louis J. Volpicelli

**Derby-Shelton Lions Club**
Francis Klos
Andrew Sabetta
Anthony Terrasi

**Devon Lions Club**
Richard E. Dowin
Roger W. Martin

**Easton Lions Club**
Paul Diana
Anthony Giannetta
John Morris
Richard Schwartz

**Fairfield Lions Club**
Donal M. Collimore
Howard P. Cooke
Edmund Forger
William Lopez
John J. Sullivan

**Georgetown Lions Club**
Michael Cardillo

**Greenwich Lions Club**
Martin L. Blaustein
Susan Ferris
Peter Imbres
Martin Lacoff
Douglas Masi
H. David Noble
Pat M. Pulitano
Paul C. Settelmeyer
Stanley A. Thal
Sandy Uitti

**Guilford Lions Club**
Manny Correia
Ronald C. Dougan
Donald Engstrom
Donald A. Johnson
Martin Lombardi
Joseph Londa
Bruce Murphy
William Passas
Vincent Porpora
Bud Redman
James Wright

**Hamden Lions Club**
Richard Inzero

**Madison Lions Club**
George Basler
Richard F. Borner
Joseph Henry Darling
Dana D. Doyon
Anthony P. Fappiano, MD
Ronald B. Hall
Edward Hansen
Richard Kennedy
Armand LaLiberte
Anthony F. Lazzari
Robert J. Leen
George C. Love
K. Stephen Meader
John S. Morehouse
Austin Myrick
Richard N. Passero
Henry D. Robinson II
Wiley Rutledge
H. M. (Sandy) Soars, III

**Meriden Lions Club**
John Albano
John Alfieri

Lee Barbagli
Walter Camp
George Carabetta, Sr.
Vincent Caramanello
James E. Crowell
Peter J. Gostyla, PDG
Raymond Gradwell
Edward G. Haberli
Conrad D. Kuzmich
David P. Lohman
Brian Mahon
Vincent Mule
David D. Murdy
William Panciera
Dr. David W. Parke
Franklin Phillips
William D. Phillips, PDG
Tom Raffile
Stephen Richards
William L. Roberts, PDG
Charles R. Stiegler
Michael Szymaszek
Francis H. Zygmont

**Middlebury Lions Club**
Walter K. Ahearn, PDG

**Milford Lions Club**
Joseph Elmo
Gioacchino de Nicolo
Steven Pavelko
Joseph Valerio

**Monroe Lions Club**
Omer Cyr
Peter DiCarlo
Richard Michel
Ronald Plude

**New Canaan Lions Club**
Helen Risom Belluschi
Jeroll Silverberg

**New Fairfield Lions Club**
Eugene N. Arcery
Michael Berenberg
Gail Redenz
Robert M. Redenz, PDG
Douglas Stram
Richard Von Werne

**New Fairfield Candlewood Lions Club**
Frederick J. Bourne
Lovie D. Bourne
Margaret Gallo
Richard T. Grant
Robert B. Gyle III, PDG
Alice M. Hoxie
Regina 'Jean' Knopf
Patricia E. Martin

**New Haven Lions Club**
Frank A. Abbadessa
Herbert E. Anderson
Walter A. Anderson
James B. Bennett, PDG
Joan C. Bennett
Ruth B. Carr
James J. Creamer
Kenneth P. Douglas
John E. Downs
Milton J. Foley, Jr.
Theodore F. Hyatt, PDG
John M. Lyons
Maureen C. Mazzacane
David Minicozzi
David R. Rice
E. Bernard Roop
Lawrence J. Shields

**Newtown Lions Club**
Winthrop Ballard
Clifford Blumer
Thomas J. Evagash
William Honan
Wayland Johnson
Richard T. Kovacs
Paul H. Krueger
J. Charles Lewis
George Mattegat
Sutherland W. G. Denlinger
Robert Tynan
Gordon M. Williams

**North Stamford Lions Club**
Meryl Aronin
Fred Cronenwett
Anthony Matteis, Sr.

**Norwalk  Lions Club**
Thomas Lynch
David H. McCullough, MD

**Old Greenwich Lions Club**
Paula Corrado
Isabelle Cox
Lucien Ducret
Phil Hahn
Hunter M. Marvel
Beverly Peyser
Seymour Peyser
Frank T. Cornacchio

**Orange Lions Club**
Robert Drobish
Dr. Lawrence Messina
Jeannette Phillips
Fred Turner

**Oxford Lions Club**
James Biondi
Thomas Biondi
Peter Costabile
Joseph Klanko
William Lund
Richard Mageluzzo
Gabe Mason
William Ryan

**Prospect Lions Club**
Marty Atkins
Richard Brown

**Ridgefield Lions Club**
Emelie M. Howard
Harold Hval
Jill C. Johnston
Leo Lardie
Michael Liberta
Anna A. Lossius
Linda Maggs
Gary C. Smith

**Seymour Lions Club**
Robert Frink
Toby Konowitz
James Lane
Andy Martin
Andy Mathews
Ted Metz
George S. Ostaszeski
Ted Rogol
Ronald Rossetti
Debra Santora
Ellie Sessa
Richard Spatafore
Rose Marie Spatafore, DG
Ugo Zullo

**Southbury Lions Club**
Anne Nanavaty
Krishnalal Nanavaty, PDG
Arthur E. Ulman

**Stamford/Springdale Lions Club**
Joseph L. Gerardi
James 'J' Scott

**Stratford Lions Club**
Thomas B. Coughlin
Larry De Libro
Harold D. Gaa
Robert J. Sebas

**Trumbull Center Lions Club**
Thomas E. Johnson
Gene G. Poulos, Sr., PDG
Chester Sobolewski, PDG

**Trumbull Lions Club**
Michael Del Re, Jr., PDG
Irving Dietz
Alan Hildred
William G. Mosseau

**Waterbury Lions Club**
Harold Ashley, PID
Stephen C. Briotti
Robert D. Cameron
Barbara Davitt
Michael Devino
Michael Granatuk, PDG
Dr. Philip Joseph
Lisa Martin
Wendell F. McKennerney
Frank Nardelli
Lida Pelletier
Dr. Harold Perkinson
Harvey N. Wiener
Richard J. Zappone

## Wolcott Lions Club
Michael G. Ardry
Warren Barratt
James Briglia
Thomas Caisse
Nicholas E. D'Agostino
Michael Denegris
David Desaulniers
John Gagain, PDG
John Gagain, Jr.
Rose Gagain
Richard Helaire
Joseph Hutnik
Joseph Minervini
Herman Mueller
Joseph Paulo
Walter H. Sherman III
Rene Wisler

## Yalesville-Wallingford Lions Club
Michael Kraskowski

## Lions Clubs of District 23-B

## Avon Lions Club
Donald E. Griswold, PDG
Russell C. Peckham
Richard A. Stahl

## Barkhamsted Lions Club
Francis Lattizori

## Berlin Lions Club
Milton Abrams
David Alkas
Robert Anderson
Marilyn Asal
Robert Asal
Thomas Basile
William Bighinatti

Robert Boryczki
Theodore Boryczki, PDG
Stephen Bruno
Tamlyn Campanelli
Armand Catelli
Robert Christensen
Robert Dabrowski
Thomas Dennis
Edward DeVivo
Anthony Di Mugno
William Diskin
Joseph Dornfried
Robert Dornfried
Fred Ferrero
Robert Ferris
Carmen Gagliardi
Anthony Gandolfo
Donald Geschimsky
Warren Glatz
Matthew Gut
Carmelo Guzzardi
Ernest Hall
Thomas Hall
Clifford Hamilton
Peter Hansen
Harry Hillstrand
Earl Johansen
Donald King
Richard King
Paul Kristopik
Clifford Landry, Jr.
William Lennehan
Felice Lupia
Norman Martinelli
Louis F. Marzi, Jr.
Jeff Matson
Richard Miller
George Ondrick, PDG

Joseph Pegolo
Harry Pentore
Roger Perno
Robert Peters
Christopher H. Porter
Robert Randall
Raymond Riggot
Burton Robinson
Robert Robinson
Anthony Rosso
Albino Simeone
Nicholas Stefanou
Thomas Stregowski
Dominic Tamburro
Raymond Victor
Robert A. Weiss, PDG
Henry Welna
Gordon Wicke
Earl Wicklund
Cliff Williams
Richard Yale
Alfred Yukna

**Bethlehem Lions Club**
Patrick Harte

**Bloomfield Lions Club**
Cynthia S. Bercowetz
Thomas A. Hubbs, PDG
Sydney T. Schulman, PDG

**Bristol Lions Club**
Arline Frankowski

**Canaan Northwest Lions Club**
Marilyn Minacci, PDG

**Colebrook Lions Club**
Peter DiMartino
William R. Hayes
Theodore H.J. Veling

**East Granby Lions Club**
Henry G. Ernst
George A. Lomnitzer, PDG

**East Hartford Lions Club**
James Gould
Michael McGuiness

**Glastonbury Lions Club**
George C. Perron

**Hartford County Fidelco Lions Club**
James O'Rourke, M.D.

**Hartford Evening Lions Club**
Luis R. Centeno
Francesco Medina, PDG

**Hartford Multi-National Lions Club**
Elba Cruz Schulman

**Hartland Lions Club**
Constance G. Baril
Paul Crunden
Ann Parmelee

**Harwinton Lions Club**
Dave French
Joseph J. Kulhowvick
David Neri
Regina Neri
Alfred Rondano
Francis Rossbach
Harry R. Schuh
Robert E. Seifel
Colleen Tomasko
J. Matthew Tomasko
Robert W. Wesneski

**Marlborough Lions Club**
Donald Lack
Glen Warstock

**New Britain Evening Lions Club**
Kenneth V. Olson, PDG

**New Britain Lions Club**
Frank Aparo
Todd Bower
Alan Daninhirsch, PDG
Judy Daninhirsch
Joseph Gustin
Maryann Lagocki
Michael E. LaRose
Frank Marrocco
Helen McInerny
Vincent Mercadante
John Miller
Faith Ondrick
Dr. Stephen Polezonis, DG
Harriet Raffel
Otto P. Strobino, PID
W. Keith Wuerthner, PDG

**New Milford Lions Club**
George C. Fitch, PDG
Robert L. Southworth, PDG
Elmer Worthington

**Norfolk Lions Club**
Paul Hosch

**Plainville Lions Club**
Anthony Caparrelli, PDG

**Plymouth Lions Club**
Cecile Dzielinski

**Rocky Hill Lions Club**
Gina Barry
Jacqueline Fischer
Raymond Flebeau
Frank C. Frago
William Speed

**Sharon Lions Club**
Carl Marshall

**Simsbury Lions Club**
Richard Bahre
John H. Bannan
Marianne D. Bannan, PDG
Jeffrey Carlson
Harolyn J. Erickson
Robert C. Gauthier
George R. Matt
D. Randall Packer
Lewis Tolan

**South Windsor Lions Club**
Betty Osborne

**Southington Lions Club**
William Adams
John Ausanka
Michael Bohigian
Michael Bunko
Richard Burbank
Carole DiPietro
Joseph DiPietro
Robert Gray
Robert F. Hubner
John J. Kania
David Kelley
Joseph Krajewski
Richard P. Muth
George Sanchez
M. Edward Sauer
Edward Schlegel
Norman Schoeler
Edward S. Smith, PDG
Robert St. George
Donald Voorhees

**Terryville Lions Club**
David J. Barbieri
Arthur Blum
Kevin Ceritello
William Custer
Richard Foote, PDG
Wayne Hunt
Russell E. Jacobs
Leonard C. Johnson
Deborah McGrane
Robert C. Nelson
George C. Skilton
Oscar Suarez
James Walker
George Wartonick
Thomas Zagurski

**Torrington Lions Club**
Elaine M. Dzurnak
Jean Gelormino

**Unionville Lions Club**
Merrill Carpenter
Richard Leide
Ralph Tallmadge

**Watertown Lions Club**
John J. Barrett
Bernard C. Beauchamp
Tina M. Bertotti
Walter M. Bertotti
Ronald Blanchard
Richard O. Clark, Sr.
Kenneth DeRego
Allan W. Dodge, PDG
Andy Gionta
David W. Jean
Robert H. LaBonne, Sr.
Craig Lamphier
Henry L. Long, Jr.

Peter C. McHale
ONeil St. Onge
William E. Taylor
Daniel A. Uitti, PDG
Anthony J. Varuolo

**West Hartford Lions Club**
Joseph Balboni
C. Gregory Burt
Craig Carucci
Edward J. Dillon, PDG
Gerard Gosselin
William F. Hedges
Edward Krakauskas
Ernest Moseley III
Arthur W. Ney
Lucy Ann Raffa
Gerald Sandler
Richard Violette

**Windsor Lions Club**
Angelo J. Salvatore, PDG

**Windsor Locks Lions Club**
Fern Alderman
John J. Boscarino
Brian S. Brennan
Richard W. Brennan
William C. Hamilton
Patricia Julian
Carolyn A. Messier, PDG
Normand J. Messier, PDG
David Renouf
Polly Ann Storms
Ronald F. Storms, PDG
Scott A. Storms, PID
James Wrinn

**Winsted Lions Club**
E. Joan Capitanio

**Woodbury Lions Club**
John (Jack) Naylor

**Lions Clubs of District 23-C**

**Bolton Regional Lions Club**
Yvonne Bass
Virginia Bergstrom
Donna Caliskan
Barbara Gouchoe
Margaret Maneggia

**Colchester Lions Club**
David Dander
Lori Dickinson
Norm Dupuis
Leo Glemboski
Eric Jacobson, PDG
Joseph Korostek
Paul Picard
Irving Plotkin
George Salpietro
Aaron Turner

**Columbia Lions Club**
Charles K. Ailinger
Henry Beck
Myron Berkowitz
Robert Bogue
Wesley Burnham
Thomas P. Cantara
Marc J. Czarnowski
George Evans
John Evans
James W. Falconieri
Norman A. Jolie
Richard P. Lange
William C. Maine
Carol Marchigiano
Edward F. Mathieu

Richard Z. Mlyniec
William D. Osmond
George E. Peters
Gary Pillion
Alfred Schatz, Jr.
Joseph Szegda
Dean T. Toepfer
Raymond Trainor
Merton Wolff

**Coventry Lions Club**
Dick Giggey
William Kelleher
Al Langner

**Cromwell Lions Club**
Frederick Curtin, PDG

**Danielson Lions Club**
David P. Burgess, PDG
Herb Elliott
David St. Martin, PDG

**Deep River-Chester Lions Club**
Arthur J. Davies, PDG
Lenny R. Divis, Jr.
Pidge Gill
Paul Knudsen
Michael Nucci
C. Talcott Scovill
Mark Tarpill
Silvio J. Zanni

**East Haddam Community Lions Club**
Virginia Bowman
Linda Bradshaw
Marion Canfield
Dena Czapiewski
Dorothy B. Davies
Celia Delehanty

Audrey Martin
Diane (Pettit) Bielski, PDG
Alice Sabo

**East Haddam  Lions Club**
Walter Bielot
Edgar H. Bishop
Raymond Churchill
Tim Curtis
William Delehanty
Edwin DesRosiers
Frederick G. Gagnon
Walter Golec
John Kromish
Paul Maxwell
Albert Sievers

**East Hampton Lions Club**
Joseph Becker, Jr.
Ronald G. Brady
Ron Christopher
Friedrich "Fritz" Hecht
Theodore Krogh
William McLaughlin
Frank Mott
Ralph V. Nesci
Charles Nichols
Donald Shurtleff
Robert B. Tourville, PDG

**East Hampton Village Lions Club**
Mary Krogh, PDG
John Robida

**Essex Lions Club**
Kurt Battey
David Brainard
James Bross
Daniel J. Burnham

Hon. Edward Domnarski
Edward S. Domnarski, Jr.
William Hawke
Phil Lombardi
William J. Moran III
Gino Origlia
Robert J. Vitari

**Griswold Regional Lions Club**
Bruce Atwater
Lindsay Atwater
William D. Graham
Claire Maynard
Lawrence A. McLean, Jr.
Joel Zuckerbraun

**Groton Lions Club**
William Foreman
Stacy A. Haines
Perley L. Kent, Jr.
R. B. Kent
Jan Miller
Henry O'Reilly, Jr.
Henry O'Reilly, Sr.
David P. Rose
Kenneth R. Smith
Ron  Stoven
John Nicholas Utz
Mark  Williams

**Haddam Lions Club**
Ray Dennis
Dave Esposito
Mark Stephens

**Hebron Lions Club**
Bernice Barrasso
Charles Barrasso
Dr. Steve Beauchene
George Blain

Philip Bradley
Peter Cafazzo
Ramon Campbell
Donald David
Donald Dion
Norman Dorval
Betty Dove
Peter Fleig
Wayne Fruke
William Garrison
Catherine Gerke
Richard Griswold
John Johnson, Jr.
Martin Kalhok
Bruce Kalom
Richard Keefe
Mike Kozyra
Joseph P. Krist
Simon Lebo
Robert Lee
William Levy
Robert M. Musson
Ted Powell
Ernest J. Reed
Aaron (Steve) Reid
Robert Schadtle
Robert Schadtle
Marian Severn
David Snow
John Soderberg, Jr.
John Soderberg
Richard Spadarzewski
Donald Spragg
William Stelzner, Jr.
Tony Sylvester

Duane Totten
Jeffrey Watt
Janina Wasilausky

**Lebanon Lions Club**
Francis Adamcewicz, PDG
Thomas Conley, Sr.
James Kenneth Craig, PDG
Ronald Drum
Gregg LaFontaine
Richard Lataille
Richard Tanger
Joseph Thibeault

**Ledyard Lions Club**
Eileen G. Akers
Barbara Bostwick
Theodora Grayson
Marjorie Heath
Garnet Hubley
Lee Kennedy
Barbara A. Lewis
Lynne Magee
Carol McKeehan
Peter Olsen
John E. Provencal
Peter J. Roberts
Heidi A. Ross
Frank J. Rowe
Thomas A. Santos
James H. Seaton
Dorothy Smith
Duncan R. Smith
Roger S. Van Dyke
Sally J. Van Dyke
Judith A. Zeppieri
Ronald Zeppieri

**Lyme-Old Lyme Lions Club**
Tom Clements
Kenneth Kitchings
Frank Maranda
William McCaffrey
Donald M. McCue
Marilyn L. Rubitski

**Mansfield Lions Club**
Gordon B. Allan
Albert C. Bollen
Hartley Fitts
Donald M. Nolan
George R. Norman

**Middlefield Lions Club**
Donald Birdsey
Russell E. "Cy" Fowler
John Tabor

**Middletown Lions Club**
Raymond Daniels
Wallace Haas
Kent Hasbrouck
Cyril C. Jackson
George V. Keithan Sr.
Martin Knight
Joseph E. Milardo, Jr.
Thomas H. Moore
Audrey J. Scotti

**Montville Lions Club**
Patricia Dougherty
Phyllis J. Eichelberg
Bruce Engelman
Donna Ganong
Alexandra Gregory
Diane Grise
Albert H. Ouellette, Jr.
Marion H. Ouellette

Herb C. Plotnick
Shaun Tine
Richard L. Wilson
Theodore T. Wisniewski, Sr.

**Mystic Lions Club**
William V. Abt
Rudolph Brandt
Arthur R. Bray
Nanette Burdick
Brian E. Cote
Mark J. Densmore
Herbert A. Holmstedt
Paul E. Jalbert
Alan R. Jensen
Frederick Leonard
Patricia McSorley
David U. Page III
Abby F. Parkinson
William F. Shea, PDG
Robert Valenti

**New London Lions Club**
Samuel-Jay Linder
Joseph L. Raub, PID

**Niantic Lions Club**
William K. Allen II, PDG
Richard (Ken) Balaska
Gerard P. Burkhardt
Terry Carucci
James E. Curley
Ralph Fortuna
Howard W. Parkhurst
William L. Tamburro
Angela R. Tanguay
Edgar J. Tanguay
Thomas W. Walsh, Jr.
Shirley P. Ward
James S. Zoldy

**North Stonington Lions Club**
Warren Edward Bishop

**Norwich Lions Club**
Rubin Bokoff
William Bomomi
William Bonomi
Henry Congdon
John Connor, PDG
Henry Daigneault
Robert C. Denesha
Joyce Dereski
Peter Dereski, Jr.
Nazzario DiBattista
Thomas J. Fitzpatrick
Charles E. Gagne
J. Clifford Gagne
Mark Gagne
Albert Gualtieri
Dino Gualtieri
Mario P. Gualtieri, PDG
Arthur F. Hawkins
Benjamin J. Kustesky
Theodore Levitsky
Abraham E. Lorinsky
Sidney Nagel
William F. O'Neil, Jr., PDG
Witter O'Neil
Joel J. Ragovin, PDG
Sue J. Ragovin
James E. Sheehan
Rose M. Slaga
Walter Teper
Victor Walka
Donald Zuccardy
Norwich LionessClub
Ida DiBattista
Flora O'Neil

**Old Saybrook Lions Club**
Shirley  Annunziata

**Pawcatuck Lions Club**
Deane Beverly
David Capizzano
John Finegan
Calvin L. Jones
William McGaw
Jeffrey McKernan
Belsita Miceli
Angelo S. Miceli, PDG
James P. O'Boyle
Joseph A. Pescatello, PDG
Stanley Prachniak

Plainfield Lions Club
Thomas Beausoleil
Edward W. Chviek, Jr.
Henry Daley
Arthur L. Nadeau

**Pomfret Lions Club**
Clifford F. Buttermark

**Portland Lions Club**
Guy Lardizzone
Richard Larke
Edward Pinunsky
Bruce Schoenbern

**Putnam Lions Club**
Ed Briere
Bernard Gilbert
Francis Gregoire, PDG
Ronald A. Hemingway, PDG
Denise LaFleur

**Salem Lions Club**
George Ziegra

**Waterford Lions Club**
Arthur Perry
Earl Peters
James Radack

**Waterford Regional Lions Club**
Judy L. Dousis
Sandra Welles

**Westport Lions Club**
Robert E. Moss

**Willimantic Lions Club**
Richard Case, PDG
Edwin Fisher, PDG
Susan Fisher
Roger Hence
Fred LeBeau
Keith Lemire
Frank P. Mauro, PDG
Shirley Mauro
Richard Oat
Richard Quinones
Gunnel Stenberg
Cynthia Tillinghast

## Appendix J—LCIF Melvin Jones Fellowship Recipients

### Lions Clubs of District 23-A

**Ansonia Lions Club**
Peter Aquila
Thomas M Duffy
Harry Feinberg
Henry J Gambaccini
Brad Harris
Michael J Impellitteri Jr
Joseph A La Rocco
Peter Lovermi
Delbert H Rau
Constandino Tomasella

**Beacon Falls Lions Club**
Richard Card
Patsy Delvecchio
Leonard Greene
Joseph A Poirier
Peter Rydzik
Raymond Shea

**Bethany Lions Club**
Arnold Cary
Donald W Duman
Bruce Hescock
George Mc Donnell
Edward Rostowsky Jr
Russell Von Beren

**Bethel Lions Club**
Thomas E Babcock
Tulio Belardinelli
James Mannion
Charles Steck III

**Branford Lions Club**
Amos Barnes
Pamela Burgh
Steven Burke
John Cushing
James Dornfeld
William Dornfeld
David B Dziura
Donald C Erickson
Edward Farley
Walter C Flesche
Craig Fuchs
Ralph Fuller
Ralph Gagliardi
Richard G Hyder
Brian Thomas Lynch
James H Mendillo
Jerry J Osochowsky
Alex Palluzzi Sr
Debbe Parisi
Hugh J Plunkett Jr
David A Reed
Howard Reitman
Arthur J White
John Wilkinson

**Bridgeport Beardsley Lions Club**
Pat Notarnicola
Louise M Smith

**Bridgeport Host Lions Club**
Theodore H Bresky
Milton S Cohen
Joseph J Feher

Philip G Flaker
Joseph W Ganim
Robert W Logan
John A Lynn
John B Mc Kiernan
Patrick A Pallotto
Elaine M Phillips
Mark A Schickler DPM

**Bridgeport North Bridgeport Lions Club**
Dom Di Camillo
Robert Dortenzio Sr
Frank J Duzy
Richard H Krodel
William Minty

**Brookfield Lions Club**
Richard Amorossi
Ernest J Bendana
Patrick M Blanchfield
Richard B Blessey
George R Brown Jr
Robert Dougherty
Alan P Gereg
Robert E Hoxie
David C Keefe
Francis Kerwin Jr
James D Kovacs
Richard Lacava
Anthony G Licursi
Mark S Lyon
Ronald H Mattson
David J Moissonnier
Gerald J Nindorf
Candice Smith
Allan D Sniffin
Robert Sorisio
Raymond T Sullivan

**Cheshire Lions Club**
Andrew G Anderson
Colette M Anderson
Theresa B Canas
Carol A Erasmus
Marjorie Jerin
Judson W Moore
Temah Reisenberg
James Rodgers
Edward C Stalmann
Agnes T Strobino

**Danbury Lions Club**
Mohammed R Alam
John J Allen
Thomas H Barnola
Keith R Beaver
Joan G Bielizna
Howard Blayney
J Thayer Bowman Jr
R Milton Boyce
Christopher Burns
Edward G Butterfield
John J Casamento
Richard S Casden
John K Cooper
Frances J Evans
Beth Ann Fetzer
Thomas A Frizzell
Charles Frosch
Emil J Fusek
S Louis Ginsberg
Catherine Golankiewicz
George E Good
Eric Gottschalk
Morris Gross
Crawford H Harmon
Ernest C Harrington
Ervie S Hawley Jr

Gerald J Hofmann
Joseph D Hornak
James Humphreville
Cathleen G Huse-Burns
John E Hyatt
Daniel P Jowdy
Bernadette M Kallas
Michael A Kallas
Warren Levy
Boyd O Losee
Robert E Lovell
Nancy E Manion
Louis G Matthews
Emanuel A Merullo
Lyn R Meyers
Harold L Michael
Doris F Miloscia
Frank P Molinaro
Paul Mooradd
Hubert V Morgan
John J Murphy
George F Nicol
Thomas Nolan
Peter J Olivo
Vincent P Pannozzo
Carl A W Rogers Jr
Noel C Roy
Kenneth G Saloom
J Roger Schmiedel
Michael R Seri
Kathleen S Shea
Wayne J Shepperd
Harry V Sturdevant
Carl Susnitzky
Kenneth A Taylor
Helene V Thompson
Nerville H White
Arthur E Wilson

Robert J Yamin
Dianne E Yamin

**Darien Lions Club**
Thomas E Bauder
William M Carello
Rocco S Cingari
William Mills
Robert Roth
Frank W Sherwood
William Ward
William Ziegler

**Devon Lions Club**
Alan J Donaldson
Richard E Dowin
Perry Kokeno
Roger W Martin
Pauline Martin
Russell Palaia

**East Haven Lions Club**
Thomas Sudac

**Easton Lions Club**
G Stephen Glaser
John W Harris
Charles W Lynch
Robert Monk

**Fairfield Lions Club**
Michael Gelormino
Joseph L Lavieri
Robert Loftus
William A Lopez
Philo S Shelton
Henry F Smith

**Georgetown Lions Club**
Michael S Cardillo
Patrick Fortin
Edward J Mc Carty
Fred Miller

Louis John Nazzaro
Carmen Nazzaro
Anthony J Nazzaro
Barry L Reade
John Howard Slade

**Greenwich Lions Club**
David Albert
Bruce Gordon
Peter Imbres
Stanley J Klein Jr
H David Noble
Halford Park,Jr
Pat M Pulitano
Eugene R Salvatore
Stanley A Thal

**Greenwich Western
Greenwich Lions Club**
Joseph P Filanowski
John Retzler

**Guilford Lions Club**
Alan Browne
John Offredi
Winfield A Redman
Frank Salzano

**Hamden Lions Club**
Charles Aitro
Thomas G Athan
George Conquest
Mario A Cusano
Gennaro De Lucia
Alfred Marzullo

**Madison Lions Club**
George A Basler
Richard F Borner
Harold E Cantrell
Burton R Chalker Jr
Marinus deJongh

David T Dean
Anthony Fappiano Md
Ronald B Hall
Ronald B Hick
Richard E Kennedy
Anthony Lazzari
David M Longobucco
R Russell Martin Md
Thomas Mc Carthy
Henry Robinson II
Harold Soars III
Louis Tresselt Jr

**Meriden Lions Club**
Lawrence M Biller
George Carabetta Sr
Joseph Crowell
Peter J Gostyla
Vincent T Mule Sr
David W Parke
William D Phillips Jr
Rene H Tompkinson

**Middlebury Lions Club**
Walter K Ahearn
Donald E Regan
Paul J Shea

**Milford Lions Club**
Gioacchino De Nicolo
Ronald M Goldwyn
Ann Valerio
Joseph Valerio

**Monroe Lions Club**
Raymond Mc Padden Sr
Albert Stoccatore

**Naugatuck Lions Club**
Dominic Alegi Jr
Patrick Joseph Farrell
John Kenworthy Jr

Robert E Lauer
Kanayo N Rupwani
Mario V Schiaroli
Richard Schiaroli

**New Canaan Lions Club**
Curry E Ford
George Friedrichs
David Van Buskirk

**New Fairfield Lions Club**
Gene Arcery
Joseph R Bates
Nicholas Bisaccia
Philip A Cammarano
Donald Cleary
Michael J Gillotti Jr
Al Gouveia
Richard T Grant
Frank Machado
Wesley G Marsh
Robert N Matarazzo
Robert M Redenz
John Rooney
Francis Shea
Richard Smith
Theodore Tegmier Jr
James V Trotta
Wayne Van Treuren

**New Fairfield Candlewood
Lions Club**
Frances Allan
Donna Bassriel
Hillery Bassriel
Frederick J Bourne
Lovie D Bourne
Robert L Farella
Robert B Gyle III
Jean Hazard

Alfred P Hazard
John Hodge
Alice M Hoxie
Regina M Knopf
Marlene F Lamendola
Gerald Platania
M Jodi Rell
Martin Steinberg

**New Haven Lions Club**
Frank P Abbadessa
Lewis W Adams
Herbert E Anderson
Walter A Anderson
Alan C Bennett
Alan M Bennett
James B Bennett
Joan C Bennett
Peter C Bennett
Salvatore G Brancato
Albert E Carman
Ruth B Carr
Luca E Celentano
Kenneth P Douglas
John E Downs
Milton J Foley Jr
Lester E Hintz
Theodore F Hyatt
John M Lyons
Walter H Palkowski
Edward J Popkins
David R Rice
E Bernard Roop
Lawrence J Shields
William J Smith
Paul J Strawhince
James E Traester

**Newtown Lions Club**
Paul Arneth

Winthrop Ballard
Gerald Frawley
Thomas Goosman
William A Honan Jr
Paul H Krueger
Carl Swanhall
Robert Tynan
Gordon Williams

**North Haven Lions Club**
Marie-Anne Barnhart
Michael A Pace,Jr
Robert B Petrie

**Norwalk Lions Club**
James M Bryson Jr
Joseph T Daley
John Dunlop
Edward Farris
John Jablonski
Donald J Miloscia
Alex Rissolo
Roy Rumore
Andrew J Santella
Thomas H Stein
John Thompson

**Old Greenwich Lions Club**
Benjamin H Bryon Jr
Robert E Button
Douglas N Carlson
Isabelle Cox
Warren J Dennison
Linsley Dodge
C Carleton Gisborne
Henry D Hubbard
Benito A Menegon
Allen O'Farrel
Edwin J O'Mara Jr
Paul P Palmer

D Gifford Reed
William B Zboray

**Orange Lions Club**
Antonette Carollo
Robert M Drobish
Marian Drobish
Robert J Gambino
Peter Leonarz
Marion Nugent
William A Phillips
Jeannette V Phillips
Frederick Pucillo
James M White

**Oxford Lions Club**
James Biondi
Thomas P Biondi
William H Lund

**Prospect Lions Club**
Rick Brown
Jeff Slapikas

**Ridgefield Lions Club**
Jerry Ambrose
Diane Brautigam
Roy Cogswell
Irene A De Mita
Lewis J Finch
Mary Foyt
Harold N Hval
Robert L Johnson
Leo Lardie
Michael J Liberta Jr
Anna A Lossius
Linda Maggs
Edward J Martin
Romeo Petroni
Francis Segesman
Gary C Smith

Lou Ann Smith
Henry R Wilson
Peter V Yanity

**Seymour Lions Club**
Alice Carroll
Frank De Leo
Toby Konowitz
Theodore Rogol
Rose Marie T Spatafore

**Southbury Lions Club**
Henry J Bassett
Francis J Guarrera
Krishnalal Nanavaty
Anne Nanavaty
George Stone Sr
Edwin P Wilson

**Stamford North Stamford Lions Club**
James H Bryson
Kenneth C Sachs
Salvatore Zaccagnino

**Stamford Springdale Lions Club**
David R Pia
Clark Robertson
James Scott

**Stratford Lions Club**
Ralph Fladd
Frederic C Kaeser
Harold C Lovell Jr
Edmond Owen

**Trumbull Lions Club**
Michael J Del Re Jr

**Trumbull Center Lions Club**
Stephen B Brickel
George M Fraina

Thomas E Johnson
J Robert Lutz
Mark Smith
Chester A Sobolewski

**Waterbury Lions Club**
Edwin F Couch
Michael Granatuk
Robert P Lyman
Francis A Petrillo
Gary L Rosengrant
William J Summa Jr
William L Tobin

**West Haven Lions Club**
Edward Voss

**Westport Lions Club**
Fred Garrington
Harold J Mc Gill

**Wolcott Lions Club**
Louis Albert
Michael G Ardry
Vernon Bedell
Brian Borghesi
Thomas Centinaro
William E Chasse
Nicholas E D'Agostino
James Dolan
Gene Fercodini Sr
John R Gagain
Joseph Hutnik
Raymond Mahoney
John Mazurek
Herman F Mueller
Raymond O'Connor
George M Phelan
Richard Renkun
Joe Santos
Walter H Sherman III

Joseph Silva
Brian Tynan
Edward Wilensky

**Yalesville-Wallingford Lions Club**
Peter G Pfau
Frederic A Pfau
George E Talbot
Joyce Wruck
Gunther W Wruck

**District 23-A**
Bette Mc Loughlin
Gene G Poulos,Sr

**Lions Clubs of District 23-B**

**Avon Lions Club**
Robert B August
Dominic P Bogino
Maurice A Dutcher
George W England
Donald E Griswold
Ruth A Griswold
Russell C Peckham
Richard W Price
Ernest I Rettig
Rene A Ruez
Otto R Ruppert
Duane E Starr
Jeffrey K Suter
Louis Tremblay
Raymond Zacchera
Heidi Zacchera

**Berlin Lions Club**
Milton Abrams
Robert R Anderson
Robert Asal Sr
Thomas Basile Jr

William Bighinatti
Theodore S Boryczki
Tamlyn Campanelli
Armand Catelli
Robert P Dabrowski
Valier J Daigle
Edward De Vivo
Thomas E Dennis
William Diskin
Robert Dornfried
Robert A Ferris
Carmen O Gagliardi
Donald P Geschimsky
Warren W Glatz
Edward Goodrow
Matthew Gut
Thomas Hall
Ernest F Hall
Clifford H Hamilton
Harry Hillstrand
Earl Johansen
George Keithan
Chester F Kelpinski
Donald C King
Ralph King
William F Klein
Clifford A Landry Jr
Felice Lupia
Joseph F Lutkus
Norman Martinelli
Jeff Matson
William J Mayer
Ernest E Mildrum
George M Ondrick
Frank O'Rourke
Joseph Pegolo
Harry Pentore
Arnold Pfeil
Christopher Hale Porter

Robert Randall
Raymond Riggott
Anthony Rosso
Nunzio Rosso
Vincent Tedeschi
Raymond Victor
Robert A Weiss
Henry Welna
Gordon Wicke
Earl H Wicklund
Cliff Williams
Joan M Williams
Richard S Yale
Alfred Yukna

**Bethlehem Lions Club**
Donald Banks
John D Botelle,Sr
T Stanley Doran
Robert A Overton
George A Precourt
Herbert I Reichenbach
Arthur L Severson
Sherwood Wright

**Bloomfield Lions Club**
Cynthia Bercowetz
Thomas A Hubbs
Sydney T Schulman
Ronald H Wolpoe

**Bristol Lions Club**
Le Roy Anderson
Michael Nestico
Ralph R Strong

**Burlington Lions Club**
Earl P Carini
Cecil B Turton

**Canaan Northwest Lions Club**
Marilyn Minacci

**Canton Lions Club**
Gerald A Coutu
Don Lannon
Donald K Scott
Joseph Sokolowski
Stella Sokolowski

**Colebrook Lions Club**
William R Hayes
Jeannette Jakubiak
Theodore Vaill,Jr
Theodore H J Veling
Raymond A Winn

**East Granby Lions Club**
Roger Baillargeon
Ernest D Chagnon
Chester M De Gray
Francis Del Principe
Lee P Echert
Henry G Ernst
Gordon Granger
Charles F Hunderlach Jr
Joseph Illouz
W Victor Jensen
George A Lomnitzer
Anna P Lomnitzer
Charles E Moritz
Francis A Rinaldi
Robert J Roncari
Benjamin Rosenberg
Louis Seymour

**East Hartford Lions Club**
Kenneth Carrier
Steven Crecco

Raymond T Donovan
Donald S Gale
James K Gould Jr
Pamela E Howes
Herbert O Johnson
John Johnston
Gerard Mogielnicki
Kathleen Randall
John Reilly
Russell W Richards
Donald Samartino
David Schwartz
Harvey H Sirota
Clifford L Symington
Gary L Vrooman
Richard Willard

**East Windsor Lions Club**
Sidney B Balf
Donald Bartlett
Walter E Colton
Daniel T Golden
Shep Kiernan
Anthony J Muska
John F Parda
Charles Rybeck
Thomas J Sargent
Richard Stathers
John Texeira
H Stuart Woodard

**Elmwood Lions Club**
Lucien A Beaumier
Walter J Matt

**Enfield Lions Club**
Joseph F Cimino
Gordon Holmes
Patricia C Holmes
Jim Hosey
Ronald E Jones

**Farmington Lions Club**
Charles H Kaman

**Glastonbury Lions Club**
Philip J Baribault Jr
Richard Belmont
Raymond J Buckley
Frank B Dibble
John P Goyette
J Wallace Hart
John R Heacock
Michael Mc Guiness
Thomas J Mulryan
Paul Pagliughi
George C Perron
Richard M Skiba
Brian Tyrol

**Goshen Lions Club**
Edward G Dailey
Otto W Goepfert
Fredric W Wadhams

**Granby Lions Club**
Thomas Sullivan

**Hartford Evening Lions Club**
Luis R Centeno
Lillian Centeno
Robert D Clark
Juan R Colon
Carlos Cruz
Wilfredo Cruz
Nora E De Leon-Clark
Francesco Medina
Maria A Ortiz Medina
Manuel Reyes
Nelson Rodriguez
Raul Rodriguez
Miguel Satut
Gerardo Zayas Jr

## Hartford Host Lions Club
Allen Beavers
Ervin Booker
Marshall William Elman
John Carlock Laflin
Edward Nordstrom

## Hartford Multi-National Lions Club
Aurelia R Hicks
Theolyn Hicks-Young

## Hartland Lions Club
Gerald E Baril
Paul J Eseppi
James Parmelee

## Harwinton Lions Club
John H Audia
Walter T Bell
David French
Andrew Kasznay Jr
Bruce Mosher
David Roger Neri
Frank A Rondano
Lloyd T Shanley
Robert W Wesneski

## Kent Lions Club
Charles J Tremont
Robert A Ward

## Litchfield Lions Club
Clarence Baldwin
Joseph Frascarelli
Donald K Peck

## Manchester Lions Club
George De Cormier

## Marlborough Lions Club
Robert J Farley
Donald Lack
Richard Shevchenko

Robert Vontell

## Morris Lions Club
August J Seeholzer

## New Britain Lions Club
Louis Amodio
Louis Gerald Amodio Jr
John P Amodio
Steven D Anderson
Frank M Aparo
Douglas B Bray
Martin S Cherlin
Paul T Czepiga
Richard D'Ambrosio
Alan Daninhirsch
Judith Daninhirsch
Elizabeth Elia
Seth Feigenbaum
John W Fisher
Joseph J Grcevic
Joseph J Gustin
T Wesley Hickcox
William E Hopke
Kenneth Kollmeyer
Susan Kuchman
Michael E La Rose
Frank D Marrocco
Helen M Mc Inerney
Vincent D Mercadante
John Miller
Judith E Olson
Faith Ondrick
Lewis M Platt
Harriet Raffel
Spencer B Reynolds
Abbott Schultz
Wayne Schultz
Donald W Schulze
Arnold P Schwartz

Robert C Soule
Robert J Stadler
Otto P Strobino
Craig K Welch
Keith Wuerthner

**New Britain Evening Lions Club**
Kenneth V Olson

**New Hartford Lions Club**
Carl A Cassella
Donald Govotski

**New Milford Lions Club**
John Buczek
Robert A Carlson
Charles J Chapin
George C Fitch
Maurice Grossenbacher
John Jack Moore
J Russell Nicolas
C Robert Ohmen
Sal Passarelli
Benjamin H Stone
Gabor Szilagyi
Joe Tobin
Charles Toussaint
William B Tremont, Sr
Edmund Turner
Michael James Wilcox
Joseph Wiser
Mark Wiston
Elmer Worthington

**Newington Lions Club**
Raymond Beauregard
Adrianne Brown
Kenneth T Brown
Paul J Goines
Leopold M Guertin
Warren F Hall

Karen Hall
John Igielski
Stanley Martinelli
Leonard J Montanari
Burton R Wixson

**Norfolk Lions Club**
Roy Johnson
Sidney W Toomey

**Plainville Lions Club**
Harry Appell
Michael T Blanchard
Anthony Caparrelli
George Hutchinson Cooper Jr
Donald C Green
Kragg F Kysor
Melvin E Lyons
Edward A Munn
Stephen N Polezonis
Bruce Smyth
Wilfred L Zerfas

**Plymouth Lions Club**
Lois B Barnes
Viola Dzielinski

**Rocky Hill Lions Club**
Raymond Barrett
Gina Barry
Neil F Ciarcia
Paul G Delaney
Raymond P Flebeau
Neil Gerald Gordes
Natalie Longo
Eugene P Rohr
Phillip Theroux

**Simsbury Lions Club**
Richard A Bahre
John H Bannan
Marianne Bannan

Vern Ferwerda
Bernard E Francis
George R Matt
Lewis E Tolan

**South Windsor Lions Club**
Edward John Curtin
Sia Dowlatshahi
John Habif
Raymond Neal
John Olem
Donald Padegimas
Richard Plank
Mark Saternis

**Southington Lions Club**
Alfred H Bussett
William S Jerin
John Kania
Joseph Z Krajewski
Ralph S Laribee
Edward S Smith

**Suffield Lions Club**
Francis B Christian
Ronald C Corriveau

**Terryville Lions Club**
William O Allread
David J Barbieri
Charles R Bombard
Timothy L Ceritello
Glenda J Conopask
Steve Daigle
Gerald E Doty
Richard J Foote
Frank L Fuller Jr
Leonard C Johnson
Robert W Johnson
Linda Konopaske
Stephen Kopcha

Robert Leroux
Deborah J Mc Grane
Robert Pelz
Francis M Scott
Kevin Squires
James Walker

**Thomaston Lions Club**
Robert Brink
Joseph Lizotte

**Torrington Lions Club**
Ray Archambault
Donato Di Virgilio
Ralph Dolan
Phil Dzurnak
John Gelormino Jr
Paul Herrick
James Hillman
Nelson Hilpert
Adelbert Latulipe
Norman E Ne Jaime
Rocco Palladino
Marilyn A Plaskiewicz
Herman Weingart

**Trinity College Lions Club**
Andrew W Szilvasy

**Unionville Lions Club**
Everett Arnold
Weston L Barnes
David Borg
David Merrills
Walter C Nicksa Jr
John J Smolen
Ralph H Tallmadge
Elsie Tallmadge

**Watertown Lions Club**
Donald C Atwood
John J Barrett
Bernard C Beauchamp

Walter M Bertotti
Ronald M Blanchard
Stephen W Bormolini
Anthony J Brody
Roger A Chace
Richard O Clark
Allan W Dodge
Richard Feliciani
H Dewey Frenger
Andrew Gionta
Philip P Grayeb
Rudolph S Graziano
Eleonora Panvini Grimaldi
Kathleen Hanson
Richard B Harris
David W Jean
Herbert J King
Robert H La Bonne Sr
Joel Labonte
Craig A Lamphier
Henry L Long Jr
Russell A Marcy
Donald R Martell
Peter C Mc Hale
Robert Minicucci
Joseph W  Moody Jr
Gregory Rutledge
O'Neil St Onge
William E Taylor
Daniel A Uitti
Anthony J Varuolo
Raymond E West
George H Wilber
Raymond E Zawislak

**West Hartford Lions Club**
A Fred Basil
Joseph Belanger
Clinton F Billups Sr

Yolanda M Burt
Robert B Clement
Sid Daffner
Edward J Dillon
Nicholas D  Ippedico
John S Lyons
John J Re
James Schwarzhaupt
George E Wolf Jr

**Wethersfield Lions Club**
Gerald S Baxter
Thomas M Leonard
John T Marenholtz
William F Shea

**Windsor Lions Club**
James Babb
Joseph P Bak
Angelo Salvatore

**Windsor Locks Lions Club**
Howard H Aspinwall
Robert F Barberi
Ann Barberi
Joseph Barile
Albert E Barrett
Richard T Barthel
Pamela Bennett
Roderick Bennett Jr
Glenn D Boglisch
Richard W Brennan
Brian S Brennan
Alma Brennan
Albert J Campanelli
Lyle Cate
Ruth M Cate
Wayne Chapple
Cynthia B Cooper
Frederick B  Cousineau

Kathryn E Cousineau
Joseph R D'Alessio
Hugh Donagher
Barbara Donagher
Charles Dugdale
Gary T Fairwood
Edward Ford
Dominick Frank
Saul Goldfarb
Ruth Goldfarb
Douglas Hamilton
William Hamilton
Roger Ignazio
Michael F Jordan
Patricia Julian
Frank Julian
John J Kennedy
Bernard Kulas
John J Lee
Ralph W Leiper
Frank W Logan
Patricia W Marinone
Norman J Messier Jr
Carolyn A Messier
Robert Methot
Barbara Methot
George J Mumblo
Roland Murdock
Roger E Nelson
Richard J O'Leary
Brian S O'Leary
Joseph D Ouellette
William F Pfaffenbichler Jr
R Clifford Randall
David Renouf
Kenneth D Roach
Michael Russo
Robert Santamaria

Sebastian Shonty
Walter F Skrabal
Alan Stegman
Ronald F Storms
Scott A Storms
Dale Storms
Polly Ann Storms
Drew M Storms
Kyle M Storms
William F Sullivan
Edward Tobiasz
Jules Van Schelt
James E Wrinn
Robert P Zdun

**Winsted Lions Club**
Milan M Knight
Virginia Merrill
James Rogers
Blanche Sewell

**Woodbury Lions Club**
William C Barthelmess
Robert Cowles
Ken Deschino
Edward P Grudzien
Donald Heavens
Robert P Keating
Karl Lindahl
Roland L Manzi
John Naylor
Charles J Rehkamp
Ernest F Schempp
Frank Shepard Jr
James Trompeter

**District 23-B**
Eugene R Flaxman
Roberta C Kaman
Sandra Uitti

## Lions Clubs of District 23-C

### Bolton Lions Club
Rodolfo A R Coralli
David J Killian Jr
Loren H Otter

### Bolton Regional Lions Club
Yvonne Alice Bass
Virginia Bergstrom
Bruce S Davies III
Barbara Gouchoe
L Margaret Maneggia

### Clinton Lions Club
Arthur Schubert

### Colchester Lions Club
Marjorie T Adamcewicz
Rita A Anastasio
Edward J Anastasio
Dave Anderson
Virginia Boughton
Fred Briger
Arthur H Brown
Ruby Cohen
Aram Damarjian
William Dickerson
Lori Dickinson
Jack Faski
Leo Glemboski
Joseph Huron
Susan Jacobs
Eric C Jacobson Sr
Barbara K Jacobson
Joseph Korostek
Janet Labella
John A Mc Nichols
Morris W Nirenstein
Charlene Picard
Paul Picard
Irving Plotkin

Cindy Prescott
George J Salpietro
Marie Salpietro
Janet M Saternis
Greg Scott
Edward Sefchik
Edward Rick Sharr Jr
Steven Marvin Shiff
Julianne M Shilosky
Jerome Squire
Arlene R Stover
Frank Suroviak
Aaron Turner
Irene Watson

### Columbia Lions Club
Charles Ailinger
Howard Bates
Norman A Jolie
William D Osmond
Alfred Schatz

### Danielson Lions Club
Rosalie M Boire
David P Burgess
Thomas E Kohl
Earl J Ledoux Jr
Charles Prest
Paulette Sawyer
John T Smith

### Deep River-Chester Lions Club
Douglas Carlson
Arthur J Davies
Margaret Davies
David Thorpe

### Durham Lions Club
Rafael Garcia, Jr
David Gatonska
Philip Slight

## East Haddam Lions Club

Richard Allen Ballek
George F Ballek
Robert Ballek
Edward Barry
Jonathan Bennett
Walter J Bielot
Edgar H Bishop
John Bradshaw
Timothy Cahill
Raymond Churchill
Thomas Comer
Tim T Curtis
William Delehanty
Edwin Des Rosiers
Richard Fiala
Frederick G Gagnon
Vincent Garofalo III
Walter J Golec
Scott Goodspeed
Donald Goss
Mike Halle
Scott W Jezek
Frank X Kehoe
John Kromish
James D Martin
Paul L Maxwell
Thomas Morrison
William Nelson
Michael Pear
Duane Perreault
James Prue
William Quinn
David Roczniak
John Russell
Walter Shields
Albert Sievers
Edward Veselak
John Yeomans

## East Haddam Community Lions Club

Diane D (Pettit) Bielski
Patricia Blaauboer
Barbara A Davis
Eva Davis
Jean M Gagnon
Shea Jezek
Gloria Sikorski
Christina A Sikorski
Dorothy C Wocl

## East Hampton Lions Club

Joseph Becker Jr
Ronald Christopher
Friedrich A Hecht
Theodore Krogh
Arthur Marsden
Ralph Nesci
Robert B Tourville

## East Hampton Village Lions Club

Mary M Krogh
Sandra S Nesci
John Robida

## Essex Lions Club

Joseph G Bombaci
Walter R Budney
Richard F Budney
Gilbert C Burke
Daniel J Burnham
Edward Domnarski Jr
Phil Lombardi Jr

## Griswold Regional Lions Club

Betsy M Arpin
Bruce Atwater
Phyllis R Brown

John Cadarette
William D Graham
Gail M Lemay
Claire R Maynard
Adele Sulik
Joel Zuckerbraun

**Groton Lions Club**
Hugh D Casey
Stacy A Haines
Peter James
Richard B Kent Sr
Perley L Kent
Jan A Miller
Henry O'Reilly Jr
John A Pescatello
Frank Ricci
Edward Stebbins
John N Utz
Domenic L Venditti
James A Zeppieri

**Haddam Lions Club**
Edward D Stites

**Hebron Lions Club**
Charles A Barrasso
Bernice M Barrasso
Steve Beauchene
George O Blain
Peter Cafazzo
Ramon Campbell
Everett J Clark
Donald David
Wilbur Dennis
Donald D Dion
Robert J Dixon Jr
Norman J Dorval
Betty Dove
Wayne P Fruke
R William Garrison

Richard M Griswold
Martin Kalhok
Bruce Kalom
Richard A Keefe
Joseph P Krist
Robert E Lee
Bruce R Mac Bryde
Michael B Mac Bryde
Robert M Musson
John O O'Sullivan
Ernest J Reed
Aaron Reid
Robert Schadtle
John A Soderberg Jr
Richard Spadarzewski
Frederick L Speno
William R Stelzner Jr
Anthony T Sylvester
Duane Totten

**Killingly Quiet Corner Regional Lions Club**
Rosemarie Lee
Timothy Dean Pratt

**Killingworth Lions Club**
Bruce Dodson
Charles Martens
John W Mc Mahon
Charles Morgan
Les Riblet
John Speicher

**Lebanon Lions Club**
Francis A Adamcewicz
Arthur Bender
Charles A Bender
Edward O Clark
Thomas E Conley
Harry Flegert
Christian Hofmann

Alfred A Krause
James A Peay
Philip L Segal

**Ledyard Lions Club**
Leo E Barron
Melvin C Bates
Luther Bess
Donald M Cola
William E Daimler
Raymond Forest Hackett
Harold W Heal
Howard G Kaminske
Walter F Keach
Roger Le Blanc
Edward Lewis
John D Mairs
Alvin M Manter
Leonard J Matzdorff
Donald A Nason
Stephen M Novic
Peter I Olsen
Donald H Pinckney
Ernest V Plantz
John E Provencal
Peter J Roberts
Frank J Rowe
Thomas A Santos
Daniel Sasur
Morris M Smith
Hubert G Sokolski
Richard Tashea
Gordon W Thomson
Roger S Van Dyke
Sally J Van Dyke
Roy K Wagner
Alfred G Williams
Thomas B Wilson
Harold F Zimmermann

**Lyme Old Lyme Lions Club**
James Graybill
Richard Hurley
Raymond Magaldi
Francis J Maranda
Philip E Parcak
Richard Pettit
Robert Regan
Elaine O Wells
Robert A Whitcomb
Barry Williams

**Mansfield Lions Club**
Gordon B Allan
Donald M Nolan
George R Norman
James E Stallard

**Middlefield Lions Club**
Debi S Berry
Thomas G Spencer
Kenneth C Twombly
Alexander Wallach

**Middletown Lions Club**
Cyril C Jackson
Martin George Knight
Audrey J Scotti

**Montville Lions Club**
A Carleton Eichelberg
Phyllis J Eichelberg
Bruce A Engelman
Donald L Fuller
Diana Grise
Robert H Krajewski
Albert H Ouellette Jr
Marion H Ouellette
Herb C Plotnick
Shaun C Tine
Richard Wilson
Theodore T Wisniewski

## Montville Mohegan-Pequot Lions Club
Jacqueline L Becker
Charles Spicer

## Mystic Lions Club
Willaim Abt
Rudolph R Brandt
Nanette Burdick
Raymond Densmore
Mark Densmore
Herbert A Holmstedt
Paul Jalbert
Alan R Jensen
David U Page III
John P Read
William F Shea
Robert Valenti
Russell E Welles

## New London Lions Club
Charles D Fisher
Samuel-Jay Linder
Edward B Neilan
Anthony N Pero
Joseph L Raub
Lawrence H Strickland

## New London Ocean City Lions Club
Lydia L Main

## New London Whaling City Lions Club
R Thad Carmean

## Niantic Lions Club
William K Allen II
R Kenneth Balaska
Gerard P Burkhardt
James E Curley
Ralph Fortuna

Wayne L Fraser
James S Harris
F H Hunt
Gary W Lakowsky
Howard Parkhurst
Robert L Senkow
William L Tamburro
Edgar Tanguay
Angela R Tanguay
Samuel L Vara

## North Stonington Lions Club
Bob Boissevain
Maurice F Browning
Hilaire S Cote
William Holub
Donald R Judge
James H Patton Jr
Charles Robinson

## Norwich Lions Club
Rubin Bokoff
John J Connor
Robert C Denesha
Peter M Dereski
Nozzario Dibattista
William Dougherty
Mark R Gagne
Mario Gualtieri
Albert Gualtieri
Theodore F Levitsky
William F O'Neil Jr
Joel J Ragovin
Susan J Ragovin
Rev Daniel P Reilly
Marvin L Sears
Rose M Slaga
Ernest A Zachae
Donald L Zuccardy

**Old Saybrook Lions Club**
Julia Bernay
Richard Campbell
Kathleen M Delaney
John Peppas

**Pawcatuck Lions Club**
David Capizzano
T Joseph Connors
Ken Craig
Toffie Deeb
John A Fusaro Sr
Calvin Jones
Angelo S Miceli
Belsita T Miceli
Joseph Pescatello
Joseph J Tudisco

**Plainfield Lions Club**
Thomas Beausoleil
Judith Beausoleil
Paul Beausoleil
William Bellavance
Richard L Brisbois
Theodore Coolidge
Robert V Erickson
Roger L Melanson
Arthur L Nadeau
Debra E Pepin
Raymond Theroux

**Pomfret Lions Club**
George Brock
William B Hull
John T Mac Donald

**Portland Lions Club**
Frank L Distefano

**Putnam Lions Club**
Richard Bennett Jr
Edward J Briere
Leia Faucher
Joseph O E Gadbois
Bernard Gilbert
Francis R Gregoire
Gregory King
Douglas King
Armand R Lafleur
Raymond R Le Clair

**Somers Lions Club**
Kenneth Schloss
Ronald Trevena
Robert Trombly

**Stafford Lions Club**
Thomas Borovicka
Robert Bourque
Silvio Dadalt
Dennis Dadalt

**Taftville Lions Club**
Stephen B Eaton
Nancy Miclette

**Thompson Lions Club**
Donald F Antonson
A David Babbit
Marcel Beauregard
Louis P Faucher Jr
Paul Franklin
Rene Morin
Daniel P Roy
Sherman L Waldron

**Tolland Lions Club**
Roger Bissell
David J Serluco
Robert G Stewart
George Tornatore

**Vernon Lions Club**
Steven Diana
Wayne Johnson
John M Risley
Helen Syriac

**Waterford Lions Club**
George Paul Abbiati
Donald Callahan
Gerrit Deurloo
Antonie Deurloo
Donald Frink
Leroy W Jordan
Arthur J Perry Jr
Howard Stillman
Robert Thornley Jr

**Waterford Regional Lions Club**
E Peter Bendfeldt
Marie Church
Caroline R Diehm
Judy L Dousis

**Willimantic Lions Club**
David W Bergmann
Gloria Bergmann
Edward Bussiere
Rocco Cancellaro
Edwin C Fisher
Susan Fisher
Wilfrid J Lebeau
Nancy E Lebeau
Keith M Lemire
James L Mackey Jr
Frank P Mauro
Shirley A Mauro
Richard Oat
Gunnel Stenberg

**Woodstock Lions Club**
Theodore Demers

**District 23-C**
Ronald A Hemingway

## Appendix K—Membership Key Award Recipients

### Lions Clubs of District 23-A

**Beacon Falls Lions Club**
Adamaitis, Richard
Egan, Kenneth
Fredericks, William
Genz, Jonathan
Kersten, Stanley H
King, John
Mis, William
Poirier, Joseph A
Rydzik, Peter
Shea, Raymond
Siemenski, Edward
Trzaski, Thomas J

**Bethany Lions Club**
Ash, Marian N
Cavaliere, Tom
Duman, Donald W
Ferretti, John
Hescock, Janet B
Johnson, Dwight R
Kelly, Robert H
Mc Clure, Kimberly A
Mc Donnell, George
Montalto, William
Stahl, Craig
Viets, Robert G

**Bethel Lions Club**
Babcock, Thomas E
Bach, John
Belardinelli, Tulio
Clausing, Richard D
Greco, Hugo F

Haitsch, Aurel
Hawkins, John F
Jagush, Jan Maria
Rasamny, Khalil
Rotella, Frank
Steck, Charles

**Branford Lions Club**
Burke, David
Burke, Steven
Carbone, Angelo
Cushing, John
Dornfeld, James
Dornfeld, William
Dziura, David B
Farley, Edward
Fuller, Ralph
Gillispie, Carol
Glynn, Richard
Krista, Kenneth R
Lawton, William J
Maresca, Perry
Mendillo, James H
O'Brien, Richard J
Osochowsky, Jerry J
Parisi, Debbe

**Bridgeport Host Lions Club**
Bhatia, Anand P
Bresky, Theodore H
Carroll, James R
Carroll, William J
Cohen, Milton S
Flaker, Philip G
Lynn, John A
O'Donnell, Charles

Pallotto, Patrick A
Parnoff, Laurence V
Pickens, Dorothy
Pickens, Stephen H
Porto, Richard
Schickler DPM, Mark A
Schurman, Albert G

**Bridgeport North Bridgeport Lions Club**
Dortenzio, Robert
Eisler, Eric V
Framularo, Nicholas
Minty, William

**Brookfield Lions Club**
Amorossi, Richard
Bendana, Ernest J
Blessey, Richard B
Campbell, John
Christy, Glenn
Collins, Francis J
Dougherty, Robert
Keefe, David C
Licursi, Anthony G
Lyon, Mark S
Missigman, Gary
Nepomuceno, Ernie F
Nindorf, Gerald J
Smith, Alan E
Sniffin, Allan D
Sullivan, Tom

**Cheshire Lions Club**
Anderson, Colette M
Canas, Theresa B
Derganc, Lillian

Erasmus, Carol A
Jerin, Marjorie
Manthey, Bill
Remillard, Peter A

**Danbury Lions Club**
Alam, Mohammed R
Bagley, Bernard
Barnola, Thomas H
Boyce, R Milton
Bull, Stephen
Burns, Christopher
Campbell, William J
Erdtmann, Eric
Evans, Frances J
Frizzell, Thomas A
Gottschalk, Eric
Humphreville, James
Losee, Boyd O
Manion, Nancy E
Michael, Harold L
Molinaro, Frank P
Morgan, Hubert V
Murphy, John J
Nadeav, Eric
Nolan, Thomas
Oligino, John
Plecity, John
Roy, Noel C
Schmiedel, J Roger
Schulze, Howard W
Shepperd, Wayne J
Yamin, Dianne E
Yamin, Robert J
Zaleta, Donald J

**Darien Lions Club**
Curtis, Harold S
Daigle, Peter
Esposito, Mark
Flaherty, Martin J
Hughes, William
Martin, Robert
Musitano, Robert R
Smith, Paul

**Derby Shelton Lions Club**
Klos, Francis A
Rondini, Henry
Terrasi, Anthony

**Devon Lions Club**
Donaldson, Alan J
Dowin, Richard E

**East Haven Lions Club**
Bucci, Barbara M
Burton, Donald J
Limoncelli, Robert
Sudac, Thomas
Van Deusen, Phil
Vitale, Marilyn

**Easton Lions Club**
Glaser, G Stephen
Monk, Robert
Turner, Sherman F

**Fairfield Lions Club**
Cooke, Howard P
Loftus, Robert
Lopez, William A
Shelton, Philo S
Smith, Henry F

**Georgetown Lions Club**
Clark, Robert F
Mc Carty, Edward J

Nazzaro, Louis John
Pilato, Michael
Slade, John Howard
Spearman, John H

**Greenwich Lions Club**
Albert, David
Devine, Barbara
Gordon, Bruce
Klein, Stanley J
Masi, Douglas
Noble, H David
Pulitano, Pat M
Tella, Chris S
Thal, Stanley A
Waterbury, Susan J

**Greenwich Western
Greenwich Lions Club**
Boensch, Warner
Nearing, Jack

**Guilford Lions Club**
Browne, Alan
Correia, E Manuel
Engstrom, Donald D
Londa, Joseph
Redman, Winfield A
Salzano, Frank

**Hamden Lions Club**
Hurlburt, Nancy
Inzero, Eric J
Inzero, Richard
Sola, Janet S

**Madison Lions Club**
deJongh, Marinus
Longobucco, David M
Martin, R Russell
Ruggiero, Robert

Tresselt, Louis
Tscholl, Ekkehard J

**Meriden Lions Club**
Alfieri, John
Barba, Richard N
Carabetta, George
Carabetta, George
Crowell, Joseph
De Rosa, Edward G
Gostyla, Peter J
Haberli, Edward G
Jaliela, Daniel R
Mule, Vincent T
Murdy, David D
Murdy, William
O'loughlin, William
Park, Howard
Phillips, William D
Seitlinger, David
Stern, Robert F
Stiegler, Charles R
Szymaszek, Michael
Tompkinson, Rene H
Verdolini, Mario J
Zerio, Stephen T
Zygmont, Francis

**Middlebury Lions Club**
Allen, William S
Pietrorazio, Raymond
Regan, Donald E

**Milford Lions Club**
Goldwyn, Ronald M
Moll, Nell
Patterson, Kathy Lynn
Valerio, Ann
Valerio, Joseph
Valerio, Michele
Weise, Roberta

**Monroe Lions Club**
Berger, Leonard F
Bohm, Robert
Orr, Richard
Plude, Ronald
Stoccatore, Albert
Whiteley, Donald

**Naugatuck Lions Club**
Alegi, Dominic
Farrell, Patrick Joseph
Milo, Michael
Newman, Robert

**New Canaan Lions Club**
Belluschi, Helen Risom
Lazzaro, Ralph
Tippman, Walter

**New Fairfield Lions Club**
Arcery, Gene
Barbuti, Judy
Cammarano, Philip A
Cleary, Donald
Disarro, Doug
Gillotti, Michael J
Gouveia, Al
Hadad, John
Kappes, Krystyna
Kerner, Suzanne
Logan, Steve
Marsh, Wesley G
Matarazzo, Robert N
Redenz, Gail
Redenz, Robert M
Rooney, John
Shea, Francis
Smith, Richard
Stram, C Douglas
Tegmier, Theodore
Van Treuren, Wayne

**New Fairfield Candlewood Lions Club**
Allan, Frances
Bourne, Lovie D
Gyle, Norma
Gyle, Robert B
Hazard, Alfred P
Hodge, John
Hoxie, Alice M
Knopf, Regina M
Lamendola, Marlene F
Walsh, Seamus

**New Haven Lions Club**
Anderson, Herbert E
Bennett, Alan C
Bennett, Alan M
Bennett, James B
Bennett, Joan C
Brancato, Salvatore G
Calzetta, Frances A
Carr, Ruth B
Douglas, Kenneth P
Downs, John E
Hyatt, Theodore F
Lupone, Salvatore
Lyons, John M
Minicozzi, David
Rice, David R
Roop, E Bernard
Swann, Paul R
Traester, James E
Wade, Roy

**Newtown Lions Club**
Arfaras, George
Arneth, Paul
Berliner, James

Brown, David E
Christensen, Jon E
Cole, Gerard L
Corey, Kevin M
De Lucia, Frank
Denlinger, Sutherland W G
Evagash, Thomas J
Ferris, Donald L
Krueger, Paul H
Mounts, Gordon
Williams, Gordon

**North Haven Lions Club**
Barnhart, Marie-Anne
Lazaroff, Arnold L
Lewis, Sidney
Parrett, Richard

**Norwalk Lions Club**
Bryson, James M
Daley, Joseph T
Farris, Edward
Lynch, Thomas
Pramer, Joseph
Rissolo, Alex
Stein, Thomas H
Thompson, John

**Old Greenwich Lions Club**
Button, Robert E
Corrado, Paula
Ducret, Lucien C
Hahn, Philip M
Menegon, Benito A
Palmer, Paul P
Stafford, Caroline G
Watts, Sterling E
Woods, Clifford C

**Orange Lions Club**
Andruskiwec, Edward
Bencivengo, Nicolas
Drobish, Marian
Drobish, Robert M
Lenz, Kenneth E
Messina, Lawrence
Phillips, William A
Turner, Frederick R
Turner, Leatrice
White, James M

**Oxford Lions Club**
Costabile, Peter
Goldberg, Robert
Lund, William H
Maciog, Robert
Ryan, William

**Prospect Lions Club**
Mirabelle, Dom
Sciavola, Mike

**Ridgefield Lions Club**
Chaplin Johnston, Jill
Di Acri, Donna
Hancock, Charles
Hval, Harold N
Johnson, Robert L
Liberta, Michael J
Ligi, Joyce
Lossius, Anna A
Martin, Edward J
Meyer, Arthur
Slade, Ann
Smith, Gary C
Smith, Lou Ann
Velez, Colleen G
Yanity, Peter V

**Seymour Lions Club**
Lane, James
Spatafore, Rose Marie T

**Southbury Lions Club**
Cognato, Thomas
Guarrera, Francis J
Heebner, Edmund R
Stone, George

**Stamford North Stamford Lions Club**
Aronin, Meryl W
Petersen, Rick
Sachs, Kenneth C
Topper, Harold Tip

**Stratford Lions Club**
Gunther, George L
Kleindienst, Priscilla
Penny, Richard J
Wahlberg, Kent

**Trumbull Lions Club**
Daley, John J
Furze, Lyle
Rogalewski, E J

**Trumbull Center Lions Club**
Lutz, J Robert
Mingrone, Nina
Okrepkie, Ralph
Whelan, Barbara

**Waterbury Lions Club**
Briotti, Stephen
Daly, Lynn H
Davitt, Barbara
Granatuk, Michael
Leidel, Victor H
Levin, Harry G
Martin, Lisa

Mc Kennerney, Wendell
Pelletier, Lida A
Summa, William J

**West Haven Lions Club**
Canadeo, Gerard
Panza, Edward S
Voss, Edward
Voss, Mary Ann

**Wolcott Lions Club**
Albert, Lawrence G
Ardry, Michael G
Barratt, Warren F
Carrah, Michael J
Chasse, Clifford
D'Agostino, Nicholas E
Desaulniers, David J
Gagain, John R
Helaire, Richard A
Hutnik, Joseph
Marino, Anthony J
Mazurek, John
Phelan, George M
San Angelo, Richard
Sherman, Walter H
Wilensky, Edward
Wisler, Rene A

**Woodbridge Lions Club**
Fries, Robert
Johnson, Kenneth W

**Yalesville-Wallingford Lions Club**
Eccles, William T
Pfau, Peter G
Santos, Maryann
Thibodeau, Sandra
Wruck, Joyce

**Lions Clubs of District 23-B**

**Avon Lions Club**
Donato, Joseph T
Dutcher, Maurice A
England, George W
Griswold, Donald E
Price, Richard W
Rettig, Ernest I
Ruppert, Otto R
Starr, Duane E
Tremblay, Louis
Zacchera, Heidi

**Barkhamsted Lions Club**
Beauchene, Paul
Lattizori, Francis J

**Berlin Lions Club**
Asal, Marilyn F
Asal, Robert
Blasko, Andrew
Dabrowski, Robert P
Demko, Jon Paul
Dennis, Thomas E
Dimugno, Frank
Diskin, William
Dornfried, Robert
Frisk, Kenneth
Geschimsky, Donald P
Glatz, Jeffrey P
Hall, Thomas
Hamilton, Clifford H
Hillstrand, Harry
Johansen, Earl
Karp, Stephen J
Keithan, George
Kloskowski, Eugene S
Lupia, Felice

Martinelli, Norman
Pentore, Harry
Porter, Philip C
Riggott, Raymond
Schmidt, Edward L
Weiss, Robert A
Wicke, Gordon
Wicklund, Earl H
Williams, Cliff
Yale, Richard S

**Bethlehem Lions Club**
Gustafson, Clayton
Overton, Robert A

**Bloomfield Lions Club**
Bercowetz, Herman
Hunter, Howard
Johnson, Perry
Kulig, Frank
Schulman, Sydney T
Wolpoe, Ronald H

**Bristol Lions Club**
Brzezinski, Irene
Frankowski, Arline
Frankowski, Raymond
Funk, Arthur
Latvis, John
Lyons, Vincent E
Pinto, Ricardo
Shafran, Sidney L

**Burlington Lions Club**
Brunoli, Albert E
Hoyt, Jamison
Martin, Tommy
Scheidel, Theodore C
Tracy, Michael

**Canaan Northwest Lions Club**
Minacci, Marilyn
Tadiello, William
Zucco, Carol A

**Canton Lions Club**
Alonzy, Gerald G
Bahre, Jared
Coutu, Gerald A
Miller, William G
Scott, Donald K

**Colebrook Lions Club**
Bremer, Brad
Gray, George C
Hiller, William
Kenneson, Douglas
Seely, Kent
Winn, Raymond A

**East Granby Lions Club**
Hunderlach, Charles F
Short, Karen M

**East Hartford Lions Club**
Crecco, Steven
Donovan, Raymond T
Gould, James K
Howes, Pamela E
Johnston, John
Mogielnicki, Gerard
O'Brien, Arthur
Precourt, George A
Randall, Kathleen
Samartino, Donald
Schwartz, David
Vrooman, Gary L

## East Windsor Lions Club
Bartlett, Donald
Boutin, Karen
Butenkoff, George G
Butenkoff, Marilyn
Cormier, Robert J
Mazur, Ann M
Nevers, Peter J
Parda, Carol J
Parda, John F
Parker, George W
Sargent, Thomas J
Sherman, Richard
Stathers, Dolores
Stathers, Richard
Sylvester, Margaret

## Enfield Lions Club
Cimino, Joseph F
Holmes, Gordon
Holmes, Patricia C
Hosey, Jim
Putzel, Sterling

## Glastonbury Lions Club
Dummit, Paul J
Fleet, John P
Manuck, William
Pagliughi, Paul
Skiba, Richard M
Tyrol, Brian

## Granby Lions Club
Conroy, Tom
Garrity, Phillip
Guarco, Michael B
Maher, Robert J
Main, Phillip D
Pierce, Harold F
Smith, Paul E
Spatcher, John

## Greater Hartford West Indian Lions Club
Barnaby, Winsome
Gibson, Joanna
Levy, Baldwin O A
Linton-Williams, Faye

## Hartford Evening Lions Club
Centeno, Lillian
Centeno, Luis R
Clark, Robert D
Cruz, Carlos
De Leon-Clark, Nora E
Medina, Francesco
Ortiz Medina, Maria A.
Reyes, Manuel
Rodriguez, Raul
Tobon Ramirez, Mariano

## Hartford Hispanic Seniors Lions Club
Hernandez, Mercedes
Rivera, Carmen N
Vicuna, Maria B

## Hartford Host Lions Club
Anderson, Curtis
Beavers, Allen
Elman, Marshall William
Laflin, John Carlock
Robinson, Curtis D
Stern, Andrew E

## Hartford Multi-National Lions Club
Aparicio, Norma
Carty, Anna
Chupas, Fidelina
Ossa, Lucy
Pacheco-Ayala, Sonia
Schulman, Elba Cruz

Vater, Susan
Wilson, Millicent

**Hartland Lions Club**
Baril, Constance
Baril, Gerald E
Davis, Robert P

**Harwinton Lions Club**
Bell, Walter T
Bigos, John
French, David
Kasznay, Andrew
Nejaime, Michael
Neri, David Roger
Tomasko, Colleen
Tomasko, Matthew
Walters, Allen
Willey, Dana B

**Kent Lions Club**
Adams, Bruce
Bain, David
Davis, Gary C
Garrity, Chris
Hanley, Mark
Hock, Robert
Jacobsen, George W
Jalbert, David M
Matson, Edward L
O'callaghan, Sean
O'rourke, Randy
Tobin, Joseph G

**Litchfield Lions Club**
Baldwin, Guy
Bower, James
Bunnell, Frederick B
Carpenter, Peter D
Crampton, Jim
Filippini, Ronald J

Fisher, Frank E
Fogarty, William V
Hill, William A

**Manchester Lions Club**
Becker, Timothy H
Garoppolo, John T
Gorman, Ed C
Rodny, William M

**Marlborough Lions Club**
Fortin, Mark
Reiser, Tom
Vontell, Robert

**New Britain Lions Club**
Anderson, Steven D
Bernacki, Maria G
Bray, Douglas B
Daninhirsch, Alan
Feigenbaum, Seth
Glowiak, Stanley
Grcevic, Joseph J
Marrocco, Frank D
Platt, Lewis M
Polezonis, Stephen N
Schultz, Abbott
Story, Kristine
Wiatr, Frank M
Wuerthner, Keith

**New Hartford Lions Club**
Creamer, James J
Seitz, Geraldine F
Seitz, Thomas

**New Milford Lions Club**
Buczek, John
Carlson, Robert A
Chapin, Charles J
Conn, Walter
Coppola, Robert

Dunleavy, Kevin
Dupree, Keith W
Fitch, George C
Layton, Richard
Nicolas, J Russell
Peitler, Arthur
Szilagyi, Gabor
Toussaint, Charles
Turner, George
Wilcox, Mike

**Newington Lions Club**
Brown, Adrianne
Guertin, Leopold M
Martinelli, Stanley
Montanari, Leonard J

**Norfolk Lions Club**
Bachman, Robert
Evans, Alexandria
Gourley, Dave
Moore, Lynn
Moses, Anne R
Mulville, Barbara A
Tracey, Barbara A
Veronesi, Joseph

**Plainville Lions Club**
Boukus, Elizabeth
Czerepak, John
Morris, Bruce
Spielman, Paul

**Rocky Hill Lions Club**
Frago, Frank C
Rogers, Sherman
Rohr, Eugene P

**Sharon Lions Club**
Clark, Linda
Heacox, Edward

Murtagh, Brian M
Perotti, John F
Prindle, Barclay W

**Simsbury Lions Club**
Bannan, John H
Bannan, Marianne
Gauthier, Robert C
Matt, George R
Tolan, Lewis E

**South Windsor Lions Club**
Dowlatshahi, Sia
Grillo, Robert
Habif, John
Hintz, Ernest
Kasevich, Lawrence S
Lebowitz, Steven
Neal, Raymond
Olem, John
Osborne, Elizabeth M
Padegimas, Catherine
Plank, Richard
Ryan, Robert
Simao, Frank A

**Southington Lions Club**
Bohigian, Michael
Bunko, Michael C
Burbank, Richard R
Galante, Frank
Gingras, Gerald
Gray, Robert J
Kelley, David P
Manning, Francis
Rechenberg, Otto
Sauer, Edward

**Suffield Lions Club**
Corriveau, Ronald C

## Terryville Lions Club
Allread, William O
Barnes, Lois B
Bondeson, Russ
Ceritello, Timothy L
Conopask, Glenda J
Custer, William
Daigle, Steve
Doty, Gerald E
Foote, Richard J
Fuller, Frank L
Jacobs, Russell E
Kosikowski, Theodore
Le Roux, Bonnie D
Leroux, Robert
Mc Grane, Deborah J
Nelson, Robert
Pajeski, John
Scott, Francis M
Scott, Jeffrey
Squires, Kevin

## Torrington Lions Club
Archambault, Ray
Bruni, Fred P
Canino, Debbie
Di Virgilio, Donoto
Dolan, Ralph
Dzurnak, Phil
Gelormino, Jean M
Gelormino, John
Hilpert, Mary Ann
Knight, William
Latulipe, Adelbert
Ne Jaime, Norman E
Palladino, Rocco
Plaskiewicz, Marilyn A
Quartiero, Elizabeth
Yuchunas, Michael

## Trinity College Lions Club
Razzano, John

## Unionville Lions Club
Arnold, Everett
Collier, Donald R
Gray, Jackalyn
Leide, Richard
Lieberman, Stephen
Merrills, David
Peltier, James
Rogers, Richard
Tallmadge, Elsie
Tallmadge, Ralph H
Wendell, Robert

## Washington Lions Club
Collum, Rex K
Kaylor, Richard
Korpalski, Adam
Miles, David S
Wright, Harry

## Watertown Lions Club
Baker, Matthew
Beauchamp, Bernard C
Blanchard, Ronald M
Clark, Richard O
Dayton, Richard A
Feliciani, Richard
Frenger, H Dewey
Fuller, Robert V E
Graziano, Rudolph S
Hanson, Kathleen
Jean, David W
La Bonne, Robert H
Long, Henry L
Mc Hale, Peter C
Porto, George T
St Onge, O'Neil

Taylor, William E
Uitti, Daniel A
Varuolo, Anthony J
Zeman, Andrew

**West Hartford Lions Club**
Belanger, Joseph
Krakauskas, Edward
Lyons, John S
Pane, Claudio M
Re, John J

**Wethersfield Lions Club**
Bates, David
Baxter, Gerald S
Leonard, Thomas M

**Windsor Lions Club**
Babb, James
Bak, Joseph P
Cohen, Joshua
Coleman, Timothy E
Fullana, John J
Groenstein, Theodore A
Kirk, Edward
Leland, John
Lombardi, John C
Lombardo, Benjamin R
Marci, Matthew
Martin, Thomas G
Miller, William L

**Windsor Locks Lions Club**
Aspinwall, Howard H
Barberi, Robert F
Barile, Michael
Boglisch, Glenn D
Boscarino, John
Brennan, Brian S
Brennan, Richard W
Bruneau, Arthur E

Cate, Lyle
Chapple, Wayne
Cooper, Cynthia B
Cooper, George H
Donagher, Barbara
Donagher, Hugh
Famiglietti, Philip F
Fuentes, William A
Goldfarb, Saul
Hamilton, William
Harvey, Robert E
Ignazio, Roger
Jordan, Michael F
Julian, Patricia
Kokofski, John
Leary, William C
Lee, John J
Leiper, Ralph W
Marinone, Patricia W
Messier, Carolyn A
Messier, Norman J
Mills, Steven
Murdock, Roland
Puia, Victor J
Ruggiero, Gary
Savoie, Lawrence E
Stegman, Alan
Stegman, Gale
Storms, Dale
Storms, Ronald F
Storms, Scott A
Uchneat, Jean
Westerman, Wayne
Wong, Hallie

**Winsted Lions Club**
Brennan, Marilyn
Knight, Milan M
Lemelin, Judy
Sewell, Blanche

**Woodbury Lions Club**
Barthelmess, William C
Deschino, John
Deschino, Ken
Doran, Philip
Grudzien, Edward P
Heavens, Donald
Kaloidis, Constantine
Lindahl, Karl
Manzi, Edward J
Manzi, Roland L
Rehkamp, Charles J
Rogers, Christopher
Shepard, Frank
Trompeter, James
Worden, Walter
Wylie, Hal

**Lions Clubs of District 23-C**

**Bolton Lions Club**
Killian, David J
Madore, Joseph D
Neil, Robert W
Rivers, Carl F

**Bolton Regional Lions Club**
Bass, Yvonne Alice
Caliskan, Donna
Davies, Jane
Gouchoe, Barbara
Minicucci, Janet

**Canterbury Lions Club**
Cook, Russell
Gray, Thomas
Levesque, Harold
Shinkiewicz, Raymond C
Vining, Sharon K

**Clinton Lions Club**
Adams, David
Bernier, Charles
Borg, Dave
Bugg, Gerald
Cuoco, Mike
Davis, Jeffery M
Hogan, Tim
Luciani, Louis
Lupone, Mario P
Reynolds, Dave
Santanelli, Richard
Schubert, Arthur
Sipples, Peter
Sliva, David
Vece, Daniel

**Colchester Lions Club**
Anastasio, Rita A
Cooper, Pamela E
Dickinson, Lori
Faski, Jack
Gallicchio, Anthony
Gillis, Steve
Glemboski, Leo
Hajdun, Michael
Hirsch, Shelly
Jacobson, Eric C
Labella, Janet
Macbryde, Cindy
Mc Nichols, John A
Nolan-Thibault, Margaret
Picard, Charlene
Plotkin, Irving
Salpietro, George J
Salpietro, Marie
Shilosky, Julianne M
Squire, Jerome
Turner, Aaron
Watson, Irene

## Columbia Lions Club
Austin, Arthur T
Beck, Henry
Czarnowski, Marc J
Lange, Richard
Mathieu, Edward F
Osmond, William D
Toepfer, Dean

## Coventry Lions Club
Barry, Barbara
Barry, Thomas F
Giggey, Richard Edward
Harris, Robert
Holinko, Eric J
Kelleher, William

## Cromwell Lions Club
Curtin, Fred D
Megos, Nicole M
Penepent, Donald

## Danielson Lions Club
Burgess, Betsy
Burgess, David P
Cheng, William
Griffiths, David
Pomposelli, Joyce
Sawyer, Paulette

## Deep River-Chester Lions Club
Carlson, Douglas
Davies, Arthur J
Di Pietro, Joseph
Gill, Raymond Pidge
Scovill, Arthur J
Scovill, C Talcott
Thorpe, David
Thorpe, Rita
Zanni, Silvio

## Durham Lions Club
Huntington, Jay
Pasieka, Richard
Slight, Leo

## East Haddam Lions Club
Ballek, Richard Allen
Bishop, Edgar H
Des Rosiers, Edwin
Gagnon, Frederick G
Golec, Walter J
Goodspeed, Scott
Jezek, Scott W
Kromish, John
Maxwell, Paul L
Nelson, William

## East Haddam Community Lions Club
Bielski, Diane D (Pettit)
Bradshaw, Linda
Davis, Barbara A
Jezek, Shea
Sabo, Alice D
Wocl, Dorothy C

## East Hampton Lions Club
Anderson, Dave
Chapps, Gary G
Christopher, Ronald
Distefano, Thomas L
Dixon, Gregory S
Emmons, Lawrence E
Krogh, Theodore
Marsden, Arthur
Nesci, Ralph
Nichols, Charles B
Parsons, Lawrence

## East Hampton Village Lions Club
Knotek, Jeanette H
Krogh, Mary M
Robida, John
Schlosser, Theresa
Vezina, Sandra L
Wilson, Donna M

## Essex Lions Club
Bombaci, Joseph G
Budney, Richard F
Burnham, Daniel J
Comey, Peter
Domnarski, Edward
Guffey, Marilyn
O'Connell, John

## Franklin Lions Club
Avila, Charles
Avila, John
Churchill, Douglass M
Hall, Richie

## Griswold Regional Lions Club
Graham, William D
Mansovr, Marion
Maynard, Claire R
Mc Lean, Lawrence A

## Groton Lions Club
Bartinik, Peter
Casey, Hugh D
Haines, Stacy A
Kent, Perley L
Kent, Richard B
Millas, Wayne
Miller, Jan A
O'Reilly Jr, Henry

Stebbins, Edward
Stoven, Ron
Tomsky, Wayne

## Haddam Lions Club
Banach, Fred
Cross, Kevin
Dennis, Ray
Esposito, David
Kapitulik, Dave

## Hebron Lions Club
Barrasso, Bernice M
Barrasso, Charles A
Clark, Everett J
Dixon, Robert J
Dumas, Richard
Garrison, R William
Kalhok, Martin
Kalom, Bruce
Keefe, Richard A
Kozyra, Michael
Krist, Joseph P
Lee, Robert E
Reid, Aaron
Schadtle, Robert
Soderberg, John A
Spadarzewski, Richard
Speno, Frederick L

## Killingly Quiet Corner Regional Lions Club
Smith, John T

## Killingworth Lions Club
Carroll, James J
Dodson, Bruce
Doyle, Terry
Folger, Jay
Gannon, Timothy E
Kempter, John F

Mc Mahon, John W
Morgan, Charles
Riblet, Les
Smith, Charles F
Speicher, John
Spencer, Dale L
White, Mark

## Lebanon Lions Club

Drum, Ron A
Lafontaine, Gregg
Petro, Ronald A
Russo, Roland
Scaplan, William
Slate, Robert M
Tanger, Richard
Teller, Harry
Walsh, Jody
Wentworth, Timothy

## Ledyard Lions Club

Brown, Terrill L
Congdon, James E
Daimler, William E
Howard, Linda J
Kaminske, Howard G
Kaune, Nancy E
Novic, Stephen M
Novic, Teresa Y
Olsen, Peter I
Plantz, Ernest V
Provencal, John E
Rowe, Frank J
Santos, Thomas A
Scott, John F
Thomson, Gordon W
Van Dyke, Roger S
Van Dyke, Sally J

## Lyme Old Lyme Lions Club

Carnese, Gregory P
Collins, John A
Cotton, Daniel T
Graybill, James
Hurley, Richard
Maranda, Francis J
Oliveira, Frank
Parcak, Philip E
Sjursen, Arnold

## Mansfield Lions Club

Allan, Gordon B
Duff, Lloyd T
Nolan, Donald M
Norman, George R
Passmore, Edwin
Passmore, Joyce C
Stallard, James E
Stearns, James W
Woody, Charles O

## Middlefield Lions Club

Berry, Debi S
Didato, Judy Ann  M
Fowler, Russell
Gribko, Mark
Tabor, John W
Wallach, Alexander
Wallach, David J

## Middletown Lions Club

Biega, Joseph E
Daniels, Raymond
Gionfriddo, Stephen T
Haas, Wallace
Hasbrouck, Frederick K
Knight, Martin George
Milardo, Joseph E
Moore, Thomas
Salafia, James

## Montville Lions Club
Bigornia, Joseph
Dougherty, Patricia A
Eichelberg, A Carleton
Eichelberg, Phyllis J
Engelman, Bruce A
Grise, Diana
Krajewski, Robert H
Ouellette, Albert H
Ouellette, Marion H
Plotnick, Herb C
Pomazon, Todd F

## Montville Mohegan-Pequot Lions Club
Becker, Jacqueline L
De Ragon, Hilda
Tucker, Nancy

## Mystic Lions Club
Abt, Willaim
Burdick, Nanette
Conway, Kevin W
Densmore, Raymond
Finlayson, George
Holmstedt, Herbert A
Jensen, Susan
Mc Sorley, Patti M
Parkinson, Abby
Valenti, Robert

## New London Lions Club
Cook, Milton L
Donovan, William
Esposito, Rudolph
Fisher, Charles D
Linder, Samuel-Jay
Neilan, Edward B
Pero, Anthony N
Van Verdeghem, Jack

## Niantic Lions Club
Allen, William K
Burkhardt, Gerard P
Carucci, Craig
Carucci, Teresa
Curley, James E
Denesha, Ted
Fraser, Wayne L
Genung, Paul F
Gidman, Robert G
Hallisey, John J
Harris, James S
Hunt, F H
Lakowsky, Gary W
Parkhurst, Howard
Rupar, Donald J
Senkow, Robert L
Stockford, Particia
Tamburro, William L
Tanguay, Edgar
Wagner, John F

## North Stonington Lions Club
Judge, Donald R
Kimball, Robert H
Mullane, Nicholas H
Paradis, Lee Ann
Patton, James H
Robinson, William Z

## Norwich Lions Club
Bokoff, Rubin
Denesha, Robert C
Dereski, Peter M
Diagneault, Henry
Gagne, Charles E
Gualtieri, Albert
Gualtieri, Mario
Kustesky, Benjamin

Ragovin, Joel J
Slaga, Rose M

**Old Saybrook Lions Club**
Campbell, Richard
Goodnow, Elizabeth
Peppas, John
Skeffington, Beverly
Tiezzi, Sharon

**Pawcatuck Lions Club**
Capizzano, David
Daly, James
Jones, Calvin
Miceli, Angelo S
Pescatello, Joseph
Prachniak, Stanley
Venditti, Rudolph J

**Plainfield Lions Club**
Bartlett, Linda
Beausoleil, Ann
Beausoleil, Thomas
Bellavance, William
Boski, Daniel J
Brisbois, Richard L
Chviek, Rosamond
Coolidge, Theodore
Erickson, Robert V
Matteau, Clement
Pepin, Debra E
Quintal, Robert
Tarkowski, Robert

**Pomfret Lions Club**
Breen, Michael
Hull, William B
Mc Nally, Timothy W
Patenaude, David
Pohlman, Eric W
Schlehofer, Glenn A

Wolchesky, Michael W

**Putnam Lions Club**
Bleau, Kathleen
Chubbuck, Barbara
Farner, Steven
Faucher, Leia
Faucher, Stephen
Gregoire, Francis R
Hemingway, Ronald A
King, Gregory
La Fleur, Denise
Lafleur, Armand R
Le Clair, Raymond R
Otero, Daniel
Wade, Lorna

**Salem Lions Club**
Fogarty, James D
Kennedy, John F
Martin, William
Miller, Vivian
Ziegra, George

**Somers Lions Club**
Casciano, Tony
Kinney, Scott
Ladue, James
Lipton, Jeff
Meunier, Franklin
Schloss, Kenneth
Weingartner, Richard

**Stafford Lions Club**
Armelin, Anthony
Bourque, Robert
Campbell, Robert
Casagrande, Richard
Denunzio, Albert
Dewey, Richard H
Pisciotta, Richard

## Taftville Lions Club
Browne, John F
Eaton, Joan C
Eaton, Stephen B
Rizzuto, Diane
Terault, Mary E

## Thompson Lions Club
Babbit, A David
Beauregard, Marcel
Blackmer, Randolph
Cunha, Kirby
Despelteau, John B
Hoening, Paul
Masters, Paul A
Morin, Rene
Morse, Richard
Naum, James
Nedzweckas, Peter J
Roy, Daniel P
Trudeau, Richard
Valade, Kevin C

## Tolland Lions Club
Charbonnler, James A
Layman, David
Mathews, Duane
Salois, Andre
Serluco, David J
Tornatore, George

## Vernon Lions Club
Du Baldo, David
Foss, Carol S
Johnson, Wayne
Peterson, Richard
Taverne, Fred

## Waterford Lions Club
Radack, James
Stillman, Howard

## Waterford Regional Lions Club
Dousis, Judy L
Jones, Arlene

## Willimantic Lions Club
Barron, Robert
Bergmann, David W
Correll, William K
De Vivo, Thomas
Donovan, Kim
Fisher, Edwin C
Fisher, Susan
Hence, Roger F
Lebeau, Wilfrid J
Mauro, Frank P
Mauro, Shirley A
Mustard, Robert
Reardon, Patricia Caton
Rice, Colin Keith
Santucci, Leo J
Stenberg, Gunnel
Tillinghast, Cynthia

## Woodstock Lions Club
Azzone, John
Bond, Jeffrey
Emma, Philip
Harrington, Joseph Edward
Moseley, William
Seney, Edmond L
Wolf, Paul